S. Thomas lane
Turnecas la.
Toure royall
S. Thomas Apostel
Bredstreat
Huggin lane
Timle lane
Garl hyll
Whytyngton Colleage
S. Iohne in Walbroke
S. Mariebutol
Tames streate
S. Martin
Dowegate
Queenehyue
Thre Crans
The Bearebayting

CARR AND CARMAN

Carr and Carman
has been published
in a Limited Edition
of which this is

Number 56

[signature] August 1989.

O, London is the place for all
In love with loco-motion!
Still to and fro the people go
Like billows of the ocean;
Machine or man, or caravan,
Can all be had for paying,
When great estates, or heavy weights,
Or bodies want conveying.

Thomas Hood: *Conveyancing*

Her Royal Highness, the Princess Royal, Master 1986–1987, was portrayed for the Company by Richard Stone. (CC)

CARR AND CARMAN

The Fellowship of St Katherine
the Virgin and Martyr of Carters

An illustrated record by

Clive Birch FSA FRSA

assisted by

Lt Col Geoffrey Pearce MBE FRNS FCIT

with drawings by

Alan Percy Walker

BARON

in association with
The Worshipful Company of

CARMEN

London

MCMXCIX

PUBLISHED BY BARON BOOKS OF BUCKINGHAM
FOR THE WORSHIPFUL COMPANY OF CARMEN
AND PRODUCED BY REDWOOD BOOKS LIMITED

© Clive Birch 1999

The author has asserted his moral rights

ISBN 0 86023 658 7

All rights reserved. No part of this publication may be reproduced, stored in a retrieval system, or transmitted, in any form or by any means, electronic, mechanical, photocopying, recording or otherwise, without the prior permission of Baron Books.

Any copy of this book issued by the Publishers as clothbound or as paperback is sold subject to the condition that it shall not by way of trade or otherwise, be lent, re-sold, hired out or otherwise circulated without the Publisher's prior consent, in any form of binding or cover other than that in which it is published, and without a similar condition including this condition being imposed on a subsequent publisher.

By the same author

The Book of Amersham (with L. Elgar Pike)
    Aylesbury
    Chesham
Yesterday's Town: Amersham (with Nicholas Salmon)
    Beaconsfield (with G & E Elbay etc)
    Chesham (with John Armistead)
In Camera: Buckingham
    Chalfont St Giles
    Around Chesham
    Chiltern Thames
    Chorleywood & Chenies
    Around Milton Keynes
    Old Milton Keynes
    The Missendens
    Vale of Aylesbury
Wish You Were Here: Buckingham
    Chesham
Remember Chesham
A Chesham Century (with Arnold Baines)
On the Move (the RHA 1945–1994) (with Len Harper)
The Freedom: City and Guilds of London (with Valerie Hope etc)

CONTENTS

ACKNOWLEDGEMENTS	6
FOREWORD by Her Royal Highness The Princess Royal	7
PREFACE by the Rt Hon the Lord Mayor, The Lord Levene of Portsoken	8
INTRODUCTION	9
1 CITY WHEELS	10
2 GENESIS	18
3 LESSONS	25
4 CONFLICT	35
5 INTO BATTLE	42
6 STOUT BODYES	57
7 TAXING TIMES	68
8 FLOREAT CARMEN	87
9 INTO ACTION	115
10 WINNING WAYS	135
11 FELLOWSHIP	147
MASTERS	177
CLERKS	178
AWARDS	179
PLATE & POSSESSIONS	181
SWORD WINNERS	182
BIBLIOGRAPHY	183
SUBSCRIBERS	185
INDEX	187

ACKNOWLEDGEMENTS

Throughout the preparation of this book, the Court has given its unstinting support. The historic story owes much to the author of the previous book, Eric Bennett, whose thorough record put old documents onto a new page; he relied on the painstaking research of a past Assistant Clerk, H.C. Johns.

The modern story was facilitated by the diligence and precision of my colleague, Geoffrey Pearce, who also contributed so much to that story during his splendid Clerkship.

Many underlying facts and truths about past carr and Carman owe their survival to Thomas Day, an earlier Clerk and Master, who copied old documents from earlier times.

In our own time, many have given to this Fellowship, some of them to this book. Our Senior Past Master, Frank Coxhead, has offered tactful advice and invaluable recollections. The Father of the Company, Charles Lloyd, his brother Dick and nephew Wyn, have provided useful information. Beside them sits a truly rumbustuous Carman, John Wells, who has delved into his 50 years of Fellowship to good effect.

Other Liverymen have been no less helpful and I am indebted to both our modern Lord Mayors, Christopher Leaver and Peter Levene, for sparing time and taking trouble. Past Sheriff Jeremy Gotch has kindly helped me too, as has past Assistant Bernard Evan Cook.

The Company and I are honoured that our Past Master, the Princess Royal, has graciously contributed the finishing touch to this record of our past.

In other ways, others have assisted – Marsha Rae Ratcliff with her lovely artwork, our Clerk, Robin Bawtree, and Assistant Clerk, Mark Pulvermacher, with information, access and courtesy when their time and office were invaded. Past Master John Ratcliff generously provided the special notice about the book.

Guildhall Library's Sharon Tuff made records readily and speedily available, and guided me through labyrinthine files, Lynne MacNab in the Print Room put herself out to help my quest for relevant illustration, while Jeremy Smith facilitated copies and copyrights. In Guildhall Record Office Jim Sewell identified and helped me to interpret original papers, including our foundation document. Other individuals and organisations have been gracious with their loans, as the picture credits demonstrate.

Artistically we all owe thanks to my old friend Alan Percy Walker, for his delightful, specially commissioned chapter head sketches.

Last but not least, all those Carmen and others who subscribed to the book before seeing a word or a picture, by their support have helped us to publication, and themselves become part of the record.

As familiar faces so often hide names momentarily escaped, so memory may have overlooked some who have contributed. If so, forgive me, for I know what I did, but not always with whom or how I did it.

BUCKINGHAM PALACE

A lifetime with horses and a heavy goods licence may seem incompatible. If you want to ride in competitions up and down the country, the best way to get the horse where it is wanted is to drive it there yourself. I have competed for many years and still need to move horses around, so perhaps it is no surprise that I should find myself in the company of Carmen.

From my clothing at Guildhall to a memorable year as Master, I found my fellow Carmen friendly and, despite their turbulent past, fairly governable! I enjoyed myself - I hope they did too.

Now Carmen have this new book, which brings their story up to date, and adds a good many pictures of carrs and carmen to their record.

In the belief that if you know where you have been, it is easier to know where to go next, I believe it will guide and inform them, root and branch. I hope so and I offer your Royal Past Master's best wishes for the future to all my fellow Carmen.

Anne

The Right Honourable The Lord Mayor

The Lord Levene of Portsoken, KBE

THE MANSION HOUSE LONDON EC4N 8BH
TELEPHONE 0171-626 2500
FACSIMILE   0171-623 9524

I have always felt part of the City. There was the family connection, work and many friends. When I had the chance to join a company, I chose the Carmen. Partly through friendship, partly through instinct, it seemed a good choice. So it has proved.

As our Company's eighth Lord Mayor, I have made transport one of the strands of my year – that first day, Carmen joined me to make the Lord Mayor's Show memorable. Transport has been part of my working life – from armoured vehicles to light railway.

So I welcome a new book about our Company, and I am glad it is a thoroughly modern book too – with a brisk text and plenty of pictures. I commend it, not only to Carmen, but to all those interested in the City and in transport. It will serve as one more way of reinforcing the high repute, charitable work, and good fellowship of our ancient Company.

SCITE, CITO, CERTE

Skill, speed and safety typify the transport ideal. These are the Carmen's watchwords. We have tried to bring them to bear in these pages.

The skills of Clerks past, other writers of records, photographers and artists are self-evident. I hope the story moves apace. In adding to it, I have safely turned to proven records and Carmen with long memories.

The origins and development of our Fellowship are here set out in national and City context, with parallel information about related Guilds and transport change, and with exemplary illustration.

I have not shied from dispute, for Carmen have been ever disputatious, and it would be unseemly to ignore modern conflict. Nonetheless, I have tried to handle this with tact and sympathy.

There are gaps. Not much survives from the 14th and 15th centuries. The minutes from 1970 to late '81 are incomplete. Perhaps that will be corrected. We also hope that our Company, a very living thing, will maintain its published past like this, from time to time, so that future Carmen may enjoy a continuous record.

There are several strands to our story, which opens with a scene-setting chapter on the City and its transport. Overall, Carmen are robust servants of trade. Throughout they are seen to be innovative. They are charitable. Theirs is very much a family fellowship. One particular strand, long considered frayed two centuries ago, is now seen as continuous – the heirs to the Woodmongers bring the Carmen's wheel full circle in this new record.

We have enjoyed making this book; we hope you enjoy reading it.

Finally, we extend the hand of fellowship to all our fellow Carmen, who have bound us thus in token of our marriage to the Company. We have long enjoyed the union, and hope this book is to their advantage, and that of our ancient Company.

Buckingham 1999

KEY TO CAPTION CREDITS

AH	Tony Hart	FC	Frank Coxhead	MS	Missions to Seamen
BL	Bodleian Library	GG	Gerald Golder	MT	Michael Taylor
BM	British Museum	GL	Guildhall Library	PL	Lord Levene
CB	Author	GR	Guildhall Record Office	PA	Peter Acton
CC	Carmen	JD	Julian Dunn	PM	Pepys Library
CH	Christ's Hospital	JG	Jeremy Gotch	RS	Richard Straus
CL	Christopher Leaver	JW	John Wells	SA	Society of Antiquaries
CM	Coachmakers	LL	Lloyd family	SHF	Stanley H. Freese Collection
EB	Eric Britt	LT	London Transport	SB	Stainer & Bell
		ML	Museum of London		

The original St Paul's sits three streets from the City wall; Alder's Gate is north of the spire (destroyed in 1561) in this 1575 map by Braun & Hogenburg. (ML)

1
CITY WHEELS

In the ordinary way traders are
the only people to visit Britain

Julius Caesar: *The Conquest of Gaul* 52 BC

London is a child of trade and transport. The City is its historic heart. That City is not today's agglomeration of ancient villages and new Metrolands, but the Square Mile, guarded by its ancient gates.

Twenty feet below the pavement lies the original town. Legend once had it founded by Brutus. Evidence points to Rome, yet Roman *Londinium* echoes Celtic *Londinion* and ancient man left his mark along the river valley – over 100,000 years ago.

Early man was here, the nascent settlement may have been Celtic but the first urban men were Roman, probably traders some 30 years *anno domini*, possibly at Queen Hithe, where they might have built a quay and storehouses. Eighty-plus years before that, Julius Caesar crossed the Thames in battle, possible 'only at one place', or so wrote Tacitus.

He added that *Londinium* 'did not rank as a Roman settlement, but was an important centre for business-men and merchandise'.

Caesar may have crossed near the later London Bridge, at the low tide shallows at Westminster or even at Chelsea. He may also have built a bridge before he left. In AD 43 Claudius came, conquered and created 'a place filled with traders'. That was built at Cornhill, and grew there and on the other hill forty feet above the Thames – Ludgate.

Neolithic man had nurtured crops and navigated his narrow world by simple trackways, to exchange goods and services. Ridgeways and greenways followed the contours, and henges were built, using horse-drawn sleds and waterborne rafts. Most travelled by foot, some used the packhorse but there is no evidence of carts. The wheel existed, but apparently not here.

By 2000 BC metals were mined and worked, and Bronze Age man must surely have fashioned wheels, as he did jewellery, and travelled tracks that presaged the Romans' roads, by swifter, surer means to move between the new ports and centres of trade. His successors, the Iron Age Celts, rode in horse-drawn chariots.

By AD 50 the colonists had bridged the Thames. In AD 60 Boudica razed their township to the ground. It rose again and by AD 80 had its own basilica – by the second century that was the size of our St Paul's. There were temples, palaces and a twelve acre fort at Cripplegate for 1,500 men.

When the Romans came, they drove roads which were not challenged for more than a millennium. They drove them straight because a straight line is the shortest distance between garrison and port. They also bent them when it was easier to improve an existing track or to circumvent obstacles. Navigable rivers were their other highways.

Cicero copied Celtic two-men carriages; the resulting Roman *Cisium* was drawn by one horse, the *Essedum* by two. Careless drivers were penalised. Railway track follows the stage coach axle width, and that was derived from the *Cisium*. The *Carpentum* was the four-wheeled baggage waggon, originally a Gallic vehicle, also used as a private carriage. The *Plaustrum* was a four-wheeled flat dray drawn by oxen.

London would have known these early vehicles. Roman carters would have used them, though the Thames was the City's main trade artery.

By AD 122 London was home to 45,000 souls but, when the Romans left, it declined, was deserted and became derelict until 604 when Mellitus built the first St Paul's. By 730 Bede called it 'the mart of many nations'. (The) Queen('s) Hithe was the Saxons' first proven dock.

In 851 the Danes destroyed the Saxon *Lundenwic*. Twenty years later they so liked the place they sailed up the Thames and took over, to be dislodged by Alfred. When Danish Cnut reigned, London became our capital, with some 12,000 inhabitants.

The city civic stems from Saxon ealdormen, the King's Portreeve and the first Shire Reeve. The Frithgild and Cnihtengild presaged later mediaeval fellowships. In 1066, whereas Edward had built his Abbey at Westminster, William raised three castles – The Tower, Baynard's and Montfichet near Ludgate. He also chartered London's liberties and perpetuated 'your laws and customs'.

When the Romans left, the roads wore out. Waggons and packhorses served Saxon settlements. Locals tended to stay put; merchants travelled. The Church moved about a bit, collecting rents, and its religious guilds maintained the roads. In 1285 government decreed that highways were to be enlarged and travellers afforded some protection. Pilgrims proliferated. Horses were the preferred mode of transport. Horse litters, two-wheeled farm carts and four-wheeled springless carriages conveyed nobility, goods and the better-off. Ordinary people walked.

Over three centuries, fire stimulated new building, criss-crossed by streets. Two Sheriffs ran the City until the first Mayor was appointed in 1192, when Prince John offered the City a Commune in his brother's crusading absence. ('Lord' was added in the 15th century). In 1215 Londoners won the right to choose their own man and Magna Carta made him one of 25 supervising barons.

Freemen appeared in 1230, some 5% of the population, and apprentices in 1275. Their status was crystallised through guilds. These guilds (gild [Anglo Saxon] = payment) evolved from the many City churches' charitable fraternities. Trades and crafts were concentrated on given areas like Poultry, Smithfield, Bread and Threadneedle Streets so that, when they organised, they did so through these fraternities.

The great guilds provided aldermen – and Mayors – meeting at the Court of Husting, or House Meeting, to transact commerce and deal with property. With 'wise and discrete' men chosen from their wards, the Court of Common Council emerged.

In Tudor England travel was better organised. So were Carmen. Maps were made. Road books were created, the first in 1577. Post-horses were the Ferraris of their day. These carried the mails from post to post, usually inns. They were also for hire at threepence a mile and ten mph. Coaches and carts were slowly improving; parishes were charged with highway maintenance.

With the Stuarts, travel was trouble. The roads fell apart without formal care and with transport growth. Robbery, narrowed carriageways. metres of mud, conspired to daunt all but the most heroic traveller. Legislation permitted 70 cwt loads on four-wheeled carts drawn by ten-plus horses. The roads buckled. Despite all, couriers cantered, the poor were potholed and the rich made travel an end in itself.

London's sedan chairs and Thames watermen were competing with the hackney coach, and carts hired from stands so that the streets were 'pestered with the unnecessary multitude of coaches therein used.'

By the 1640s stage coaches had emerged – joining London to main towns within 40 miles. Flying coaches followed, increasing distance and speed. In 1635 a Master of the Posts was appointed. Postage now meant letters, not travel.

The City took against the King in the Civil War, and civic trained bands played a significant role in his defeat. In 1666 the Great Fire scarred the City's fair visage, razing 80%. By 1706 the Carmen had found a degree of independence.

The 18th century saw little improvement in the country's roads. They were clogged with carriers, cattle and coaches. They were poorly surfaced and barely maintained. Turnpike trusts tackled sections of main road; parishes paid lip service to local lanes. Contractors cheated and the roads themselves went where the money pointed rather than where they were needed.

By the 18th century London housed 26,897. The City now evolved into a financial centre and distribution nexus. In mid-century 1,000 hackney carriages were licensed to stand in London streets. Banks and docks dominated.

By 1725 the Livery at large assembled for elective purpose. Livery denoted uniform, and liverymen, as their companies' senior members, were drawn from the yeomanry, or freemen. Governing courts had emerged in the 17th century. The companies, authorised and milked by Royal charter, grew in power, wealth and influence, providing troops, ships, loans for the Crown, settling disputes, helping the needy and laying the foundation for modern marketing with their lavish displays, like the (Lord) Mayor's procession, today's annual Show.

London moved outside the City walls, but the City civic stayed within, where it was in control. It led the way with care and education, church and entertainment.

In the eighteenth century there was a challenge to the wheel. Canals were created to serve the growing commerce of the first industrial age – corn, coal, iron were cost-effectively carried by the new network of national waterways, for the rivers which carried imports inland and moved goods out were navigably limited. Harnessed by the railways, the canals co-existed for some years but, once steam got up a commercial head, their days were numbered too.

As the 19th century dawned, London's docks moved, and Carmen faltered. By the 1820s light, two-wheeled cabs were competing with the hackney coach. In 1834 Hansom invented and Chapman improved the two-wheel 'hansom' which dominated the trade for sixty years. In 1853 cabs were licensed by the police.

Mail coaches gradually replaced post-boys, stage coaches competed with the armed-guarded mails, and by 1836 700 mails, 3,000 stage coaches, 150,000 horses and 30,000 men provided a nationwide service. Four-wheeled post-chaises drawn by two horses sped from town to town. Telford and McAdam revolutionised the roads with their smooth, hard-wearing surfaces in the 1820s.

Then came steam. Steam coaches emerged in 1827. Then the turnpike trusts and anti-speed laws priced the newfangled device off the roads. In 1821 the Stockton and Darlington railway was born, to be horsed or steam-hauled. Steam won when it opened in 1825. The railways fought their way through obstructive landlords, Parliament and public prejudice to network the nation.

Nationally, the railways maimed the roads. Coaching declined. Then came the bicycle, to offer the first personal transport revolution, and one which has oft since bedevilled urban highways.

In 1829 the first recorded omnibus brought serious public transport to Britain. In 1861 the first tramway opened in London. Two horses provided power. After 1870 legislation, 200 miles of tramways were planned. The busmen objected, the Corporation refused, and the City stayed tram-free.

In the late 19th century, Corporation and Companies were criticised, cross examined, but survived. Technology took its toll of ancient crafts, but trades adapted and the Livery lived on. Electricity powered, not only trams, but the underground trains that gave London the leading public transport network in the world.

In 1905 there were over 100 motor 'buses in London. The Unic pioneered the motorcab era. After the Great War, surplus Army trucks saw horse replaced by lorry. Docklands depended on freight transport to get goods from metropolis and by now Carmen were thin on the ground.

By the 1930s road haulage was firmly established with over half a million trucks in use on the eve of World War II. Carmen regrouped, grew and prospered. In 1933 London Transport was born, and the days of the independents were numbered. Trolley buses succeeded trams. When man rose above the earth and started to fly, a new challenge to the wheel emerged, but this did not radically change transport in the Square Mile.

In the post-war years, diesel became the preferred option for truck, 'bus and cab. Trolleys disappeared, freight and passenger services nationwide were regulated, nationalised, privatised and deregulated. Motorways, ring roads, orbitals, park and ride, one-way systems, 'bus lanes, ro-ro, channel tunnel, mini-cabs, JIT juggernauts and the inexorable rise of the private car have produced a motorised matrix without which modern man seemingly cannot survive.

The millennial challenge lies in the conundrum of how to move more and more people and things more and more quickly, safely and with confidence. Scite, Cito, Certe.

Romans used LEFT: the adapted Celtic *Cisium* one-horse gig and RIGHT: the larger Gallic-style *Carpentum* baggage wagon. (RS)

ABOVE: King Alfred saved London: his 'London' penny was found in the mud at the first quay and carmen's port of call at Queenhithe. (GL)
BELOW: The mediaeval White Tower was built by William the Bastard; watermen ply their craft alongside the quay in 1742. (GL)

ABOVE: Down came the Cross in Cheapside in 1643, during the Civil War, recalled here in the *Gentleman's Magazine* of 1764. (CB) BELOW: Civic pride – Mansion House by Thomas Bowles c1751, with carts, livestock, private carriage and several hackney coaches. (GL)

ABOVE: Civic splendour – Guildhall early in the 20th century. (CB)
BELOW: London Bridge – the first crossing – seen from the south bank in 1749. (CB)

The Carmen form up – this is the 1517 original Carmen's contract with
the City: part of the first page of the foundation document, formalised
on 19 March. (GRO)

2

GENESIS

clothed in o liveree,
of a solempne and greet fraternitee.
...Wel seemed ech of hem a fair burgeys,
To sitten in a yeldhalle on a deys.

Chaucer: *The Canterbury Tales* 1389

A carman is a man who drives a carr, a carrier or carter; the place he plies for hire, a carroom or standing. The carroom became synonymous with a licence to carry goods.

Trade and commerce depend on transport. Carriers have plied between wharf and market since Romans built *Londinium*.

Ships docked above the tidal reaches that lapped the Roman bridge at today's Upper Thames Street. Saxons laid today's street pattern, focused on the market streets of East and West Cheap.

Streets attracted trades, tradesmen lived side by side, churches served their needs and, as wards emerged from soke and burgh, church guilds evolved as umbrella organisations for mutual self-help. The early trade guilds grew out of those religious fraternities.

Clothmakers formed the Weavers in 1130 but, of the Carmen, there is no mention – until 1277. Legend alone claims a Fellowship that century, but that year did see transport on record – 'no cart serving the City, bringing water, wood, stones etc, be shod with iron.' Edward I was hammering the Welsh at the time, but his instincts leant towards law and order – eight years later he decreed that 200 feet should be cleared on each side of the highway to protect travellers and he appointed the first Justices of the Peace to make it stick.

Though wood was the principal source of London's fuel, open-cast coal had been used by the Romans, and was still in use. It was known as sea-coal, or pit-coal if mined, as against charcoal, another common fuel. In 1228 Sea-coal Lane went on record. In 1257 ships were offloading coal at London's quays.

By 1249 Aldermen were no longer drawn from a few families, but elected by ward freemen, though they still came from the rich merchant class. In 1291 a fishmonger infiltrated the closed circle of vintners, goldsmiths and the like., The Black Death came and went, taking nearly half the population, rivalries grew between guilds, taxes increased and the peasants revolted, Mayor Walworth knifing rebel Wat Tyler to death at Smithfield. In 1319 Edward II gave London the charter that established the guilds, reinforced the freedom, and encouraged liveries and prosperity.

The earliest fellowship touching on transport may well be the oldest. The Guild of Saddlers is recorded in an 1160 Convention which refers to 'custom of old'. The first charter was dated 1272, and the Company was incorporated in 1395.

The Loriners, who produced harness accessories, were next off the mark with a transport-related guild. In 1261 the *Liber Custumarum* records their first ordinances 'for the abatement of all frauds and deceits'.

The Farriers, or shoeing smiths, were recognised in 1356, when two 'the most sufficient and best knowing' were appointed to control the trade. Three years before that Edward III ordered householders on the 'alta via' from Temple Bar to Westminster to make up the roadside and pave the centre.

Meanwhile the Paviors (*pavire* = to ram or beat) worked to ordinances which were said to be 'old' in 1302 when four were 'sworn to make the pavement...most commodious for the public'. In 1479 proper ordinances were obtained.

In 1369 the City appointed four coal meters to measure coal straight from the ship. It was generally used in kilns and by smiths, who avoided burning it at night because 'an intolerable smell diffuses itself'. In 1376 a 'misterie' of Woodmongers was recorded.

In 1375 Guy de Stratford's cart was seized because it was 'Shodde with iron' against the ordinances. He was told not to drive a cart so 'shodde' in future. Two years later carts were ordered not to drive faster when empty than loaded. In 1413 the Sheriffs were ordered not to take Henry Cook's two carts – he was using them for the new work at Guildhall.

In 1391 the City repeated itself and again in 1485 when Common Council banned carts with long and square-headed nails to save the pavements. Guildhall held a sample flat nail and carmen copied it or paid the consequences. A year later Richard II deposed the Mayor and Sheriffs, for a year – the City sided with Lancastrian Henry eight years after that. Henceforth the guilds gained strength, Royal charters and corporate identities – with the power to own property in perpetuity.

In 1479 Common Council acted to stop carters blocking streets near Billings Gate. The inhabitants of Thames Street and Petty Wales had complained, and the City agreed that 'the common carters' were stopping everyone, including King, Queen, Mayor, Aldermen and merchants, from making their way between the church of St Magnus and the water gate near the Tower. In 1481 the 'disorders of carmen' still caused trouble.

By the reign of Richard III there were 28 livery halls. Small guilds disappeared, others merged, great guilds fought one another – sometimes literally. In 1516 the Court of Aldermen determined the order of existing guild precedence.

Throughout all this turmoil and civic change, carts came and went, traders carried their own goods from wharf to market, yet in 1502, twenty-six carmen alone sufficed to serve the City's needs, and no transport fraternity was recorded.

Back in 1300, four cart brokers had intercepted carriers outside the City, told them the monarch's men would seize their carts, and hired them for 15 shillings apiece. Once the deal was done, they let each cart to others for 30 shillings, making 100 shillings overall. That same year the law courts were reorganised into King's Bench, Common Pleas and Exchequer.

John and Richard de Kirketon, John 'Byndere' Bulychromp and Robert Staunford were caught, convicted and sent down. Their crime was to capitalise on the Royal prerogative – not a sensible move with a monarch dedicated to the rule of law.

The Crown had always commandeered what carts it needed and the goods required. London suffered the most. Royal purveyors afflicted all trades, carmen included. Inevitably, these officials were corrupt.

The Royal seal or commission stopped a carter in his tracks; sometimes a sword did the same job. The price of release to carry on carting was high. The alternative was to lose cart, carriage and custom. Officials or simple villains, the cart takers were a costly burden, so the City acted.

There were two kinds of cart – popular 12 × 3 ft carrs on two wheels for lane and hill, and long 14 ft carts, four feet wide, favoured by purveyors and cart takers. In 1512 the City ruled there should be 15 'carts of ffreemen', that each one should also have 'a carre' and that no one should use the one without having the other. Altogether 40 carrs were authorised to ply for hire.

Like most bad laws, it was unenforceable. London carmen did not need long carts and could not afford them for occasional Kingly needs. Suburban and provincial carters did need them for long haul work, so they were the ones the King's men sought.

What goes down also comes up. Because the horses and carts 'brynging ... vitailles to the Citie' were often seized 'for the kyng's Caryage', their owners thought twice about their journeys. When they did take the risk, they charged accordingly. 'Vitailles' got to be 'dere and of more excessyve price' – the cost of living rose.

Two years later the City tried another tack to solve another problem, again at the outside hauliers' expense. The problem was muck but there was no money in it and, when the century turned with the new Tudors, money mattered as England emerged from its feudal past into an era of commerce and enterprise.

Householders and merchants tossed their sewage into the street. Ward officials raked it up. Carters removed it outside the City walls. The pay was poor, the job nasty; the filth spread, the problem persisted.

The Aldermen decided that, whenever one of them needed gravel, sand or clay, the carters hauling good, clean dirt in should take noxious, nasty dirt out. To remove such 'Rubbush ordure dung or other fylthe' they paid twopence a load 'and no more uppon payn of Imprisonment'.

The suburban carters were not at all pleased. The job was not well or often done. Then along came Thomas Newman, an Innholder, and founder-Carman.

He got together with fourteen other freemen who 'with ther horses and cartes usen and occupyen commen carryage within this Citie', offered a triple service, against the right to organise their own fellowship.

On 19 March 1517 the Fraternity of Saint Katherine the Virgin and Martyr of Carters was born. The Carmen had come to town. Good King Hal was on the throne, Columbus, Cabot and da Gama had but recently opened up the oceans; the world was turning.

In fact, each of the fourteen was already a freeman. Thomas Bonde was a Tallow Chandler, John Hatton a Skinner and Robert Anderson a Salter. Apart from Newman, Christopher Arundell and Edward Tomlynson were also Innholders – a guild established but two years earlier.

There were two Greytawyers – James Richardson and Bartholomew Worrell; Tailor John Briggs, Saddler John Scott and Brewer John Ranewyke. Thomas Cure was aptly named as a Brownbaker, while John Hills was a Coffermaker and John Wrytsam a Fuller. As a Woodmonger, Robert Hammond presaged future events.

The contract gave them the right to 'use themselves as brethren of one ffeliship and ffraternyte' to take on more freemen, to elect four of their number to govern the guild. They were given the sole right to occupy within the City 'any carre or carte for commen carriage' although other freemen could still cart their own goods.

Carters outside the City could join, and be guaranteed freedom from the King's cart takers and victuallers could also join: though their carts might still be commandeered, their horse, harness and servants would not.

The service the Carmen offered the City was threefold. Given reasonable warning, they would 'provyde horses and cartes able and sufficient to s[er]ve the Kyng in careyng his wyne ale or oder Stuff'.

To the relief of the Aldermen, they agreed to 'clense, purge and kepe clene' the streets and lanes of the City and the suburbs 'of Donge or other filth' for agreed prices.

Finally they promised to move wine, wood, oil 'and other wares and merchaundyses' from wharf to market and wherever else they were needed within the City and its suburbs, at prices to be agreed. That included 'colwood billet ffagott' but 'cooles only excepted'.

The fellowship was modelled on existing guild practice, as far as it went, but it was far from perfect. It was different in several respects, and the difference stemmed from its trade. Carting was a relatively unskilled industry, it was common to all other trades, and it was less geographically focused.

Carmen had no regulatory powers over carters who plied for hire within the City. There were no precise criteria for membership, which was uniquely open to outsiders from without the City walls. Other traders could own carts; other guildsmen could join the Carmen's fellowship. And 'coliers which dayly or weekly resorte unto the seid Citie' got a special rate of quarterage.

Two vehicle types were mentioned: 'cartes' and 'waynes'. The deal was struck between the 'Lord Mayre and his brethren' and the 'New bretherhod or ffraternyte', which was bound to the Chamberlain of London.

By 1527 the Fraternity was falling down on the job. Carmen were over-charging, there were not enough long carts for Royal service, outside carters were boycotting the City, causing shortages. The next year Scott, Anderson and Cure led moves with Royal officers, victuallers, colliers and fuellers towards new rules. In 1529 the Fraternity was incorporated by Act of Common Council.

The new regulations laid down that carters would have their carts marked 'with the sworde crowned' and on six weeks' warning, would make them available or pay a fine of 20 shillings, half of which went to the Brotherhood of St Katherine.

Carmen could no longer let their carts out, or allow anyone other than their own staff to operate them unless the Guild Wardens agreed. Woodmongers with wharves were restricted to one cart each, to be marked with 'a sworde and the sygne of a ffaggott' and had to join the Brotherhood. Those that raked the muck for a Ward had access to a cart, also suitably marked, and needs must join the Fellowship too.

Two carts were to be set aside to 'serve the chamber' and let out to no one – if they were they would be forfeited – and the Mayor and Aldermen were no longer to grant carrooms, originally cart standings from which carters plied for hire, then licences, or the right to operate for hire. No car was to be admitted or marked unless it was entered in Guildhall as well as in the Wardens' records. The cost of marking was fourpence, half to the Guild.

'The Masters of the saide Brotherhood' were to choose two 'honeste men' to bear staves and send the carts for Royal service, without bribes or favouritism, on pain of losing their jobs, and unspecified punishment. They were to be paid eightpence a week – and if they behaved themselves they had a job for life.

Thus the woodmongers and muckrakers and the materials carriers all had to join the Carmen, and the City tried to stop the grant of carrooms.

Transport crosses all trades. It is catholic in its intentions and in its activities. It was too much to hope the new Guild could cover allcomers and all contingencies. As trade grew, so did the industry, and the Carmen's Guild gradually lost control.

ABOVE: Primitive carts succeeded the sledges first used to haul freight, and lasted in southern Europe until the 19th century. (RS) BELOW: The Thames was the City's mediaeval highway, with oar and sail power evident by the Savoy Palace, recreated by Christopher Hughes. (CB)

ABOVE: Billings Gate was a principal quay for the lightermen of the middle ages – another Hughes reconstruction. (CB) BELOW: A 14th century carriage and a reaper's cart showed little advance in vehicle design: from the *Louterell Psalter*. (RS)

3
LESSONS

The Even Carriage betweene two Factions,
proceedeth not alwaies of Moderation,
but of a Truenesse to a Mans Selfe.

Francis Bacon: *The Essays or Counsells Civill and Morall* 1596

Woodmongers, forced by the same rules to join the Carmen, swamped it. Founder Hammond was a Woodmonger. Scott was one by 1528. A difficult man, he was accused of calling a Sheriff and an Alderman 'ffalse pollyng knaves' and admitted he could not remember what he said – 'I had been at the Tavern all morning'. He had to walk the streets barelegged, saying 'I was known in the City before. And now I will be better known'. He promised to provide carts for the Crown, which he did. So did other Woodmongers.

The Crown controlled imports. All dutiable cargo had to land at the Legal Quays. These twenty quays lay between London Bridge and the Tower. Here were the principal wharves, warehouses, the merchants – and the Woodmongers.

During the 16th century the number of 'official' carrs shot up tenfold – from forty to four hundred. On top of that, many carriers operated outside the system, and Aldermen flouted the 1528 rules, granting carrooms to their friends.

The Woodmongers outnumbered Carmen, so they became principal purveyors to the Crown. In 1536 they were subject to City control, for 'creating a scarcity of fire wood'. In 1546 the Court of Aldermen decreed that anyone operating a wharf big enough to operate long carts should maintain at least one (so it could be pressed into Royal service). In return the wharfinger, usually a Woodmonger, could operate two carrs – one for fuel, and the other for general carriage.

The Woodmongers virtually ignored the requirements but exploited their advantage, undermining the Carmen's trade and their Fraternity. Now there were two transport guilds and the Woodmongers were the larger. Their membership overlapped. Woodmonger Nicholas Pyggott was a warden of the Fraternity of St Katherine in 1548.

Things went from bad to worse in 1549 when the Aldermen told the Carmen 'to be obedient...and to comen redilly at all tymes at the lawfull somons of the... Woodmongers'. By then the Woodmongers shared Guildhall's responsibility for marking and recording carrs, and for registering carrooms.

It was a time of turmoil for, under Mary, Catholicism was restored, and the people were restless. At Guildhall Mary secured City support against Wyatt's rebellion – 25,000 freemen enrolled, Wyatt was crushed. In 1558 England lost Calais – the last Continental outpost of empire, and Mary died. Elizabeth Tudor reigned.

The next year the new Queen rode in majesty through the City – the streets were thronged by 'her most loving people' and 'to the high end of Cheap' lined by the liveried Companies. When she received 1,000 marks in gold she told the Mayor 'his brethren and you all' that she would be their 'good lady and queen'.

The next thirty years cost a good deal more than 1,000 marks, as the City paid and paid again for ships and soldiers and supplies for their 'good lady'. In return she kept the peace, and they prospered.

The Queen might ride in majesty. Ordinary people walked, and the wealthy were conveyed in litters or on horseback. Then the coach made its appearance, somewhat against the tide, for it was initially regarded as effete. John Lyly wrote in 1584:

'In a sin-guilt coach, not closely pent,
Jogging along the hard pavement.'

The first vehicles were waggons with decorations. Carts were even simpler.

In 1580 the Carmen's fellowship was swallowed up by the Woodmongers – but it proved an indigestible dish. Trade, unemployment, inflation, transport all increased – and so did the population. London housed less than 50,000 when the Carmen created their Fellowship; when Mary died, 90,000. By the end of the century the population touched 250,000.

That year the City sought to restrict development, after a Royal decree against new housing within three miles of the walls. Southwark was City property from 1550 but its people were not citizens of London. The restriction failed.

Within the City, control remained within the wards and through the liveries. And the City did succeed in social provision. It endowed hospitals for the sick, infirm, insane, and one for the education of orphans – Christ's Hospital. Merchants and liveries established other schools throughout the country.

In 1575 'wood being grown to dearth', coal rose in value. By 1612 it was the general fuel due to spoliation of forests and Stow reported 'the great expence of timber for Navigation...the neglect of planting of woods'. By 1640 the Woodmongers were said to be 'very much decayed' with 'not above seven persons of the whole Company that trade in wood'. Given their hold over carrs and carting, and their widespread control of wharves, this stretches credulity.

The Woodmongers had long since nominated cart takers and advised the City on regulating stands and reducing carrs. Then, in 1580 it was agreed to ratify 'certayne orders devysed by the...Woodmongers' aimed at restricting the number of Carmen and for 'better government of thyre companye and of carremen wythin the same cyttye'.

Referring to the Carmen's 'unrulynes and dysorders', the current 400 carrs were to be reduced at the whim of Lord Mayor and Aldermen. To ensure their 'better government' all Carmen were to be 'under the governance of the Master and Wardens of the Company of Woodmongers'. The Fraternity of St Katherine had lost its independence.

All Carmen were to become Woodmongers, pay them twopence quarterage, attend Woodmongers' Hall, and hire employees for a minimum term of five years. The Woodmongers also gained the power of search whenever Carmen were suspected of negligence. Draconian fines and then prison awaited any Carman who failed to appear when required, or overcharged.

The outside carters were to be eliminated – as they fell away, freemen were to replace them. No new 'foreigners' would be permitted rights of carriage within the City. Existing outsiders could only run one cart.

Carmen who failed to meet their obligations would lose their licences 'for ever' unless they produced sureties.

The Royal arrangements were reviewed. The original two long carts had somehow escalated to sixteen, used to purvey the Queen's wine. It was agreed these be halved, provided that, if the Crown proved greater need, the shortfall would be met by the Company.

Overall, the City sought to protect Carmen by imposing conditions on the Woodmongers, that they too kept the ordinances, observed the authority's price scale for fuel, and neither created nor implemented any ordinance that bound Carmen, other than those the City decreed.

Thus the Fraternity survived, if not in name, in fact, though it had lost all control of its own affairs. At the same time, for the first time, the City recognised transport as a trade, sought its regulation *a priori* over the Queen's needs and pulled the Fellowship into line with other guilds.

If the Carmen had lost control, so soon did the Woodmongers. The City coveted revenue from those who held carrooms; the Carmen coveted freedom from the oppressive Woodmongers. Once more, three individuals saw a way out.

Robert Shardlowe, William Cornewall and Edward Drane found a way to help themselves by helping others. They approached Christ's Hospital. The young school was short of income. The City was hard pressed to fund it. In 1582 the Court of Aldermen agreed that Christ's Hospital should have 'the rule charge oversyght and government of all the Carts Carres and Carmen' within the City and suburbs, and the income that the Woodmongers had enjoyed would now go to 'the relyefe of the pore children'.

Christ's Hospital took over the sealing of carrs, and that cost Carmen a penny a year. A new carr cost fivepence, for 'chip and brass', which showed the cart number and its use. Each year was signified by a letter of the alphabet, branded onto the cart.

All fines went to the school and – this was the nub of the deal – every Carman, carter or Woodmonger paid a quarterly rental of 6s 8d too.

Christ's Hospital took its duties seriously. A sealing house was built 'within the Towne diche' for the Governors and Master Carmen. A furnace was provided, irons for branding, 'three basketts of great Coles' and six quires of paper – presumably to record matters. The initial outlay totalled £10 17s 3d, most of it on the building.

Shardlowe, Cornewall and Drane were rewarded with four pounds apiece as 'certaine honest and painefull men' for their 'great travailes, expenses, painstaking forwardness' in helping the Governors and 'bringinge this benefitte to Christ's Hospital'. The trio joined the staff as pensioners, and to seal carrs and collect dues.

The school looked after its new charges too. Carman Steven Randall broke his leg when he was carrying goods on his back. 'Beeing without ffreinds and money' he was given 16s 5d. 'A poore Carremannes widow' Goodwife Greswell received 13s 4d annual relief.

A handsome profit went to the school: £153 16s 5d in the first year, £223 14s 10d by 1597–8. It was hard earned, for the Hospital found the business of running the Carmen 'verie troublesome'.

The Woodmongers acted. They went over the City's head to the Crown. They took their grievances to the Board of Green Cloth, which handled the purveyance of goods to the Royal household. The school paid annual pensions to some purveyors, and settled some phoney bills 'to satisfye' the claimants but 'not by waie of right', deftly sidestepping the issue without giving much away.

Thus stymied, the Woodmongers appealed – to the Court of Aldermen. On 2 July 1586 an Act of Common Council confirmed the 1582 decree, and expanded it. The Woodmongers were foiled.

Christ's Hospital retained control. It was to liaise with the Queen's purveyors as required. Services to the City, carrooms for long cart owners, Woodmongers' duty to provide long carts, were all renewed. Two cart takers were to be appointed. Significantly, the Royal service was for the first time sensibly limited. Long carts should not be sought 'except therebe great necessite'.

Robert Fletcher was yeoman purveyor of carriages and chief cart taker to the Queen and her successor, for thirty years. He wrote of his fellow cart takers in 1605. 'Thomas Knarisbrough, Grome, a notable bribing and corrupt carttaker' and 'Edward Coosyn, a most sly suttle and cunnine brybing wretchid fellowe, an usurer verie crewell'. John Bremell, known as Cutts, was 'a common gamster, cuning cheater'.

Cart takers commandeered carts daily 'whether there be cause or no cause', and took money 'continewally'. They would 'steale upon an ignorant carter' who had loaded up for an out of town trip, tell him to unload, load up with drink for the Court, showing their seal or commission. 'The poor man drawith his purs and payeth £5, £4, 5 marks etc' to be free of the cart taker. Commented Fletcher: 'A nakid sword were even as lawfull'.

So widespread was this practice that sermons were preached against the cart takers, in front of the monarch, and again before 'all the lords in the chapel at Whytehall, when her late majesties corps lay there not interid'.

From 1586 Carmen would serve the Queen when 'her highness doth remove from one of her howses' in London, and then only carrs would be used, 'without the ... provision of any longe Carrts'. Carmen's staff would henceforth be apprenticed – a new departure. The school would be told, and also when they moved to another master.

Even so, the Royal service could be onerous. One of the Queen's 'removes' required over 400 carts. In one year alone, 600,000 gallons of beer and ale were carried from City to Court.

Carmen's interests in long-haul traffic were explored and protected. Except for great fairs, provincial carters could not work out of London. The exceptions were Norwich, Cambridge and similar town's carriers, who regularly serviced the City with goods inward; they were allowed to take as much, and no more, back out again. By the same token, Carmen were forbidden to subcontract once outside the City gates.

Then the Act broke new ground. For the first time, transport was seen as something beyond the interest of Queen, City or carters. It touched society, affected people's lives, their safety and their wellbeing.

The City recognised new needs. Noise would be abated. No Carman might leave his cart in the street at night. Speed was dangerous. A Carman must not 'ryde or drive his horse ... in a more speedie course or pace than is usuall'. Children were at risk – and old people. Carmen should always lead their horses by the collar, 'with a speciall regarde always as well before him as behinde him as well for children as for aged people'. If he did not, he was fined twelve pence or lost halter or collar 'beside further punishment'.

Echoes of long past regulation were reinforced, to save road damage and expense, and proper servicing was encouraged. Carts shod with iron, with iron plates or nails on their wheels, or those 'heard to Creake or Pype for drines and want of greasinge in the Nave' would cost their operators special fines.

Above all, traffic congestion was addressed. 'Thames Strete and other Narrowe lanes' were 'pestered many tymes' with long carts, drays and carrs in both directions, and 'soe muche the more by wilfulness' of their operators, most of whom 'will not take paynes to put back...for the ease of one another'. Carmen simply would not give way. Offenders would go to prison, and lose their carts for a month.

Similarly, Cheapside and other streets were clogged with empty carts touting for custom, difficult to pass 'without troble and daunger to be hurte'. Accordingly, stands were specified, and the numbers of carts varied according to market days. For instance, Little Conduit in Cheap could hold four carrs at all times, but near Friday Street in Cheap only three were allowed, 'when market is done'. Great Conduit in Cheapside accommodated ten carrs, reduced to four in market time.

Stands were allocated near Broad Street, in Cornhill, towards and in Birchin Lane, at Leadenhall, Lime Street, near Fen Church, at Aldgate Pump, Gracechurch, Eastcheap, Newgate Market, and at or near the Cardinal Hat without Newgate.

Christ's Hospital was caring; rent arrears were extended, but fines were not imposed. Most of the defaulters were Carmen. By contrast, the Woodmongers had compounded their dues at £52 10s annually – the school used the cash to hire carters for the Royal service – but they lacked long carts. In 1596 the Woodmongers and wharf keepers came before the Court of Christ's Hospital to be reminded they should provide these carts according to the rules.

By 1598 the school had got tougher. Carmen were made to pay their arrears – only one per cent got away with it, where initially ten per cent failed to pay. The number of carts was reduced to fifty. Unfortunately, paying more and operating less coincided with recession. The Carman's lot was not a happy one.

In 1600 the Carmen went to court – in common cause with the Woodmongers. They won a suit in the Court of King's Bench. The details are not recorded, but the gist was in line with other judgements of the time – that unskilled trades should not be restrained.

Christ's Hospital appealed to the Privy Council. The City approved: 'that uncivell and disordered Companie of Carmen' had called into question the City's ordinances and Acts. These were sensible, carefully designed, liaised with the Crown, and had applied for seventy years, to good effect and without complaint – so long as the Carmen benefited.

Once Christ's Hospital had taken over, and profits went to help 'many poore and small children', Carmen sought 'by all meanes to overthrows theis orders'. The Court had rejected the authority of the ordinances and Acts, and thus granted Carmen 'libertie...to take what course they like best'. The result, the City said, would be no order or government at all.

Transport chaos, loss of school income and worst of all, civic anarchy would result: it was suspected that the Carmen's lead was being followed by the Horners and the Watermen, who were suing their superiors for implementing their ordinances.

'Our humble desire therefore ys that your Lordshipps would be pleased to take some spedye Course' to put the Carmen firmly back under control, so their example did not encourage 'other turbulent and contradictinge spiritts' to run amok and make a mockery of the City's writ.

The Privy Council tried to please everyone. It supported the City's ordinances and warned the Carmen that they broke the by-laws at their own risk. It took no action whatsoever against them.

Woodmongers and Carmen accordingly defied Christ's Hospital. At its 1603 Court, Carmen refused to be bound by the ordinances. For two years they 'paid nothing to the use of this house'.

Robert Shardlowe had received £10 annually out of 'profitts of the Carrs'. Now he had none. He petitioned the school and it paid him £5. Even when the Carmen departed, it kept up his salary, took in his two-year-old child and, when he died, gave his widow a lump sum. They even maintained old Carmen's pensions, even though they no longer received carr rents.

Until now, ships offloaded coal onto the wharves; as consumption grew, ships grew larger and more numerous. The quays could not accommodate them, so lighters took up the loads. The coal merchants of the century were fuellers – Woodmongers.

However, just as physical control of coal imports passed from shore-based Woodmongers to Thames-borne Watermen, so timber was being replaced by coal. Most of that came from Newcastle, by sea to London's wharves. The guild system was about to be rocked by a new brand of entrepeneur.

For the time being, the Woodmongers held most of the cards, and carrs. The Carmen wanted a limit to the carrs available. The Woodmongers did not. They wanted as many as their trade demanded, and more for hire. Given the Court ruling, which suspended the City's authority over transport, the Woodmongers exploited the market. The City had no choice. It bowed to their demands.

On 22 October 1605, the 1586 Act was annulled and the Carmen once more put under Woodmonger control, two months after they were brought together in 'one bodye Corporate'.

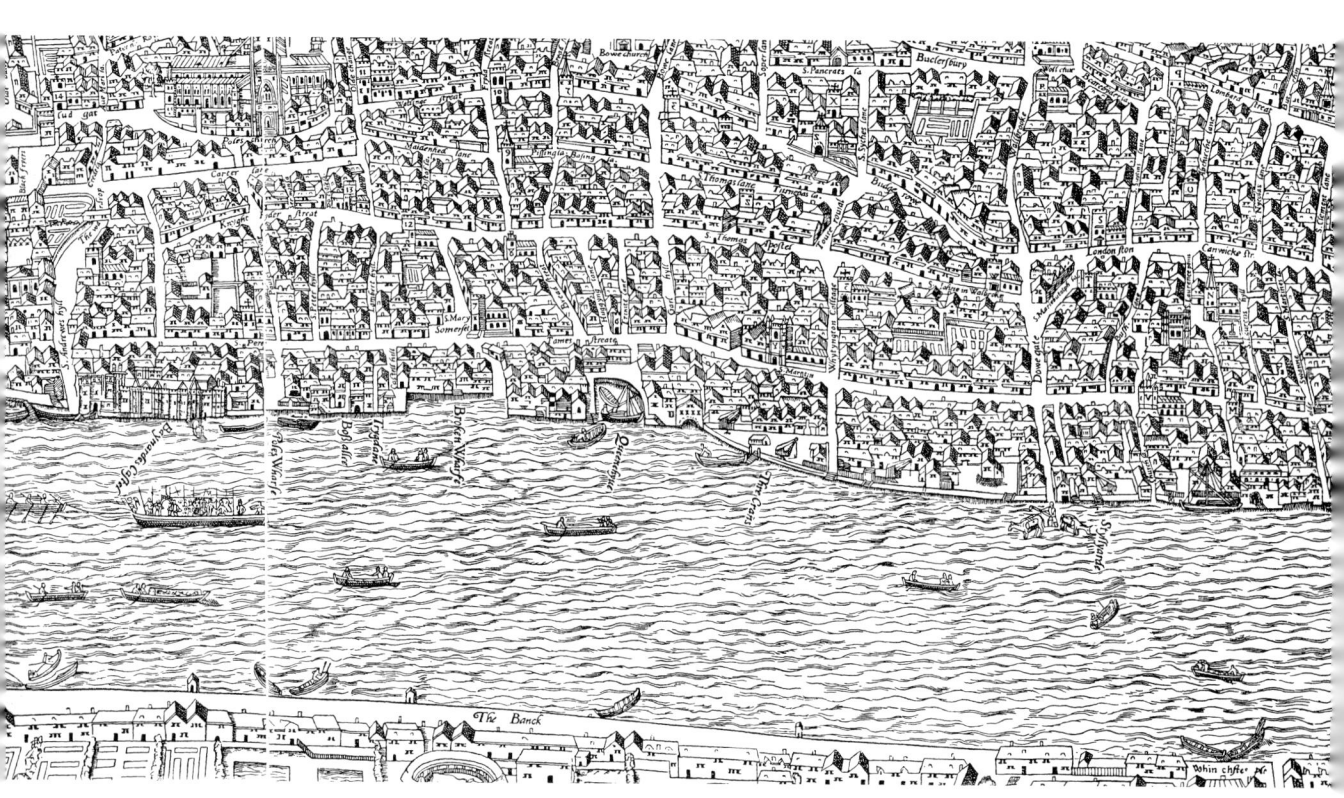

The 1562 'Agas', map shows Thames Street, the 'home' of London's Carmen, running left to right above the river. (GL)

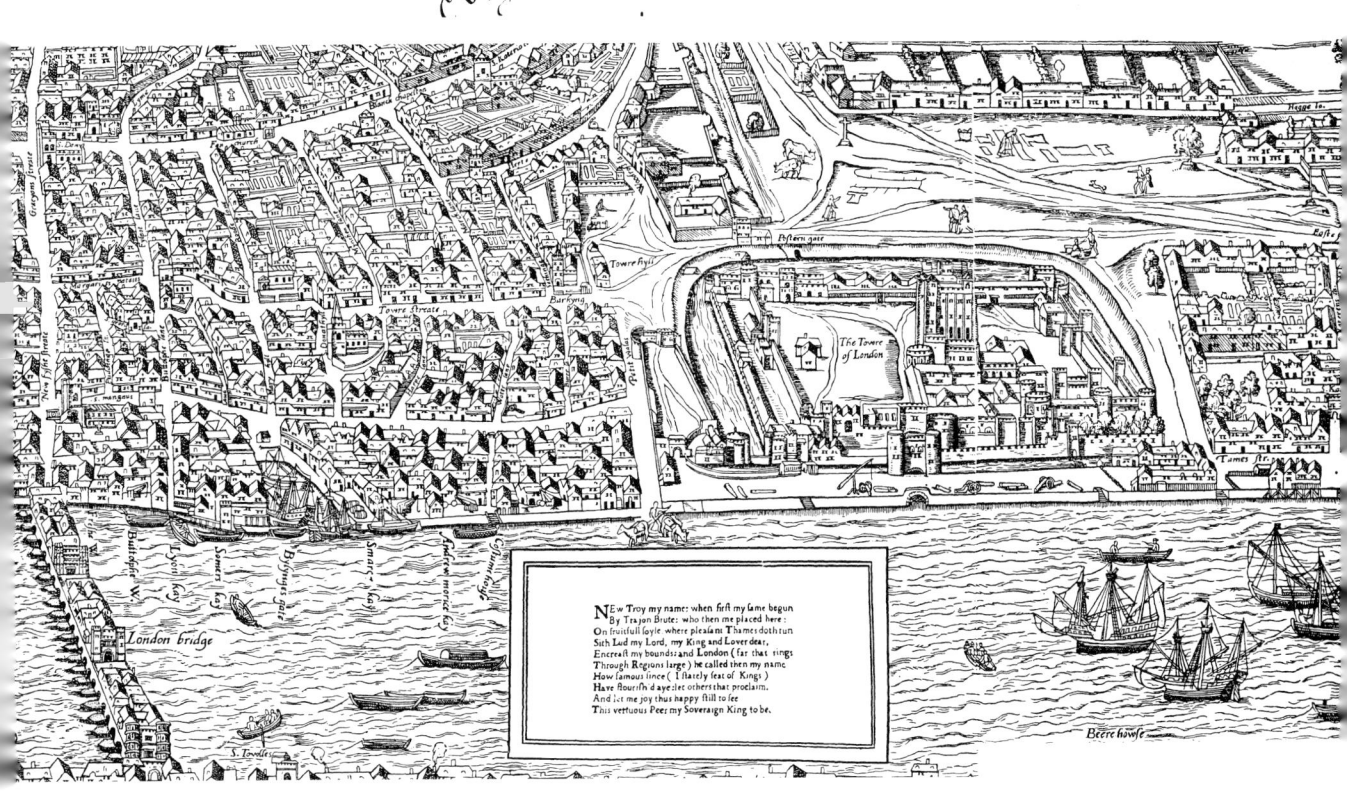

The Carmen's 1528 ordinances start like this. (GRO)

ABOVE: Details from the 'Agas' map give us (1) Harp Lane, where Carmen briefly had a hall, (2) the infamous St Magnus Corner, and (3) Woodmongers' Hall below Ryder Street. (GL) RIGHT: A later engraving shows 'Old Queenhithe Steps', the centre of the Legal Quays, and possibly the original Thames trade wharf, as it appeared in the 17th century. (GL) BELOW: The Carmen swore this Oath in 1582. (CC)

The Oath of every Person at his first Admittance into the Brotherhood or Fellowship of CARMEN *of the City of* London; *To be administred by the Wardens and Assistants of the said Fellowship or Brotherhood for the time being.*

YOU shall swear, You shall be true to our Sovereign Lord the King and his Successors. You shall be obedient to the President or Governours of *Christ's Hospital*, and to such in whom the City shall hereafter place the Government of Carrs by the Act of *Common Council*, and to the *Wardens* for the time present. You shall not discover the lawful Council of this Fraternity. You shall not take a Forreignman into your Service, but only such as use the Occupation of a Carman, or else an Apprentice duly bound without Fraud: At the beginning of their Terms or before, you shall bring and present them before the *Wardens* of the said Fellowship for the time being, and here have the Indentures to be made, and every such Apprentice to be inrolled within the first Year, as the Custom is. You shall not entice or withdraw any Man's Servant of this Society, until that reasonable departing be made with his said Master.

THESE and all other good Rules made, and to be made, not reversed; You shall keep so near as God give you Grace.

So help you God, &c.

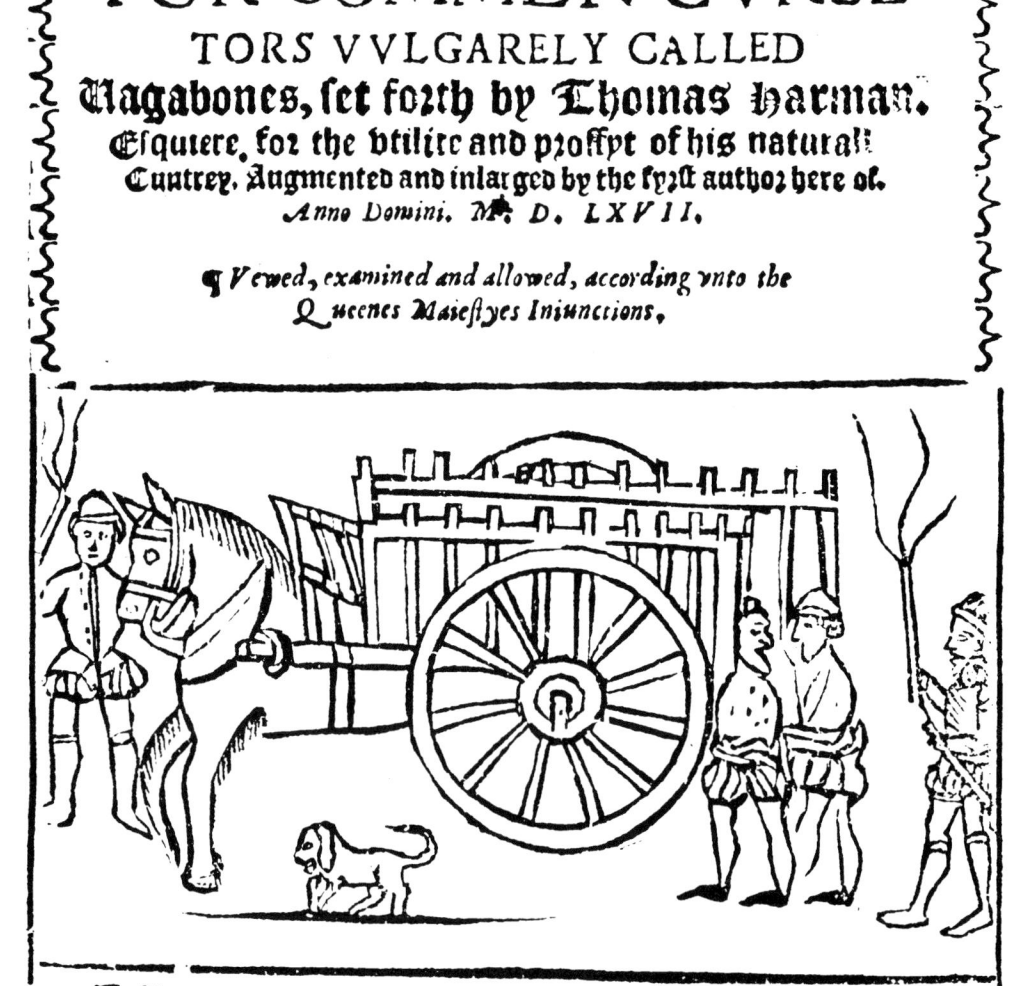

Thomas Harman's 1567 *A Caveat of Warening for Common Cursetors vulgarely called Vagabones* published 'in Fletestreete at the Signe of the Falcon: depicted a Carman's cart, at the tail of which they were whipped. (BL)

4
CONFLICT

Three Jog on, jog on the foot-path way,
And merrily hent the stile-a;
A merry heart goes all the day,
Your sad tires in a mile-a.

Shakespeare: *A Winter's Tale* 1611

The Carmen's first Royal charter was signed on 29 August 1605.

It was a false dawn. Proudly it recorded 'the humble petition of the Woodmongers and Carremen of the said Company within the Citye of London and the Suburbes thereof', and went on to state 'all and singular the Woodmongers and Carrmen' should be 'one bodye Corporate and pollitique in deede and name'.

The Stuarts now held sway, and the Bible was published in English in the 'Authorised Version'. That same year Catesby led the so-called Gunpowder Plot. When it was exposed, The City lit bonfires in 1605 in support of King James.

He appointed the first Master, Wardens and Assistants of the new Company, with the power to name their successors. They were all Woodmongers. He also gave them the gift of carrooms, and the right to regulate Carmen, while the Carmen had no choice but to obey their oaths as freemen, which forbade rebellion.

There was no route to power either, since the Woodmongers kept the number of Carmen to a minority, and that kept them out of office.

The Company paid Christ's Hospital £150 annually – less than their previous profits. Car rents were halved to 13s 4d while quarterage was fixed at 1s – a nett gain to Carmen of 9s 4d *per annum* but a transient one.

In 1606 the City ruled that any freeman carrier who refused to join would go to prison. In Newgate they could either relent, or 'become bound not to use any Carres' within the City. In other words: 'Join, suffer or lose your licence.' The Carmen wasted no time. In 1606 they petitioned the Privy Council. The Lord Mayor was not pleased: 'nothinge but manifest untruthes impudently suggested by some fewe of the Carmen' and 'scandalous false allegacons'. In 1607 the ordinances were confirmed in the King's Bench and Court of Common Pleas. That should have put a stop to any lawsuits. In 1608 the Privy Council reinforced the rules, even stating that any one who took the Company to law would have to answer to them.

That did not stop the Carmen either. They were encouraged by Henry Doyley, a lawyer of Lincoln's Inn, adviser to the Woodmongers, and an expert at playing both ends to the middle. He suggested the Carmen be sued in Star Chamber – the court for matters of illegal assembly – and at the same time became standing counsel to the Carmen too.

They paid Doyley a load of coal monthly, and he kept them posted, egging them on, saying the ordinances were 'of noe force or validitie', could be safely ignored and he himself 'would adnull and overthrowe the same whensoever him pleased'.

In 1610 Parliament attempted to negotiate terms with King James, including the removal of rights of purveyance.

In 1611 both Woodmongers and Carmen went to law. The Carmen were careful. They did not attack the Company, and did not act in concert. They backed Thomas Acres, who sued the Clerk, James Harrison. They claimed he was corrupt, evil, had been sacked from Bridewell for lewd behaviour and had got them to sign the ordinances by false pretences.

The Master, Wardens and Fellowship of Woodmongers counter-sued Richard Kitchen and other Carmen for 'unlawful assemblies' designed to 'overthrowe the Charter, ordinances and government' of the Company.

The Carmen's case was financial. Harrison, they said, had 'craftelye and deceiptfully' framed the rules to extract 'unconscionable ffees' for his own profit and that of 'his complices'. They accused him of setting the terms to extract fees, quarterage and licences of some four hundred pounds each year, and then writing this down in a book which he kept to himself.

At the Company's meetings, they alleged, he produced a different book which excluded these sums and provisions, read the revised ordinances, which were approved, 'and beinge most of them unlearned' they 'did sette theire hands and marks to the sayde writings'.

Not content with that, Harrison, the Carmen alleged, 'did corruptly and deceitfully raze the said wrytinge', altered it and inserted new penalties for those who flouted 'his' rules.

The Company took a different view. 'The disorders and abuses of Carrmen...was like to grow from badd to worse', whatever the Company did. The Master and Wardens were 'terrified from putting their said lawes and statutes in execucon' against the Carmen, who were contemptuous, disobedient and prosecuted 'malicious and unjust suits'.

Star Chamber passed the buck to the City. The Lord Mayor and Aldermen found for the Company. They found Acres' complaint 'causeles and unjust' and that Acres was a front, a mere kennel raker, pushed by others to slander the Clerk.

The Company's cause was just, the Carmen apparently 'turbulent' but, as they were 'poore men and have acknowledged their faults', no more should be done.

Star Chamber dismissed both suits. Within a year the Aldermen were dealing with an errant carpenter, Richard Wyatt, when they warned that everyone, in or out of the Company, should pay the same fees. Clearly not every carter had joined up, despite the edicts, and equally clearly, someone was on the fiddle. Two years on, the City examined the books, and Carmen had to pay their fees through the City Auditor *pro tem.*

By now the City was a significant financial player. Fifty-six companies backed the Virginia colony in 1609, and by 1612 Ireland was a centre for investment. London's growth increased freemen, and the cost of redemption fell. Patrimony meant more citizens without trade links. The companies began to turn from specific trades to social intervention and government.

In 1617 Common Council acted to control traffic. Claiming the 'disorder and rude behaviour of Carmen', the Council found that 'mann woomen and children have been indangered' and some lost their lives because carrs, carts and drays blocked the streets and passages.

They found that operators were careless. The great and good were discommoded since Carmen hindered 'great personages of the Realme' on their way to see the King. More to the point, 'Inhabitants of sondrey streetes' like Thames Street and London Bridge 'are soe pestered with the stoppinge of Carres against their shoppes' as to hinder trade and endanger their households.

The most serious complaint was that 'Carremen meeting one another in narrowe streetes... are soe churlish to one another as that they will not make waye'. The answer was the one-way street.

The rules laid down lasted for two centuries. They were long overdue. Cart stands in 1586 were near the markets; now trade focused on the docks. New stands were located in Philpot Lane, Little Eastcheap, Botolph Lane, Fenchurch Street, Mincing Lane, Mark Lane, Crutched Friars and Tower Street.

To ease congestion, loaded carts left Thames Street by St Dunstan's, St Mary, Garlick and Bread Street Hills and the hill from Tower Dock to the east end of Tower Street.

Empty carrs had to approach Tower Street by Fish Street Hill, Whittington Lane, Wardrobe Hill, and these Lanes – Water, Harp, Botolph, Pudding, St Michael's, St Martin's, St Lawrence Pountney, Bush, Trinity and Huggin.

The age-old problem of free passage from St Magnus to the Tower was revisited. Carters and Carmen were forbidden to enter Thames Street by St Magnus corner before being hired. The penalty: 2s 6d for the first offence, 5s the second, 'and to be disabled from using a Carr'. To ease pedestrian access, a bar was erected near the corner, and it was staffed at the expense of Thames Street residents; only laden carts could pass. For over a century Carmen were fined for 'coming in at St Magnus'.

Traffic was henceforth controlled on the spot. The Woodmongers were ordered to appoint three officers to handle traffic between St Magnus and the Tower, another to control London Bridge, and two more to supervise the stands.

Horses were not to be fed in the street. Carmen had to maintain a car-length gap between carts. They could not ride on their carts, let horses go unled, or use a leading rein over three feet.

The Woodmongers were told to restrict carts to 400 – and that included wharf carrs. It led to untold conflict and arguments before Lord Mayor, Common Council, King's Bench, Privy Council, the House of Commons and Star Chamber. The wharfingers wanted the right to carrooms, and the abolition of carrooms' property rights. Carmen joined Woodmongers in fighting this heresy.

Restricting carts had some merit, if the Venetian Ambassador was to be believed. In a despatch of 1618 he coupled the rude Carmen with the naughty apprentices: 'the great devils and the little devils'.

The carts 'do not choose to yield' when they meet 'the coaches of the gentry'. The imps 'that is to say shop boys' on Shrove Tuesday and May Day went wild 'committing outrages in every direction', killing people and demolishing houses, especially in the suburbs.

Of the carts 'there is such a multitude of them, large and small... it would be impossible to estimate'. City carts were largely two-wheeled and carried beer, coal, wood – or dung. The dung carters were 'the most insolent fellows'. Four-wheeled waggons from upcountry brought goods and people 'iggledy-piggledy' drawn by seven or eight horses in file, plumed, belled and with 'embroidered cloth coverings'.

As the century had turned, habits had changed. Increasing demand meant coal replaced wood and Woodmongers were sometimes called fuellers. From 12,000 tons in 1580, coal consumption rose to 74,000 tons in 1606. Wood was expensive, but charcoal and faggots from the country held prices within reason. Coal was different. It all came in through dockland. The wharfingers held a monopoly.

Coal merchants grew in power; they sought carrooms and wharves. Within the Company, Carmen and Woodmongers held all the aces. Fuellers needed their carts and they needed their carrooms. With the latest restrictions, values shot up. A carroom could fetch £50 or £60. As property they could be bought and sold, used as collateral, bequeathed – they were a good investment. Many were owned by outsiders, who then rented them to those who used carts.

Wharfingers claimed the right to move their goods independently, without licence by the Woodmongers. The Company impounded their carts. This became a way of life.

When the Company sued John Blinkorne in 1618, Lord Chief Justice Montagu ruled that 400 was the limit and any surplus 'shalbe abated and put down'. He further decreed that wharfingers should have prior claim to carrooms over other trades, but only through the Company and only within the 400 'for there are noe carroomes to be claymed as appurtenant to their Wharffs (as some would pretend)'.

Finally, he stated that those wharfingers who had legitimate carts could not 'stand with them or worke them in the streets'.

The wharfingers reacted by refusing to pay rent or capital for carrooms. The Woodmongers could not win. If they gave the carrooms away, they destroyed an asset base of £25,000, lost their own advantage in the coal trade and damaged their associate Carmen. If they stood their ground, they disobeyed the Court.

They stood their ground, and the wharfingers appealed to the King. The dispute raged for seven years. The wharfingers pushed for legislation to eliminate the system, but failed. Star Chamber broke the deadlock – and found for the wharfmen.

In February 1625 the Court confirmed 400 carrs as the maximum, and allocated a fixed number to the wharfingers – 140. The rest were retained by the Company. The wharfingers' carts were not tied to any one wharf, but they could not work the streets either.

Speculating in carrooms ceased. No one could have more than one street carr in his first four years as a freeman, and then only two until he had served as Master or Warden, when three were allowed. Carrooms could only be hired to wharfingers to carry fuel – and they lost their property rights.

When a carroom owner died, his carroom 'shalbe within fowerteene dayes disposed of' by the Company, first to wharfingers (within the 140) and last to those who had sold carrooms from their wharves and then to Carmen who had served their articles 'and be fittest men to have a roome'.

The cost of entry was held at twenty shillings, apart from the annual cost of 17s 4d. To protect Carmen's widows, they were granted a life interest on their husband's deaths – 'unless she do after marrye a fforeyner'.

Non-freemen carters must join the Company upon becoming free; wharfingers must join or forfeit their right to use carts; freemen of other companies with carts need not join, but must abide by the Company's rules.

Carters operating from Southwark and other neighbouring suburbs might 'bringe in their lodinge into the said Citty for necessary supply there of' but they must return empty, and not ply for hire. Millers and bakers were expressly forbidden from carrying fuel in their grain carts.

The dispute was over, but the Carmen were in trouble. They were already unhappy with the £2 levied to fund legal costs. There were accusations of bribery. When these were referred to the Recorder, his wife was accused of receiving a gilt cup from the

Company. Attorney General Sir Henry Yelverton was 'bought' and, when the City stepped in, the Woodmongers 'to prevent the ending of the cause proffered the Lord Mayor a bribe of great value'.

Sir William Cockaine refused to be bought, so the Company turned to the Lord Chief Justice and their accusers sneered: 'because the Lord Mayor would not take a guilt cup...hee was no more to be trusted...'.

The Woodmongers now tightened their grip on street carrs through control of carrooms. The coal trade was growing and coal merchants dominated the Company. They needed to, since they could not stop newcomers to the cart trade.

One merchant, Thomas Morley, was charged in 1607 for running a coal cartel. He was not a fueller or a carter. In 1620 he held nine carrooms. By 1625 he was a Warden of the Woodmongers.

The Company's officers used the Star Chamber decree to take over carrooms as they fell vacant, give them to friends or, and then only rarely, to Carmen who toed the line. Independent Carmen were forced out of business, for the carroom was no longer an asset but a licence; it could not be bought, sold or leased; it could be revoked. Gradually Carmen went out of business, or became dependent on the coal merchants.

When Charles I took the throne, plague hit the City. The new King needed funds to fight Spain. Parliament granted taxes – for one year only. The King needed more. The City obliged – for one year only.

The City, the nation, and the Carmen, were uneasy.

The City's 17th century taxis were wherries, powered by Thames Watermen and illustrated in this contemporary broadsheet: *The fond Lovers Lamentation for the unkindness of Silvia*. (PLM)

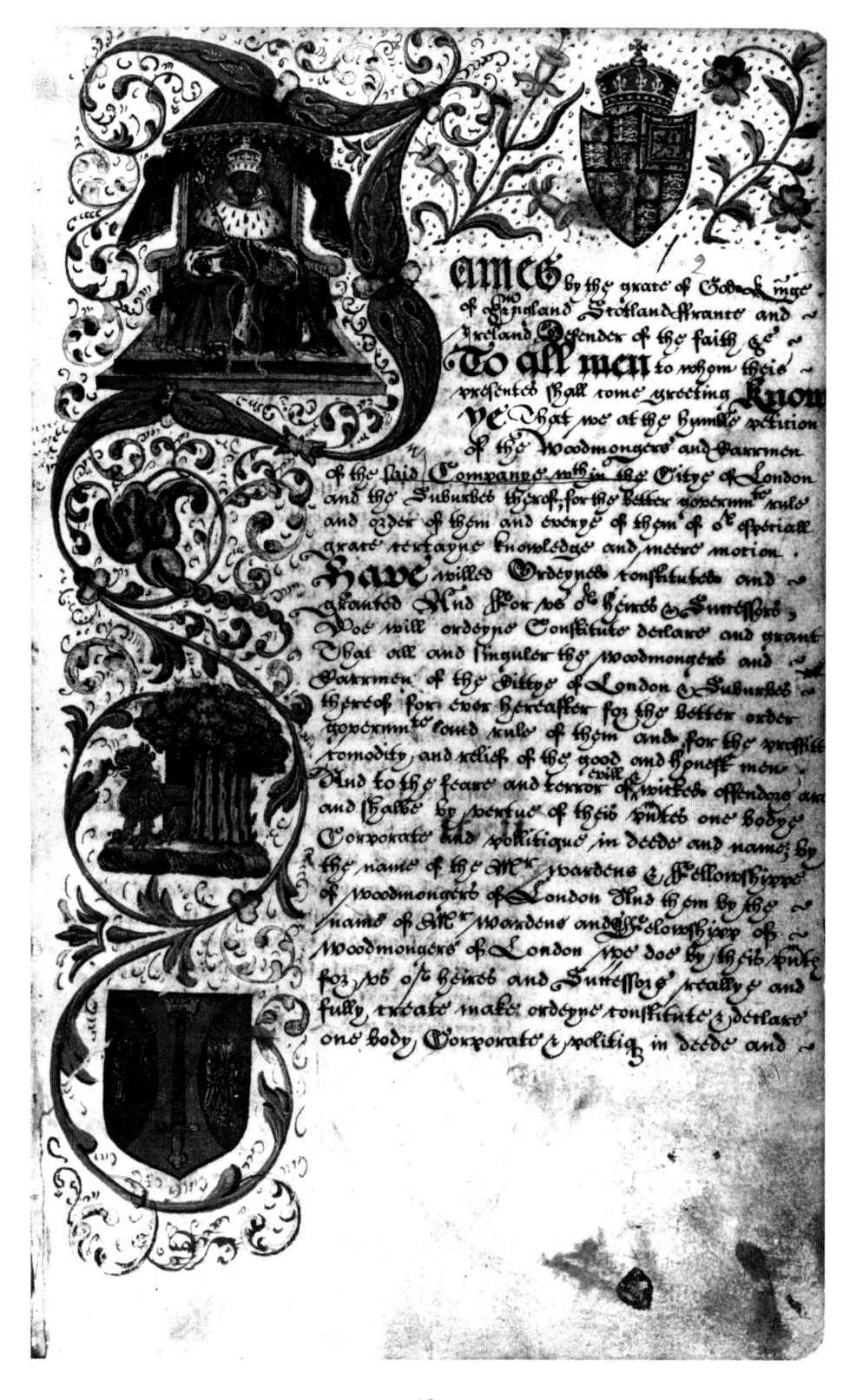

James by the grace of God Kinge of England Scotland Fraunce and Ireland Defender of the faith &c. **To all men** to whom theis presentes shall come greeting **Know ye** That we at the humble petition of the Woodmongers and Carremen of the said Company within the Citye of London and the Suburbes thereof, for the better government rule and order of them and every of them of our speciall grace certayne knowledge and meere motion **Have** willed Ordeyned constituted and graunted And for us our heires and Successors Wee will ordeyne Constitute declare and grant That all and singuler the woodmongers and Carremen of the Cittye of London & Suburbes thereof for ever hereafter for the better order government and rule of them and for the proffitt comodity and relief of the good and honest men And to the feare and terror of wicked offendors evill and shalbe by vertue of theis prntes one body Corporate and politique in deedes and name by the name of the Mr wardens & Fellowshippe of Woodmongers of London And them by the name of Mr Wardons and ffellowshipp of Woodmongers of London Wee doe by theis prntes for us our heires and Successors really and fully create make ordeyne constitute & declare one body Corporate & politiq in deede and

3. The whislinge Carman

MR. BYRDE
AUGUST 14, 1612

LEFT: 'At the humble petition of the Woodmongers and Carrmen' the King constituted them 'one bodye Corporate and pollitique in deede and name' on 29 August 1605. (BL) ABOVE: Mr William Byrde composed *The whislinge Carman*, published by Clement Matchett in his *Virginal Book* on 14 August 1612: this is the first of three folios. (SB)

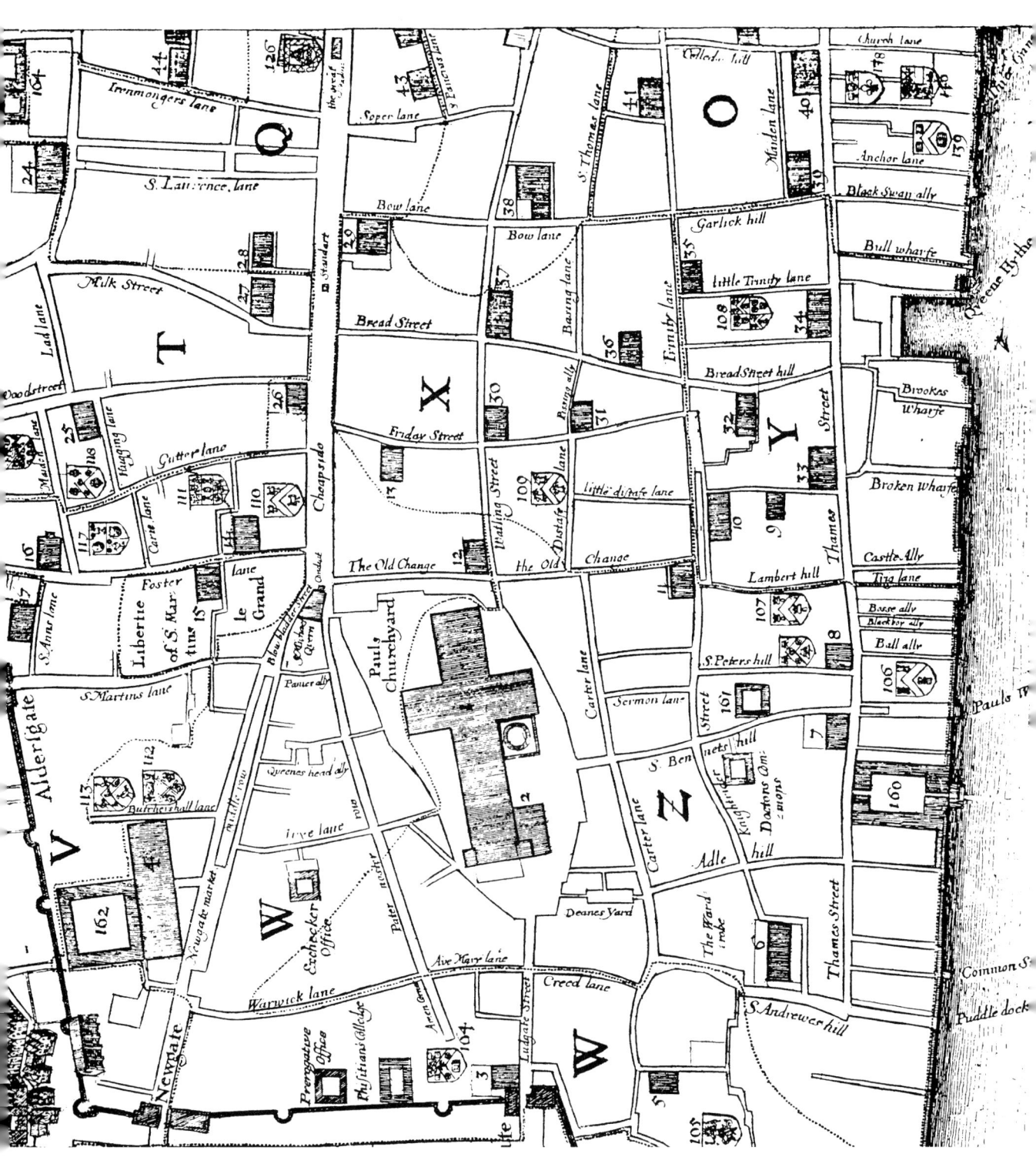

One year after the Great Fire of 1666, John Leake surveyed the City – the
wharves and alleys off Thames Street were Carmen territory. (GL)

5

INTO BATTLE

Many made a question which party had the better of the day; and either was well enough with their success.

Edward Hyde, Earl of Clarendon:
The History of the Great Rebellion 1625–1660

War with the Woodmongers erupted first; then battle was joined between carriers and Watermen; finally King and country took up arms, City against noble, squire against cousin, brother against brother.

The earliest coaches had arrived in the 1550s, mostly Royal, and replaced chariots in State processions. In 1572 a noble's coach cost £34 14s, the horses £11 13s 3d. Four passengers were drawn by two, four or six horses. By 1625 hackney coaches (*haquence* = horse for hire; Kotze = the coach's birthplace in Hungary) were used by jobbing carriers. They were often noble cast-offs.

Hackney-coaches were hired at 10s by the day. Then Captain Bailey 'hath erected...some four hackney-coaches, put his men in livery and appointed them to stand at the Maypole in the Strand' said Lord Stafford – just like the carrooms, and the later cab-rank.

Smaller 'hackney hell carts' evolved; by 1635 authority decreed they should only be used for three mile journeys out of town. 6,000 became 600. A year earlier the sedan chair was introduced. The two vehicles competed for passenger custom with the watermen, until then the sole City passenger transport.

When hackney-coaches were temporarily banned for causing congestion, Sir Saunders Duncombe made a killing out of his forty-plus sedan chairs. The chairs lasted from the 1630s to the 1820s.

The watermen complained through poet John Taylor:

'Against the ground we stand and knock our heels,
Whilst all our profit runs away on wheels.'

The Watermen had provided transport since the birth of the City, but they were not regulated until 1514 when Parliament imposed Thames fares. That changed little, so in 1555 Parliament appointed rulers of all watermen and wherrymen working between Gravesend and Windsor, requiring one year apprenticeships.

In 1598 Stow recorded 40,000 river workers and in 1603 apprentices had to serve seven years. 1626 ordinances recorded weekly pensions of 8d for 'poor and impotent freemen' though the Watermen (people carriers) and later Lightermen (goods) were not free of the City.

In 1631 the Wheelwrights and the Coachmakers made common cause, and petitioned the Court of Aldermen for joint incorporation. A year later they responded: 'many fraudes and deceipts are duly used' by both trades, with unseasoned timber in wheels and frames, deal in coachwork, and everything covered up with paint. Lives were endangered and wheels 'doe often breake in the Streets of the Citty...'.

Joiners, smiths and others persuaded the Court that incorporation was the best means to repairing these abuses and in 1633 the matter went to committee, where it rested – for forty years.

Taylor saw merit in Wheelwrights, but not Coachmakers. In his pamphlet, *The World runnes on Wheeles: or, oddes betwixt Carts and Coaches*, he praised the former: 'A Wheelwright, or a maker of Carts, is an ancient, a profitable, and a Trade' and he acknowledged the Carmen's role. 'For Stones, Timber, Corne, Wine, Beere, or any thing that wants life...should be carried, because they are dead and cannot go on foot, which necessity the honest Cart doth supply.' The coach only 'helps those that can helpe themselves'. Taylor was, of course, a Waterman and, so far, Watermen carried people, not things.

Meanwhile, wharfingers vied with Carmen to carry wine and beer, Woodmongers tried to save their trade in fuel, and merchants sought a profit on all merchandise, whoever carried it. Tonnage and poundage – import/export taxes on tuns of wine or beer and pounds of merchandise – funded wars. When Parliament restricted this support in 1625, the King dissolved it. He turned to the City, which accommodated him – but again for only a year.

The 1626 Parliament came and went – dissolved. The 1628 Parliament lasted a little longer – to 1629. Charles accepted a Petition of Right – no man paid tax without Parliament's consent; no one was imprisoned without cause shown; no military billeted in private houses; no one tried by martial law.

Government was henceforth by Star Chamber decree. Taxes, fines, sale of monopolies were among the means to funds. In 1634 Ship Money raised fixed sums, initially from ports and maritime counties, then nationwide.

In 1630 Star Chamber attacked the Irish Society and the liveries for lack of development in Ulster. In 1635 the Irish estates were confiscated and the companies fined £12,000. The establishment still served King and country, but City rank and file was disaffected.

In 1640 Parliament sat, refused funds, and stood down. The King turned to the City, demanding direct support from the richest men. They refused and four Aldermen were thrown in gaol. Others tried to collect Ship Money house to house. Only one man paid. The Liveries refused a direct appeal. Puritanism was gaining ground and citizens were questioning the power of the few.

In 1640 the Society of Coal Merchants told the King the Woodmongers were interrupting tax-paid supplies; the Woodmongers replied the coal was defective. The shippers were frustrated, and Scots skippers threatened to export coal direct to Holland. Lime kiln owners were desperate enough to offer premium prices. In 1642 Parliament decreed that no 'Wharfinger, Woodmonger or other seller of Newcastle coals' should charge more than 23s the chaldron. The Lord Mayor agreed: the reasonable price was 22s and another twelve pence to encourage winter supplies.

Several companies faced rebellion in their ranks. The Carmen were no exception. On 26 April 1641 the House of Commons gave a first reading to their Bill 'for the better government of the Corporacon...of Woodmongers of London and for the relief of the Carrmen of London' against the decrees of Star Chamber.

The Bill anulled the decree, restored the asset value of carrooms, according to 'ancient Custome and usage' and sought compensation for those who had lost their rights. It claimed the decree was made without reference to the Carmen, and should not affect them. Some had lost their carrooms to Woodmongers and to the 'greate wrong of the said Carre-men and the great oppression of divers poore Widowes and children' of dead Carmen.

Carmen also sought to stop the self-perpetuating oligarchy which ruled the Company. No one should serve as Master or Warden for more than a year and a month, and Carmen should be eligible.

Taxes, unpopular ministers, church reform, the Scottish war and finally, the Irish rebellion, drove King and Parliament to the brink. Parliament convened again. In 1641 the Grand Remonstrance recorded Parliament's work and Charles' unlawful acts. The Carmen's Bill was suffocated by the weight of larger disputes.

In 1642 King and Commons went to war.

The City elected those opposed to the King and his High Church. A City MP became Mayor, the trained bands of the City stood firm and, despite a Royal blockade in 1643, the City survived. With the King's execution in 1649, City government was diminished under Cromwell's administration.

The Carmen had not been idle during all this mayhem. When the Company allocated dead men's carrooms, they were sued by the widows. They claimed the decree was invalid and the matter *sub judice*. For the same reasons, Carmen rejected the Woodmongers' orders and demands.

In February 1649 Christ's Hospital wanted answers. The annual payment was £250 in arrears. The Company agreed the claim but pleaded 'there are 300 Carre men...that will not pay'. Fighting the Carmen's suit had cost more than £300 'besides great sumes of money' imposed by the 'obstinacie of the unruly carrmen'.

Parliament had voted to abolish the Lords, the Levellers sought an egalitarian society, puritans pamphleteered and the Carmen joined in. Stephen Spratt wrote 'The Carmen's Remonstrance or a Reply to the false and scurrilous Papers of the Woodmongers by them put out against the Carremen'.

The Carmen claimed embezzlement, fraud, false measures, price escalation and asked Parliament to give them a separate Company. In May 1650 a committee agreed, if that Company paid Christ's Hospital £150 a year. There was one more condition: the Carmen should take over some of the Woodmonger's Civil War debt.

Mayor, merchants and Woodmongers fought the Bill. It evaporated in committee in September 1651. In 1653 the Carmen tried again. Again a committee approved, but Parliament was dissolved.

That year the Woodmongers leant on the Carmen. Over forty acknowledged the Company's authority and in 1654 an Act of Common Council issued new rules. 'How abundant and continuall the disorders of Carrmen' it began. Frequent provisions had been made 'for Restraint of their unruliness' but they had 'no reverence of Lawes' nor 'remembrance of mischiefs' and many had operated outside the Company.

Once the Act got into its stride, it became strident. Carmen had pestered and annoyed others, to the 'perill...maimeing and sometimes slaughter of Children and Passengers'. Carrooms had been claimed 'against all reason and Custome' as legacies, leading to ruin for some and speculation by others.

The Act limited carrs to 420 – 140 for the wharves, 280 street carrs. Six officers would enforce one-way streets and carr stands, charges would be fixed and recorded by the Aldermen and £150 would be paid annually to the school, plus all arrears.

So far so little change. Then came innovation. Carrooms would be allocated by a joint committee of Company and Common Council. There would be no legacies, but widows could keep their late husbands' carrooms, as long as staff were apprenticed or free of the Company.

Carrooms could be hired, subject to Company approval and a dead Carman's carroom would be allocated only to Carmen free of the Company. For the first time, the Woodmongers had tried to meet the Carmen's needs.

In the temper of the times it was not enough. The Carmen petitioned Cromwell in person in 1656, to no avail. In 1658 the Woodmongers were in trouble. Their 'great abuses' were brought before Common Council. They had licensed eighty more carts than allowed.

The Company lost the right to license carts. It was handed to the Governors of the Corporation of the Poor which, founded in 1647, helped vagrants and orphans, and needed the money. Christ's Hospital still received its annual fee.

In 1657 the first stage coach appeared, leaving the George in Aldersgate for Chester. It took four days. William Dunstan, Henry Earle and William Fowler had started something.

In March 1660 hard times induced a temporary truce. Carmen and Woodmongers joined forces when 45 Carmen subscribed to Articles of Agreement. These reinstated the asset value of carrooms as negotiable, if not bequeathable. The value was set at £40.

There were provisions for income from carrooms for widows, orphans and dependants; for a committee to settle disputes; for limiting carroom hire to Woodmongers' servants, and agreement not to go to law without Company approval.

At that time, taxes were high, liveries had lost substantial loans to the Crown, and trade was depressed. On 8 May 1660 Charles II was proclaimed King by the Lord Mayor and received £10,000 from Common Council. The Lord Mayor was Sir Richard Browne. He was a Woodmonger.

With the Restoration, the Corporation for the Poor was closed and Christ's Hospital took 120 children into its care. It offered to take charge of carrooms and Carmen, but Common Council decided in May 1661 to repeal the Act of 1658 and reinstate those of 1605 and 1654. Government of Carmen and the right to issue carrooms was leased to the Woodmongers for 61 years, subject to the school's annual fee of £150. The Carmen were back where they started.

By 1662 stage coaches were operating out of London to Dover, Portsmouth, Oxford, Chester and York and there were 2,500 hackneys in London. In 1660 Commissioners were appointed for, among other things 'regulating the hackney-coaches in the city of London'. They were reduced to 400. Private coaches were proliferating. Samuel Pepys yearned for one in 1661 ; if he were rich he would 'be a knight, and keep my coach'. In 1667 he made up his mind, 'my expence in Hackney coaches being now so great'.

By 1664 the Woodmongers had alienated public opinion with their coal trade monopoly and price manipulation. A committee appointed by the Aldermen found that the Woodmongers had been buying up wharves and wharfingers, stopping them handling coal, spreading rumours about City price control, using false measures and victimising protesters.

They were accused of preventing ships from unloading 'at Smart's Key', forcing them to disgorge at their own wharves, fixing prices, cheating on weights, squeezing out other dealers and generally putting citizens 'under an intolerable grievance'.

They absented themselves in summer to artificially delay shippers, reduce prices, and increase demand. If City meters attempted to check measures, they 'fall upon them with evil and reviling language'.

The basic scam was described: 'They labour to suppress all others', imposed fines and prosecuted others, denying them carrooms and the use of carrs, punishing Carmen and seizing their carts, embargoing stored fuel or buying it in at their own prices, until they had 'engrossed the whole Store in their own hands'.

This inhibited free trade in fuel, and let prices rise well beyond 'much lower rates than the Woodmongers'. The Company stopped apprentices securing wharves and carrooms 'after their times are expired', and 'hinder the Town Carrs from carrying home the Coals of private Persons which are not bought of themselves'. One way and another they served 'their own private Gain' and 'advance of the Price of Seacoals must necessarily ensue'.

Not content with massaging supplies and prices, the Woodmongers were also accused of forcing fifty 'Carrmen of the Poorer sort' to either accept twenty pounds each for their carrooms, or find twenty pounds to retain them. In many cases, there was no choice. This was February 1665. By May the Great Plague had arrived. By September, 100,000 had perished. London was a ghost town.

In November Christ's Hospital learnt that 'several persons whose Carrs were sealed' that same year had died, and their families were 'in a miserable and deplorable condicon. They sought admittance to the rooms'. The Governors decided to admit any who could prove a will or produce other evidence.

That year Amy Beare, widow of Edward, petitioned the Hospital. Her husband had owned a carroom. He had been hauled before a committee to give evidence of carrooms during Parliament's deliberations. The Woodmongers 'taking distast thereat' confiscated his.

The Committee gave it back; when he died it went to the Corporation for the Poor. They settled it on Amy but in 1661 the Woodmongers 'did take away the same'. The Governors gave it back. Carrooms might be inherited, after all.

The Aldermen proposed to repeal or amend the 1661 Act, to allow all carrs to carry fuel. Three days later, the Woodmongers surrendered their lease and the following June the Act was repealed. The 'government of the Cars' was returned to Christ's Hospital as the plague was abating.

Thirteen Carmen who headed the 1660 peace treaty attended the school's first Court. They included Henry Marson and John Hill. In July they suggested the Woodmongers should lose their 140 wharf carrs but, if not, then they should employ the eighty 'poore persons upon their Wharfes they haveing made them Supernumery and without some reliefe must all perish'.

The Carmen also suggested four street keepers 'of absolute necessitie' to control disorderly Carmen. They nominated Henry Ingersole, Henry Moore, John Swettman and John King at £16 per annum, 'or as you shall think fitt'. They proposed to deal with fines as they claimed to have done under the Woodmongers. Christ's Hospital agreed.

The Woodmongers did not give up. In December the Carmen complained they were 'soare oppressed by the Woodmongers and other supernumary Carrs'. They claimed over 240 were operating unlicensed, and that the Company planned to take over once more. Woodmonger William Fellows told Christ's Hospital he had not claimed his carrooms because 'severall members...did perswaide him not to come in'. They were convinced the control of carrs would be 'againe settled in the Company of Woodmongers'.

The first sealing day of 1665 saw 275 carrs branded, owned by 219 Carmen. Two held four carrooms each, two held three, forty-six held two and 169 owned one. Most plied for hire by turn-keeping, like today's cabranks, on licensed stands near wharves or markets.

Some refused light loads, some made private contracts, some loaded out of turn. Inevitably there were disputes, the more so when officials intervened to enforce the rules. Merchants complained about the 'pestering of the streets'. Carmen got cross, trying to navigate heavy loads through narrow lanes.

Some regulations were pedantic and Pepys pillories Lord Mayor Sir John Robinson as 'a talking, bragging, buffleheaded fellow' whose 'precept, which he, in vain-glory, said he had drawn up himself' against coachmen or Carmen offending gentry 'is drawn so like a fool'.

Pepys used 'a hackney-coach from my Lord Treasurer's down Holborne' but the coachman 'told me he was suddenly stroke very sick.... So I light and went into another coach' on 17 June 1665. The constant use of the Thames as a highway is underlined by many diary references: 'At noon by water to the King's Head at Deptford' and 'about Grayes...we took our wherry'. By 1669 he had his own coach – 'I to my coachmaker's...and saw my coach cleaned and oyled'.

In June 1666 the Carmen asked the King for separate incorporation. The Attorney General handled the petition and heard the Carmen promise Christ's Hospital to raise annual carr-rent from 17s 4d to £1. The City opposed the petition and it failed.

In September the Great Fire swept London and consumed four fifths. Guildhall was gutted; 13,200 houses were destroyed, 44 livery halls levelled, 200,000 homeless. Only eight people died, and Carmen made a killing – evacuees cried desperately 'Forty pounds for a cart!'. Pepys 'wrote to my father this night; but the post-house being burned, the letter could not go'.

In the aftermath, Wren's grand plan for rebuilding was jettisoned but he and Roger Pratt headed six commissioners, and practical solutions emerged. One envisaged an open quayside with warehouses forty feet from the river, from the Tower to Blackfriars. The gutted Guildhall was refaced. But there was corruption and conflict and the wharfingers, predictably, eroded the quayside for storage.

Watermen's Hall at the Mansion of Cold Harbour was destroyed too, rebuilt in 1670. St Paul's took thirty-three years to rebuild, and altogether 51 churches were rebuilt by Wren, including St Michael Paternoster Royal and his finest, St Stephen's, Walbrook.

The Woodmongers were far from finished and, after the Great Fire, were instrumental in the rebuild. The City relied on them to collect the coal dues. The tax went up 1s a chaldron, then 3s in 1670. Roads were improved, wharves built, churches replaced, St Paul's rose again – coal tax paid for 80% of the 'new' City, tax which was collected by the Woodmongers.

While the cost of rebuilding was met by coal tax and the livery companies, some of those who fled never returned. London's residential nature began to change. The streets were wider, the Royal Society had contributed to the development of lighter coaches, and the coachmakers could and did build, lighter, wider, faster vehicles.

In January 1667 the Lord Mayor addressed both Carmen and Woodmongers. The Company would henceforth 'recieve and admitt the Carrmen, free to their Company, to all Common benefitts, dignities and advantages and the Carmen would comply with the Company's 'just and good government'.

Over two years, coal prices had escalated and that same month a Commons committee investigated the Woodmongers. It found that the Dutch war had affected coastal traffic but the Woodmongers had exploited this to make 200% profits. The House discussed the charter. The Clerk was arrested – he refused to produce the Company's books. It was then resolved that the charter was illegal and on 5 December 1667 it was surrendered.

Sir Edmund Berry Godfrey was the Master. Honoured for his role in the Great Plague and Fire, he was the magistrate before whom Titus Oates later swore details of the phoney Popish plot, which had London in a state of siege in 1678. Two months after that, he was found stabbed to death on Primrose Hill.

With the tide flowing strongly against the Woodmongers, the Carmen went to Christ's Hospital and asked 'that they may be a Brotherhood or Fellowship as antiently they were'. The school agreed and its Carroom Committee drew up a 'Booke of Orders' which was ratified by the City on 28 April 1668.

Seventeen articles established the authority of City and Hospital, and fifteen regulated the Fellowship.

Those who worked 'Carrs or Carts within the City of London and liberties thereof' would be known as the Carrmen of the City of London. Three should be Wardens and twenty, Assistants.

The first three Wardens would be John Hill, William Turner and John Earle, and they would serve for a year, and thereafter until an election was held.

The first Assistants were William Standley, John Standford, James Ruffhead and John Fox; Robert Hardy and Edward Oxlad; Anthony Browne, Isaac Preston and John Clarke; three Thomases – Haines, Smith and Hooker; John Cue, James Maw and Edward Benson; John Caines and Alexander Sheppard; Edwards Tucker and Lucar, and John Chitwell.

New Wardens were to be elected between 25 March and 24 June every year and, if any Warden died, a replacement could be elected to serve out his term. If anyone refused office, he would be fined £3.

Within a month of their replacement, the old Wardens were expected to render accounts and hand over all the receipts, or pay a fine of £5, and as much again for every month they delayed. The Wardens and Assistants were expected to appoint a Clerk and Beadle or Beadles, set their salaries and pay them quarterly. To pay for the Fellowship's costs, quarterage was to be levied of not more than twelve pence a quarter.

Anyone who did not attend upon the Beadle's summons was subject to a fine of not more than 2s 6d, and anyone who used 'evil, opprobrious or revolting Language in the Street' to a fellow freeman would forfeit five shillings. Naughty apprentices would be punished at the Wardens' discretion.

If language was tempered, fighting was forbidden, on pain of a ten shilling fine, though apprentices were dealt with as the Wardens saw fit. Swearing at or fighting with anyone outside the Fellowship was referred to Christ's Hospital.

'For the preservation of the Unanimity and Brotherly Love' within the Fraternity, no one should go to law against another Freeman unless he had talked to the Wardens first and secured their approval. The penalty for doing otherwise was forty shillings.

Any Freeman failing to pay fines due after being asked twice was liable to be hauled before the Lord Mayor for punishment.

Apprentices could not be bound until the Hospital authorised the Freeman concerned, and presentation cost 12d, indentures 18d paid to 'the Common Box'. Articles were set at seven years. After that the apprentice must pay 6s 8d for admittance, plus 2s 6d to the Clerk and 12d to the Beadle.

Freemen should take no apprentice until they had served four years, unless sick or lame and where a Journeyman 'is not to be had' and even then only with a licence from the Hospital and the Wardens. One apprentice at a time was the rule.

The Wardens were required to follow the rules, and ensure they were read out twice a year to the whole Fraternity. Failure to do so brought a penalty of twenty shillings.

The articles laid down the oath required of every Carman, 'to be true to our Sovereigne Lord the King…obedient to the President and Governors of Christ's Hospitall…to the Wardens for the time present'. A Freeman swore not to take on foreigners, and only Carmen or apprentices duly bound, and to fulfil the rules regarding both. 'You shall not entice or withdraw any mans Servant of this Society until that reasonable Departing be made with his said Master.'

'These and all other good Rules made and to be made not reversed you shall keepe soe neare as God give you Grace.'

'Soe help you God.'

It was a limited victory, with little power over carrooms, traffic or transgressors, but the Carmen were at last free of the Woodmongers, free to ply their trade, and free to run their own affairs – within limits. The battle, if not the war, had been won.

When Charles I came to town, the City turned out and John Taylor recorded it in *England's Comfort and London's Joy* in 1641. The Citizens appear somewhat subdued but the horses look happy. (GL)

THE CARMENS REMONSTRANCE,

OR A

Reply to the false and scurrilous Papers of the WOODMONGERS, by them put out against the CARREMEN:

IN A

Way of opposing them in getting of their Charter, and Vindication of the Carmens intentions against the Scandal of the

WOODMONGERS.

Directed to the Right Honourable, ALEXANDER GARLAND Esquire, and the rest of the Committee of Parliament Who heard the businesse between the Woodmongers and the Carmen.

And likewise to the Lord Mayor and Court of Aldermen of the City of *London*.

By STEPHEN SPRATT Solicitor for the Carremen.

Printed at London by G. Dawson 1649.

ABOVE: In 1630 Londoners were advised to leave the City to escape the Plague. In the broadside, *A Looking-glasse for City and Countrey*, people went by foot, horse, or private coach. (SA) LEFT: In 1649 Stephen Spratt let fly with *The Carmens Remonstrance, or a reply to the false and scurrilous Papers of the Woodmongers*. (GL) RIGHT: As mobility increased, mapping developed – *The Surveyor Surveyed* in 1652. (CB)

ABOVE: Came the Plague and Londoners left their homes feet first in waggons or in fear and coaches. (ML) BELOW: Carmen's carts were pressed into service in the Plague's aftermath. (ML) OPPOSITE: Long carts joined coaches as the City recovered – all in John Dunstall's 1666 *Return of Londoners after the Plague*. (ML)

BELOW: On 21 June 1665 the Corporation returned the control of 'Carrs Carts Carrooms Carters and Carrmen' to Christ's Hospital. (GL)

53

This Day the President and Govern'r of Christs Hospitall London, to whome the Rule Oversight and Governom't of Carrs, Carts Carroomes Carters and Carrmon within the City of London and Liberties thereof is comitted by Act of Common Councell made 21th day of June 1665. In the xvijth yeare of his Ma:ties Reigne exhibited into this Court a Booke of Orders Rules Direccons and Limitacons devised for the better Regulacon of the said Carrs Carts Carters and Carrmen humbly submitting the same to be allowed and confirmed by this Court According to the said Act of Common Councell and the Custome of this City.

LEFT: In Charles I's time, horses had to haul coaches like this. (RS) RIGHT: By the 1660s, coach suspension had improved and design was more graceful. (RS) BELOW: Not long after that, Christ's Hospital approved the 'Orders Rules Directions and Limitations' for 'Carrs Carts Carters and Carrmen'. (GL)

LEFT: Dunstan, Earle and Fowler sent the first stage coach on its way in 1657 – the beginning of public road transport. (CB) RIGHT: The waggon was the only means of long-haul road transport. (CB) CENTRE: The Great Fire destroyed most of the City – Londoners fled, and paid Carmen £40 a cart: from a German source in September 1666. (GL) BELOW: Among London's rebuilt churches, Wren's St Michael Paternoster Royal replaced a 13th century original. (MS)

The Wardens and Assistants of this Fellowship or Brotherhood of Carrmen this 28th of May 1668. admitted the Widdows following to the said Fellowship they being severally admitted to Carroomes by the Governrs of Christs Hospitall.

Jone Hobbs
Mary Burroughs
Rachell Bricknell
Katherine Noodham
Ellin Simpkins
Margt Slaughter
Eliz: Miles
Eliz: Briggs
Eliz: Gale
Isabel Eales
Eliz: Swadling
Alice Maismore
Frances Stratford
Eliz: Grosvenor als Godsbury
Anne Ponny
Eliz: Coleman
Mary Hackleston
Margory King
Dorothy Hale
Sarah Sheppard
Margry Wilkins
Sarah Lowsley
Isabel Clayton
Anne Edmonds
Eliz: Cursoll
Sarah Garrott

At a Meeting of the Three Wardens And all the Assistants of the Fellowship or Brotherhood of Carrmen in London. The 6th day of May Ao Dnj 1668. At ye house of Mr Burgitt in Nortonfolgate.

Present.

Mr Jon Hill
Mr Wm Turner } Wardens.
Mr Jon Earle

Mr Wm Standley Mr Jon Sandford Mr James Ruffhead Mr Jon Fox Mr Ro: Hardy Mr Edwd Oxlade Mr Anth: Browne Mr Isaac Proston Mr Jon Clarke Mr Tho: Haines Mr Tho: Smith Mr Tho: Hooker Mr Jon Cue Mr James Maw Mr Edwd Benson Mr John Caines Mr Alexander Sheppard Mr Edward Tucker Mr Edwd Lucar Mr John Chitwell Assistants.

ABOVE: On 6 May 1668 the 'Three Wardens And all the Assistants of the Fellowship or Brotherhood of Carrmen in London' met 'at the house of Mr Burgitt'. (GL) LEFT: Twenty two days later they admitted 'Widdows ... to Carrooms' and listed them. (GL)

6

STOUT BODYES

That which a Man is bred up in, he thinks no Cheating; as your Tradesman thinks not so of his Profession, but calls it a Mystery.

John Selden: *Discourses* 1689

In 1668 341 Carmen were admitted to the Fellowship; 68 were women.

The first meeting was held in Norton Folgate at Mr Burgitt's house. On 6 May 1668 Christ's Hospital Clerk William Parry became the Carmen's Clerk. Carman Henry Ingersole was Beadle. The first apprentice was Thomas Wheeler, son of Richard, husbandman of Monson in Bucks, bound to John Thompson.

The Wardens and Assistants each contributed £10 to defray members' legal costs in the recent difficulties and the Beadle gave £5; most owned a carroom, though about a hundred rented them or were journeymen. Hill, Preston and Turner held three each and Earle two. Thomas Haines held four.

John Earle and James Ruffhead had given a personal bond for £150 to John Baker of Middle Temple – he was consulted on the Royal petition for incorporation. Though that had failed, he claimed his fee now the Carmen were independent. The Wardens persuaded him otherwise, but they wanted him on their side, so they gave him £50. If and when he secured incorporation, the rest would be paid.

Women were as unruly as men: Mrs Benson accused Mrs Bates of abusing her good name and the matter went to arbitration. First to join the Fellowship, Richard Clarke was fined 1s 6d for going with three horses, and another 2s for riding on his cart. Three others were also fined, and the Beadle collected 1s 6d for his pains.

Beadle Ingersole was also appointed a street keeper. When he impounded a country cart belonging to Sir Charles Doe, he went too far. Doe sat on the Christ's Hospital Carmen's committee. Ingersole had to 'cry him mercy for the offence'.

Offences were frequent, for regulations were numerous. Loads were limited by weight and bulk, except for building stone. One ton or a butt or pipe of liquid was the maximum. No load could be refused.

Horses had to be led; carters had to keep the reins within a yard's length. There were speed limits – trotting was forbidden; full or empty, the speed must be the same. One horse power was the limit, except uphill from the riverside.

Initially horses could not be fed in the street, especially from 'prickets' – portable mangers. Later, feeding by hand or nosebag was permitted. When the carr was stationary, the carter must stand by the horse's head, and never leave the carr unattended.

No one could 'drive' a cart under the age of eighteen.

57

No one was immune from 'prosecution'. Within a week of becoming Junior Warden, James Ruffhead was fined 2s for 'goeing with three horses'; so was retiring Warden John Earle. That was May 1669.

Others were less fortunate. Widow Needham had her carroom 'cut off' for carrying a heavy load and 'railing and abusing ye Governors etc'. Widow Edwards got off scot free for 'Imploying a boy', but Assistant Haines paid 10s for two heavy loads.

Six Carmen were fined 1s each for riding their carts, though a seventh was fined twice as much. Thomas Stone was charged 5s for carting eleven barrels of raisins and Robert Bendall, 5s for overloading with four hogsheads of wine. Inevitably someone came into St Magnus corner – Richard Sheppard. He did it thrice and it cost him 6s.

For those who paid up promptly, there was a rebate. Edward Benson was fined 5s 'whereof returned back 2s 6d' and Thomas Stone likewise. Benson was Senior Warden in 1674 and Stone Upper Warden in 1683.

Wardens were only ranked in order of their swearing, though in 1677 James Ruffhead became Eldest Warden; his successor was designated Upper Warden. So it remained for a century and, with the single exception of William Smith, Master in 1788, even longer.

There were more pressing matters than office. Cleansing the streets was one. In 1671 negotiations began with the Commissioners of Sewers. Sixty Carmen volunteered at 5s a night in the City, 6s 8d outside, 10 pm to 5 am for one man, a horse and a cart.

The Commissioners, who threatened to obtain eighty extra carts to rake the streets, offered £1,000 a year for the whole contract. The Carmen refused. Up went the ante to £2,400 a year. A few Carmen obliged but the scheme was dead in the water within six months.

In 1670 the Wheelwrights were chartered, women were admitted, and in 1681 rules laid down for cart construction. 'Every Cart from henceforth...shall be in bodie...between the staves thereof four feet...and in lengths from the fore end of the shaft to the outside of the hinder Earebred thirteen foot four inches and noo more.'

While all this was going on, Common Council ordered that Assistants should be increased to forty-one. Then there were the troubles in Thames Street – again. Residents complained they were 'not able to stir out of theire houses', because of cart congestion, careless carters and surplus horses – Carmen were 'in Aleshouses when they should be at the horse heads'.

Even the Lord Mayor had his problems. In 1674 the Fellowship offered the sword bearer £25 to stop procuring their horses, but Sir John Frederick, Hospital President, asked them to 'not exasperate the Lord Mayor' until he gave them the go ahead.

With subs at £1 a carroom, the Fellowship was clearly short of cash when it determined to sell its possessions 'except the Table Cloth...with all convenient speede'. In 1679 there were ructions in Court. William Campeon asserted 'All the Assistants are Knaves' and was promptly fined 10s. Mr Clerke was elected Upper Warden, turned it down, and paid £3.

When Edward Benson was charged 10s for 'speaking reviling and scandalous words' he refused to pay and left the Court. He was not the only one. Edward Jempson refused to take the Carmen's oath – out. It cost Edward Martin 5s when he swore the Wardens were 'none but a parcel of bawling whelps'.

The worst offender was Mr Assistant William Holder. His 'gross behaviour' lay in helping Hugh Cursell, an erstwhile Woodmonger who had been refused admission. Cursell slapped a warrant on the Wardens and Holder spoke against the Fellowship at the Court of Aldermen. He was suspended.

At first Carmen met at Christ's Hospital. Then in 1668 they leased premises on the east side of Harp Lane in the Parish of St Dunstans-in-the-East. This became known as Carmen's Hall. In 1678 they moved Court to Blacksmith's Hall, then from 1680 to 1710 they met at Painter Stainers', after which they met in the Irish Chamber at Guildhall until 1728.

In 1680 the Fellowship launched an initiative to 'prevent all misbehaviour of the Carmen' and to stop minors attending carts. Two Assistants went out to 'walk the streets weekly in rotation'. This service continued for more than a century.

At that time, coffee houses were the centre of City social life. Started in Cornhill with Pasqua Rosee's in 1652, they numbered 497 by 1714 and presaged the later London clubs. Merchants used Edward Lloyd's in Lombard Street, scholars the Grecian in Covent Garden and the clergy Truby's or Child's, near St Pauls.

In 1676 the King tried to suppress them and failed. In 1680 a private penny post was launched, using coffee houses as *postes restantes*. Newsletters were produced for patrons, newspapers from 1702. Once again the City had innovated communications, and paved the way for national news distribution – personal and public.

Carmen now turned to the business of carrooms – and settling scores with the Woodmongers. Many claimed they had lost their inheritance, thanks to them. There was also some precedent stemming from the year of the plague. In October 1669 the Fellowship approached Christ's Hospital to make up the numbers of carts to 420, to suppress 'disorderly' carters, and to return confiscated carrooms to Carmen's heirs.

The school acted. One claim went back to 1646. Nineteen heirs were reinvested with their forbears' carrooms. Unlicensed Woodmongers ignored both Carmen and Christ's Hospital and continued to operate.

The Woodmongers, bereft of charter, continued as a corporate body, wealthy and influential. More often called fuellers, they fought on. The Carmen asked the Hospital to license all 420 carts to their members, offering enough carts to handle all wharf business. They listed selected operators, and the Hospital required them to 'attend any three Traders in fewell' as a test case. That failed.

The Hospital now summoned the Woodmongers repeatedly. Eventually some of them appeared and were asked why they worked carts without licence, and why they refused to carry measures as required by the City.

The Woodmongers replied that they carried their own goods, and they were not concerned with the Act of Common Council which gave Christ's Hospital powers over carts. They said they would return with counsel's opinion.

A month later, Captain Clarke, Mr Berry and Mr Irons told the Hospital they 'did desire they might be excused' from producing anything which exposed their case, as the Hospital 'is resolved to commence suite against them'.

The Carmen egged Christ's Hospital on. Their livings were at stake. King's Bench eventually decided the Act of 1665 was defective, and it was repealed. An amended version was enacted in 1677, but 'Afterwards Mr John Vere, Trader in Fuel' who sat in Common Council and had been convicted for false measures more than once 'caused the By-law...to be removed into the Exchequer, where it lay a considerable time'.

In 1680 it was approved, except for the apparent monopoly posed by the cost of admission to work a cart.

By July 1680 Common Council had drafted a new bill. The Woodmongers petitioned -- against. So did the Carmen – in favour. They recited all the old plaints, and now the

Woodmongers struggled. In desperation, they pleaded that common carriers should not carry fuel because 'the Carmen, living so remote from the Wharfs' their charges were too low to bring them out for those who wanted fuel 'at unusual hours'.

The City rejected the Woodmongers' feeble case, even though they had managed to drag it out for a year. The Hospital then tried to bring some order to the industry, but even their first prosecution was held up. Woodmongers persuaded the Lord Mayor to stay the proceedings while a committee looked into the question of wharf carrs.

By 1680, the Woodmongers, despite their loss of cartage control, and the depredations of the Watermen, were still powerful enough to buy up coals on the wharves, and resell them at exorbitant profits. In 1734 an anonymous scribe observed that Woodmongers 'lived on the Wharfs, kept Horses and Carts of their own, bought their coals at Billingsgate of the Masters of the Ships and were there plyed by the Lightermen' for carriage from ship to wharf.

When Charles II brought in *Quo Warranto*, suspending the City's charter, by-laws were questioned and, when the courts ruled for Carmen, Woodmongers used *Habeas Corpus* to move cases to Westminster. Delays were so long that 'in the meantime the Chamberlen may happen to dye or be removed from his office' and 'the action will abate'.

The Carmen also did their sums. Even if the City got judgement, the 13s 4d penalty would not cover half their costs. Yet the Woodmongers' charges would be met by their fellows and with coals 'at 24s per chauldron' and ten loads a day, they would gain by 'modest computation of their fraudes' four shillings for every chauldron. 'There is very little hopes...to suppress the use the Woodmongers make of their Carts'. The Act was useless.

Both sides knew that incorporation was the key to control. The Woodmongers petitioned James II in 1687. City and Hospital opposed the charter and on 2 July, it failed.

The Carmen thanked Christ's Hospital for its support, and then suggested that the Fellowship should 'obtaine some further authority and power'. Proposals included the power to impound carts without licence, to prosecute disorderly members, and 'to inforce Turn keeping, especially in Thames Streete' and over standings.

The means would be a Royal petition and new by-laws. The Hospital consulted the Attorney General, who took three guineas, and some time 'to return an answer'. Hospital and Carmen were unhappy with this, so the Fellowship was asked to draft its own by-laws.

The Carmen had its draft ready and waiting. It included a specific proposal to remove the Star Chamber decree: 'noe man shall be allowed...to purchase a Carroom, who is not a Freeman of the said Fellowship of Carremen' and the same carrooms 'shall descend to the Executors and Administrators of the purchaser', while the Fellowship 'shall have power to suspend' anyone who disobeyed its rules.

Christ's Hospital was surprised, and said so. It referred Carmen to previous enactments and the matter to a committee, which invited comment from Thames Street traders. These 'severall worthy Citizens' thought it to their 'gross prejudice' if the Carmen were incorporate, so the Committee 'think fitt that the said request of the Carremen be rejected'.

Other guilds were forming. The Wheelwrights had secured their charter in 1670, separately from the Coachmakers, who also found the Attorney General an expensive ally. He charged them six guineas and took five for the King, another six went to the Secretary 'for obtayneing the King's hand' and a first fee of £50 to the Clerk of

Patents; the Recorder took two guineas and the Lord Chancellor's clerk five. They secured their charter in 1677.

When the King suspended the City's charter in 1682, companies like the Coachmakers knew they were outgunned. They surrendered their charter. In 1687 a new, restrictive one was gained, but in 1688 the old one was reinstated. By 1694 there were 700 coaches in London. That same year the Bank of England was founded with £1.2m loans, at 8% interest secured on taxation.

In 1675 some fuellers proposed that 52 of their carts be sealed to ply for hire, paying £20 for each cart to be licensed. This anonymous offer was shelved by suspicious Carmen who wanted to know who was behind it. Nothing more happened.

On the supply side, Coachmakers were trying to enforce standards. In 1679 Mr Awbry was summoned 'for putting an old Carriage to the Queen's body Coach' and again 'A carriage at Mr Polehamptons – rotten cross-bars, old pearch, knotty standards, & 2 old plates belonging to Mr Obediah Bentley'.

After the Great Fire, when Carmen failed to secure contracts to carry stone to St Paul's for the great rebuilding, a contractor called Slithurst got the job. In 1686 he secured more work for other churches. Christ's Hospital protested. 'It is a prejudice to the Fellowship of Carmen.' Slithurst carried on without penalty.

In 1687 the conflict with Thames Street came to a head. It centred on turn keeping. The Carmen composed a paper to present to Christ's Hospital 'Concerning Carmens keeping Turne in the Streetes'. They confirmed the City's authorisation 'over Sixty yeares since' and that the Woodmongers had maintained the same rule.

The 1667 rule ensured that carts for 'Wharfe work, tackle work, Cranework, Shops and Merchants houses...are to stand in order and be taken in turne'. In 1686 'by the Importunity of some few traders in Thames Streete' the words 'Shops and Merchants houses' were taken out.

Turn keeping was 'a great Benefit to the Carrmen in General', to merchants, shopkeepers, people at large, and the roads. 'All Carroomes are alike to every Carrman' who paid the same rent, and should have the same work. Their carts were numbered, so they were a known quantity. Their carrooms stood surety for goods carried.

The Fellowship pointed out that the King entrusted his 'Treasures from the Custom House to the Exchequer, sometimes 18 or 20 thousand pounds at any time without any Guard upon the Carrman'. Safety depended on carts working in turn – otherwise the scramble might endanger children, the old, blind or maimed.

Working out of turn promoted carriage of heavy loads, 'which tares up the pavements and shakes the brick buildings'. Some of the Thames Street traders caused 'the Nusance they complaine off' for Carmen ran down the lane with their carts to secure their custom.

Christ's Hospital invited the traders' response. They replied with 'The objections of the Agreived Inhabitants'. There was no problem except with 'Turnkeeping in the Streetes and out of Shops'. The regulations were 'obsolete Orders of Sixty yeares standing as useless as a story out of Reynard the ffox'.

There followed a tortuous argument founded in the premise that the orders predated the Hospital's present rule and were unjust. All work effectively came out of wharf, warehouse, cellar or shop, and sometimes the first cart in turn was several away from the intending user.

Carmen used the system to impose high charges, delayed deliveries, left empty carts unattended to 'lye in Alehouses and not to be found'. Turn keeping led to undue loads, which damaged the roads.

The paper concluded with suggested new rules 'And lastly we pray that the ffellowship of Carrmen may Shew by what authority they punish one another by ffynes.' The Carmen were incandescent.

They fired off a rejoinder, suggesting 'it had been better for them to have said "the objections of halfe a Dozen agreived Inhabitants of Thames Streete"'. They then repeated all their justifications.

The traders' reply was even more tart: 'they seeme to value themselves' by the cost of carrooms, which compared unfavourably with the rents traders paid, yet spent 'Superfluous money' on 'potts of Beere'. Perhaps Carmen were paid for their attendance on the Hospital and 'for their impertinent humours'. They then reiterated their arguments.

The Hospital backed the Carmen and required 'Turn keeping be strictly observed' but the Act of 1694 allowing 120 extra carts to Woodmongers abolished the practice.

In 1689, with the more enlightened William III on the throne, the Carmen had petitioned the Crown for incorporation with the 'Reason why the Carrmen should have Authority to Governe their owne Members'.

The reasons included 'ffirst It will prevent the publick being cheated by the Woodmongers and other Retailers in ffuell', it would prevent the 'Nuisance created in the Streetes', by Woodmongers and other unofficial carters, and it would stave off ruin for 'Severall hundreds of ffamilies' who had served their time, but lost their rights.

In addition, it would stop 'unruly and Rude Drivers of Carrs' offending, Carmen would accept regulation when unofficial carters were restrained, and finally, no one governed a trade as well as the traders themselves.

William passed it onto the Attorney General, who told the Lord Mayor. The Aldermen, backed by Christ's Hospital, opposed the petition. Their committee, Sir John Lawrence, Sir Patience Ward and Sir John Moore, the Hospital's President, in 1690 presented this memorial:

'Reasons why the Carrmen should not be Incorporated arise

1. From the Rights of the City of London
2. From the nature of the persons and their Imployment
3. From the No-necessity and the inconvenience to the publick of their being Incorporated
4. From the generall Sence at Severall times of such persons both within and without the City of London as have had this matter in consideration.'

Under 1, they found incorporation 'would be a disherison to the City' of a 'great right', exercised since Edward III's reign, of 'granting, ordering, Regulating and Governing of Carrooms, and of all Carrs, Carts, Carrmen and Carters within London and the liberties thereof.'

Under 2, Carmen were labourers, not tradesmen. They were like Tankard bearers or Chimney Sweepers. Then came the damning words that have lived with the Carmen ever since.

'Their imployment requires stout bodyes and naturaly renders their minds unthinking and unheeding, rough and sturdy, untractable and ungovernable by themselves or by one another or without great difficulty by their Superiores.'

They had 'frequent Brawles and Quarrells amongst themselves' and they lacked the 'skill or temper' to redress that, or to avoid 'great rudenesse not onely in words but hurts and mischiefes' to the coaches of the gentry, other traders and even strangers to town.

There was even a so-called Tuesday Committee to hear citizens' complaints about Carmen.

Under 3, the Committee asserted that learned counsel, courts, the Governors of Christ's Hospital, Lord Mayor and Aldermen, indeed all the great and the good had laboured long and hard to effect suitable rules and regulations.

If the Carmen had their way, they would enact those rules which suited them, monopolise the carting trade, 'enhans the Rates', clog the streets and, worst of all, aspire like other liveries, to high office 'where they are not like to be more regular than thay are in the Streetes'.

Finally, under 4, they expressed 'there sence in this matter', drawn from the many conflicts of the past, Acts of Parliament, of Common Council and failed petitions, that the government of Carmen properly lay with the City, where the Carmen, if they behaved, should be 'vindicated, encouraged, assisted and protected'.

The Committee then quoted the Attorney General, Sawyer, who had ruled, even while the City's liberties were suspended by *Quo Warranto*, against the Carmen, which showed 'the sence also of those without London touching this affaire'.

The current Attorney General, Sir George Greby, accepted the Committee's findings, promised to obstruct the petition, and it failed. Stout bodyes had certainly met thinking but unheeding minds. The Hospital paid their saviour ten guineas 'as a fee for his paines'.

The Carmen not only lost the day, they had to raise taxes on carrooms to meet their costs. Sir George meanwhile was asked his opinion on a proposal to make the President of the Hospital perpetual Chief Ruler of the Carrmen. Pockets well lined, Sir George approved and the Aldermen were asked to set it up.

In 1695 the Lord Mayor appointed Sir Thomas Stampe and Sir Humphry Edwin Governors of the Fellowship. A Court had been called without the Upper Warden's consent and the election was declared void. At the next Court, the same officers were chosen, but nine Assistants were sacked – they had served no apprenticeship.

By now carrooms were changing hands at £130 a time, and not all Carmen were 'disorderly'. Past Warden William Turner died in 1690, leaving two carrooms to the Fellowship for poor members.

The Woodmongers had not been idle. They secured an Act of Common Council in 1694 allowing them 120 carts over and above the 420 licensed for the streets. The Carrmen complained that 'above 200 lycenced Carts stand Idle…for want of their Rightfull Labour'.

The Carmen again sought incorporation, in Whitehall and the Commons. They offered £400 to Christ's Hospital and £300 to Greenwich Hospital for 'Wounded, Antient and Indigent Seamen', a seemingly patriotic gesture in time of war against France. These appeals cost £600, but to no avail.

In 1697 some Woodmongers sought a meeting 'touching matters of Importance relating to the Society'. Eighteen months later, after protracted discussions, Carmen agreed to admit Woodmongers to the Fellowship and offered to sell their carrooms for £70 and to make the price up to £100 from corporate funds. Approved in April 1699, the resolution was rescinded in June.

Talks continued. A joint constitution was drafted. Come January 1700, the petition was approved for presentation to Common Council; two weeks later reference to union with the Woodmongers was suspended. Old suspicions died hard.

In 1699 someone slipped a note into the Christ's Hospital carroom book: 'Mr. Reave. I dont lay no Clame to the Carrome but I would desir you to dow it, so as the two boyes may have theare personabell parts of it as well as shee, and to make the best of it, your frend and Sarvant – John Clarke'.

This note appears, from 1702: 'Sir, if my sonn should go to sell any of my Carroomes, I will not have any of them sold by noe menes for he will Sell if he Cann pray speak to ye Governors your selfe...'. Clearly the Hospital was open to poor Carmen's pleas.

Then in 1700 the Woodmongers faced a closed shop. The Act which merged the Watermen and Lightermen stopped anyone else working Thames boats. Woodmongers could keep their lighters for their own trade, as long as that guild manned the boats. Predictably the Lightermen blocked the Woodmongers' servants when they applied to join.

A Committee of Carmen and Fewellers was set up in 1700. They sought reasonable common cause, and found it in the suburban carters. Their carts were not regulated, they practised 'ffrauds and abuses in the Coale Trade' and general goods carriage, which deprived both Woodmongers and Carmen of London 'of their Worke and Livelyhood', the remedies for all of which lay in chartering both trades in and out of London.

In 1703 Woodmongers and Carmen petitioned the City as one, 'all the unhappy differences between the said partners being now reconciled'. They sought a new charter – together. Their common cause was prompted by porters and victuallers buying 'Lighters of Coals' and reselling false measure. The public blamed the Woodmongers; the 'foreigners' carried overloads and skimmed the Carmen's trade. The petition was considered, favoured, but charter came there none.

When Aldermen and Common Council turned this down, the Carmen abandoned the enterprise, but the Woodmongers persisted. Carmen heard about a petition to the Queen in the Green Dragon tavern, Fleet Street in 1705. Others were 'confederate with them' but the Fellowship told the Aldermen it was nothing to do with them.

The Aldermen ordered that 'Mr Remembrancer do attend Mr Attorney General therein' and stop the rot. In November 1706 Mr Bowyer, Upper Warden, was asked by the Assistants to 'gratifie Mr Remembrancer for the Services he hath done this Fellowship'.

The war was over. The Carmen had no Livery, but they had seen off their rivals. The last known mention of the Woodmongers is in 1746. After that, nothing; well, not quite nothing, but not quite Woodmongers either....

OPPOSITE ABOVE: Seven years after the Wheelwrights, in 1677 the 'Coach and Coach in Harnesse Makers, were chartered by Charles II; both the Carmen's 'supply side, guilds were incorporated. (CM) BELOW: Coffee houses were communications centres, used as *postes restantes* for the new penny post, and launched first newsletters, then newspapers: Jonathan's, drawn by H.O. Neal and published in 1763 by Mr Sumpter at the Bible and Crown near Shoe Lane. (GL)

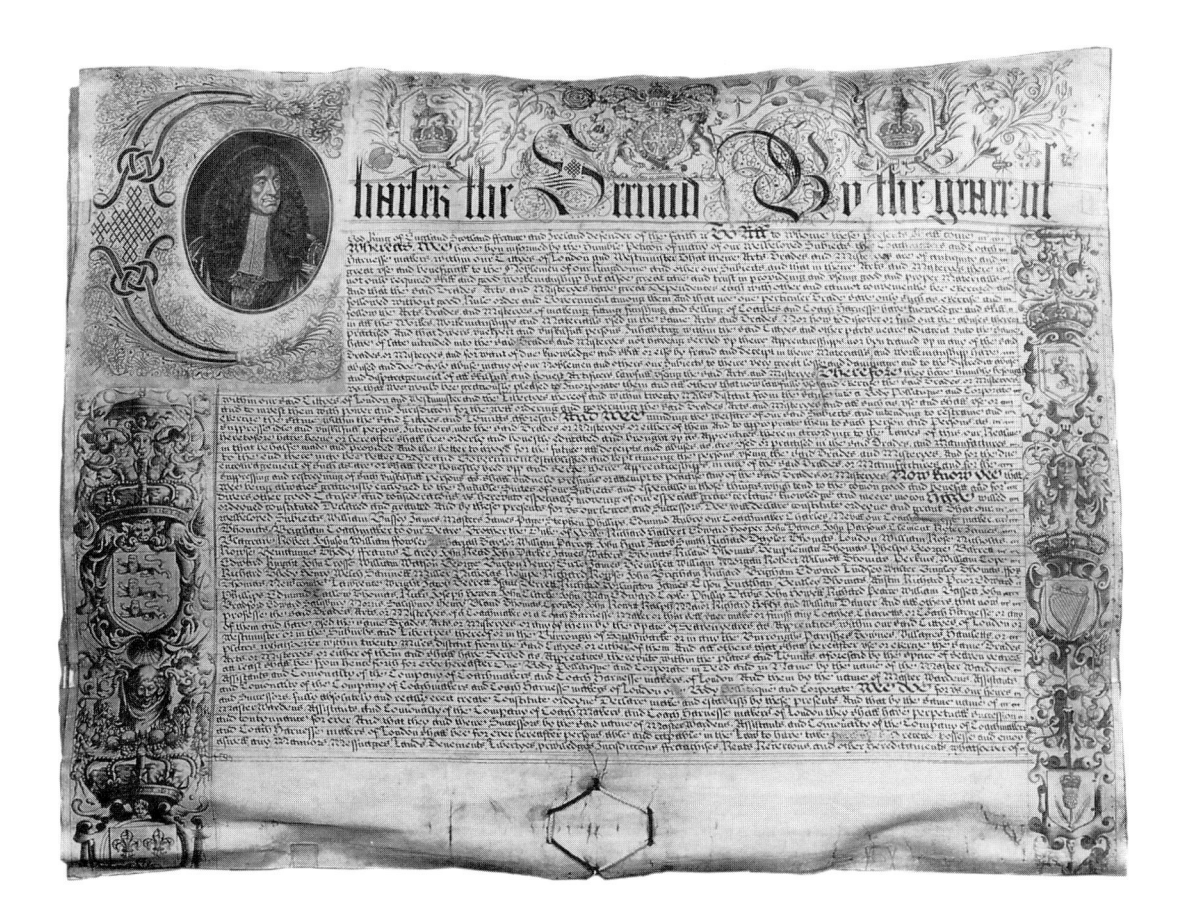

JONATHAN'S COFFEE HOUSE or an Analysis of CHANGE ALLEY
With a Group of Characters from the Life – Inscrib'd to Jacob Henriques.

The Courteous CARMAN,
And the Amorous Maid.
OR,
The Carman's Whistle.

What here is Pen'd in this same pleasant Story, || And brought her joy in midst of heaviness:
Doth only tend unto the *Carmans* Glory ; || He was Couragious, and of mettle good,
Who did relieve a Maiden in distress, || As by this Story may be understood.
To a New Tune, called, *The Carmans Whistle* ; or, *Lord Willoughby's March*, &c.

As I abroad was walking
by the breaking of the day,
Into a pleasant Meadow,
a young-man took his way,
And looking round about him,
to mark what he could see,
At length he spy'd a fair maid
under a Mirtle Tree.

So comely was her countenance,
and smiling was her chear,
As though the Goddess Venus,
her self she had been there,
And many a smirking smile she gave,
amongst the Leaves so green,
Although she was perceived,
she thought she was not seen.

At length she chang'd her countenance,
and sung a mournful song,
Lamenting her misfortune,
she staid a Maid so long:
There's many that be younger,
that long time have been wed,
Which makes me think that I shall die
and keep my Maiden-head.

Sure young-men are hard hearted,
and know not what they do,
Or else they want for Complements
fair Maidens for to woe:
Why should young Virgins pine away
and lose their cheifest prime,
And all for want of Sweet-hearts,
to chear us up in time.

The Courteous Carman And the Amorous Maid or the Carman's Whistle appeared in the 17th century – 'Now fare thee well brave Carman/ I wish thee well to fare,/ For thou didst use me kindly/ As I can well declare...'. (BL)

The young-man heard her Ditty
  and could no longer stay,
But straight unto this Damosel
  with speed he did away:
He nimbly stept unto her
  which made her for to start,
But when he once embraced her,
  he joy'd her very heart.

Sweet heart he said unto her
  why do you so complain,
If you'l be rul'd by me
  I'le play you such a strain,
As uses for to give content
  when as true Lovers meets,
It is much like to that they call
  the shaking of the sheets.

Strike up quoth she, and spare not
  I prithee use thy skill,
For why I greatly care not
  If I thy mind fulfil,
The Carman then most nimbly
  unto this sport did settle,
And pleased her most bravely
  for he was full of mettle.

When he had plaid unto her
  one merry note or two,
Then she was so rejoyced
  she knew not what to do:
O God a mercy Carman,
  thou art a lively Lad,
Thou hast as rare a Whistle
  as ever Carman had:

Now if my Mother chide me
  for staying here so long,
What if she doth I care not
  for this shall be my song:
Pray mother be contented
  break not my heart in twain;
Although I have been ill a while
  I shall be well again:

And thus this loving couple
  did oftentimes imbrace,
And lovingly did prattle
  all in that flowry place;
But now the time of parting
  began for to draw near,
Whereas this Noble Carman
  must leave his only dear,

He took his leave most kindly
  and thus to her did say,
My dearest I will meet thee
  next time I come this way:
Away this bonny Carman went
  a whistling of his Note,
And there he left this fair Maid
  a brushing of her Coat.

Now fare thee well brave Carman
  I wish thee well to fare,
For thou didst use me kindly
  as I can well declare:
Let other Maids say what they will
  the truth of all is so,
The bonny Carmans Whistle
  shall for my mony go.

Por F. Coles, T. Vere, J. Wright, J. Clarke, W. Thackeray, & T. Passinger.

RIGHT: Sir Edmund Berry Godfrey was the last Master of the Woodmongers, 'Murthered by Papists' on 12 October 1678. (CC)

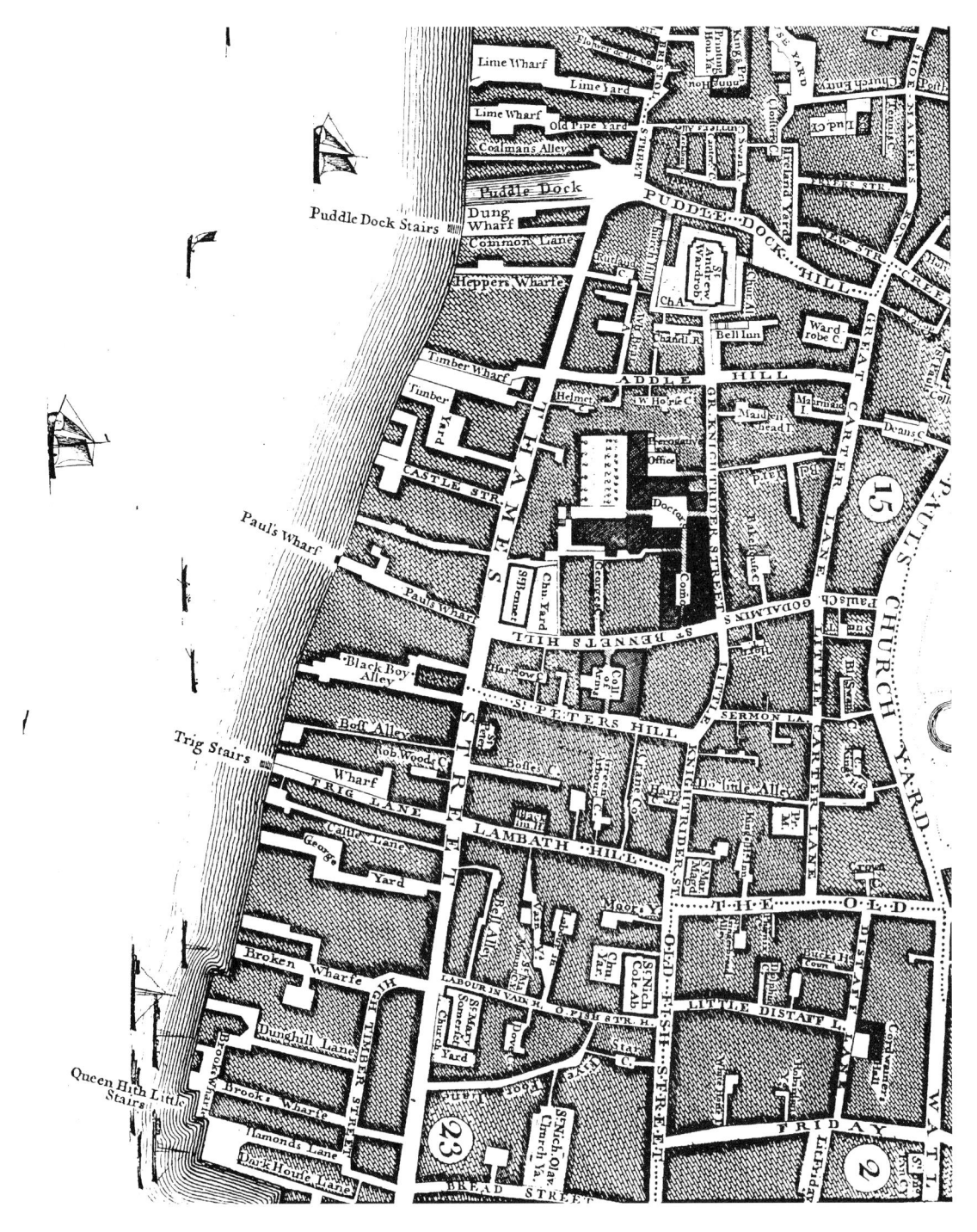

John Rocque's map of 1746 clearly shows the wharves off Thames Street – Lime, Dung, Hepper's, Timber, Paul's, Trig Lane, Broken and Brooks, next to Queen Hithe. (GL)

7

TAXING TIMES

Sir, I'd as soon have a man to break my bones as talk to me of public affairs, internal or external.

James Boswell: *Life of Johnson* 1783

Tax, war and old age drive men to drink, to charity and to end of their days. Carmen fought taxes, enjoyed their wine, and returned from armed service in need of work. Old Carmen simply died.

Under Queen Anne, Marlborough trounced the French, port meant tax-advantageous wine from Portugal, and land tax bore down on carrooms. The 1704 land tax Assessors claimed that owned carrooms were an employment of profit; leased carrooms were taxable on rents; carrooms as assets were stock or capital. A future Attorney General, Edward Northey, argued Carmen were not taxable, and they escaped.

The year before that, the Carmen's first Clerk died. William Parry had also served Christ's Hospital as Clerk since 1654. He had resigned the Carmen's Clerkship in 1677. Parry enjoyed a jar. The Common Serjeant once complained he 'was soe in drinck that he was not able to discourse'. In 1696 Thomas Day was made free; in the 18th century, his grandson Thomas was to become Junior, then Upper Warden, Master, champion of innumerable causes, and the Carmen's Boswell.

In 1703 the Coachmakers acquired their own Hall, in Noble Street, buying it from the Scriveners for £1,600, who leased it back for four days a year. The Loriners obtained a grant of livery – the last until the Carmen in the 19th century.

A year after that, William Thomas served as a mariner 'in the Service of Her Majesty', and was granted the freedom without delay, as was Thomas Hopkins in 1713, both 'to execute such Trades as they are capable of', following 'the late War'.

Many Watermen joined the Navy, most of them press-ganged. In 1700 the Lightermen, traditionally free of the Woodmongers, joined the Watermen by statute and gradually outnumbered the Watermen in their own Guild.

Carrooms grew in value to £150 by 1714 – by 1707 the Clerk earnt £20 a year and in 1709 Beadle John Moore, 'a very useful man' who 'had suffered great losses and Misfortunes...was granted £30 as a free gift'. In 1711 John Chitwell left the Court, the last of the first Assistants. Starting with one carroom, he finished up with five. The year before that, Christopher May was admitted for the now expensive fine of £30.

When the Thames froze over, the Frost Fair came to town. In 1683 stalls formed streets on ice, and coaches plied for hire between Westminster and the Temple. In 1715 'multitudes walk'd over it and some were lost by their rashness'. Coals rose to £3 10s per chauldron for lack of navigable water. Over 200,000 people now lived in the City.

Watermen were paid government grants when the river froze. They fought against theatres moving to the City from the south bank, and for 35 years stopped sedan chairs and hackneys two miles short of the river.

Private coaches and commercial carrs attracted criticism. John Gay had something to say about their effect on the City:

'Oh happy streets, to rumbling wheels unknown,
No carts, no coaches shake the floating town!
Thus was of old Britannia's city bless'd,
Ere pride and luxury her sons profess'd.'

and he added this biting comment on those with delusions of mobility:

'What walker shall his mean ambition fix
On the false lustre of a coach and six?'

and that was over a century after John Lyly's earlier strictures. Ned Ward wrote of Fleet Street that 'The Ratling of Coaches loud as the Cataracts of Nile Rob'd me of my hearing' and when he took a hackney-coach, 'By the help of a great many Slashes and Hey-ups, after as many Jolts and Jumbles', he arrived.

He described the public carriage as it 'enter'd upon London-Stones ... had no more sway than a Funeral Hearse, or a Country-Waggon, that we were jumbled about like so many Pease in a Childs-Rattle'.

Carmen still went to law. Their 1713 action was against the workers of the Brazen Rooms. These were carrooms licensed by the Tail Cart-takers of the Royal Household, under the auspices of the ancient Board of Green Cloth. Sixteen carts were marked with the rose and crown and brass letter.

Carts intended for food and drink were plying for hire, for which they were not licensed. From Lord Mayor to Queen's Bench, the action swung, with Attorney and Solicitor Generals defending the servants of the Crown. Prosecutions continued until, in 1755, Widow Brown withdrew carts marked I and K. Thus ended the Royal prerogative over Carmen.

Individual Carmen made sacrifices. In 1724 William Thompson asked to be disfranchised, so he could witness against a wharfinger – the case took four years, before Thompson was re-admitted. That same year journeymen Coachmakers rioted at their Hall, fatally wounding the watchman.

Common Council increased its powers and in 1725 the exclusive right of Liverymen to attend gained the force of law. They elected Lord Mayor and Sheriffs, the City's four MPs and influenced national policy through Common Council.

In 1722 the Lord Mayor had ordered traffic from Southwark to cross London Bridge on the west, outward vehicles on the east, perhaps the origin of driving on the left. In 1750 the City's monopoly across the river was broken – Westminster Bridge opened. The Lambeth–Millbank horse ferry closed soon after.

Fares until then had been 'Man and Horse – 2d. Horse and Chaise – 1s. Coach and two Horses – 1s. 6d. Ladened Cart – 2s.' Watermen were compensated for loss of ferries.

Carmen hid 'irregular working or abuseing of Worthy Citizens' by covering the brass number on the cart shaft, or parking close to the wall 'to the hazarding of the lives or the maiming of Persons' trying to read them. In 1728 Christ's Hospital ordered a duplicate brass on the other shaft. In 1754 Parliament decreed the cart owner's name be displayed and registered with the Commissioners for Licensing Hackney Coaches.

It was in 1728 that the Court put its own house in order. The Clerk was told to summon Assistants to meet 'at Nine o'clock in the forenoon' and to read out their names 'after the clock in Guild Hall or St. Laurences Church hath struck Ten'. Anyone who was late was fined a shilling. Assistants who missed the Court altogether paid 2s 6d. If they refused, they were liable to be thrown out.

Assistants who wanted wine on Court days had to produce a ticket; the tickets were presented to the Upper Warden to vouch for the Court's costs to the Fellowship.

In 1734 the Court expressed concern at the numbers of Carmen dining on Court days, which was 'very expensive to the Fellowship' and also 'the cause of much Riot, Confusion and Disturbance'. Guest numbers were henceforth limited, and a table laid in another room for those free by servitude or patrimony. The Upper Warden was authorised to invite those free by redemption to the Court table.

Ten years later, it was ordered that anyone attending a coffee house before Court should pay his own way – no expense was allowed for 'Coffee, Tea or Chocolate on any Court Day'.

Yet many Carmen enjoyed a boom as the century passed. When John Barber died in 1734 he owned twenty-four carrooms. By the '60s former Warden John Flexney held twelve, and Past Master William Holyland held eleven. Thomas Day himself held thirteen and worked another, while Samuel Day worked eight.

By mid-century, the Lightermen 'took the hint to do what the Woodmongers could not' and formed 'a Cabal, in which ... [they] settled the Market-Price to their own Minds'. Effectively, they stitched up the coal shippers, and skimmed their profits, cutting out the Woodmongers in the process.

'The Lightermen, called crimps, are great occasion of the high rate of coals' reported Mr Wilcox to the Aldermen. Billingsgate had become a closed market, and the Lightermen combined with the northern coal owners to rig that market. In 1730 Parliament acted, and Lightermen were barred from broking, factoring or acting as agents. Owners' lighters could carry coals, though their operators must be qualified and their lighters registered with the Guild.

Ships had to deliver in turn – shades of Thames Street – and now these successors to the Woodmongers had to allow other wharfingers access to the product. It was the story of the Carmen all over again. The ship masters could appoint their own agents, which led to the Society of Coal Factors in 1750, four years after the Woodmongers left recorded history.

On 19 February 1746, the usual committee was appointed by the City to enforce licensing of Woodmongers' carrs. There the record stops.

In 1743 John Trull introduced the fast post-chaise. Dr Johnson records 'If I had no duties ... I would spend my life in driving briskly in a post-chaise with a pretty woman'. The 1745 Turnpike Act put up the cost of cartage. As 'Jack Whipcord' was quoted in the 1747 *Gentleman's Magazine*: '... roads had but one object, namely, waggon-driving ... the gentry ought to stay at home' for one correspondent 'walk'd several miles on foot, met 20 waggons tearing their goods to pieces, and the drivers swearing for being robb'd on the highway by a turnpike'.

Supporters of the Bill argued carts would improve, and cartage costs go down. One side wanted light carts, the other broad wheels. Broad wheels won, by government decree in 1754. In 1764 Daniel Bourn of Leominster even produced a cart on rollers.

James Sharpe of Leadenhall Street made similar carts with cast-iron, two feet diameter rollers. In 1770 roller-carts were made toll-free and allowed as many horses as necessary, both of which laws disadvantaged ordinary carrs.

After repeated attempts, in 1757 the Carmen extracted new rules from the Magistrates of the City, in an Act which gave them regulatory rights, including turn-keeping for wharf, crane and tackle work.

Thomas Day recorded the events outside the minute books. 'Turnkeeping at the Public Wharfs and Warehouses is the Fellowship's Strong-Hold and whoever seeks ... to encroach upon or extend it ... is an enemy ... to the Fellowship.' Years later he claimed 'preservation of Turnkeeping, Unanimity, Regularity and Resolution' among members as 'the only means to preserving the Existence of the Fellowship'.

In 1757, sixty-five years had passed since cartage rates were fixed. Yet 'no authority existed to compel the payment'. There were many instances of flagrant abuse. Loads which were rated at 4s 10d were authorised at 2s 6d; packages were enlarged, weights increased, turn-keeping 'grievously broken through even at the Waterside'.

'This produced Quarels Animosity and Ill behaviour' and even 'Masters were not exempt from this'. Eventually, Wardens and Assistants acted. In 1756 they refused the higher rates, and insisted on payment by the 1691 tariff – 'the only legal rule they had to direct them.'

The East India Company paid at that rate, and the sugar refiners. But merchants 'met at the brown Tavern behind the Exchange' and drew up 'totally ridiculous and inadmissible' proposals. The Carmen riposted with their own rates.

One merchant asked 'But what do ye say to our proposals?' and another said 'O let the Carmen alone, it is plain they know what they are about much better than we do'. The merchants took the new rates and tweaked them somewhat, 'introducing absurdities'.

Unfortunately Richard March, the Clerk, filed the Carmen's paper, and neglected to pass it on to Edward Mayor and Thomas Day, deputed to sort the matter out. After nine months the City procured the Act which laid down the new 1757 rates.

Carmen would henceforth pay 17s 4d annual rent to Christ's Hospital per licence, plus 3s 6d licensing fee and 20s on transfer. The legal limit was raised from one ton to 25cwt, the halter increased to five feet, the age limit of drivers reduced to sixteen. JPs would impose fines for any offences, such fines to be divided between informer and parish poor. The school appointed and paid street-keepers and sealed carts. A new forge was built in 1758.

Carmen were not the only ones in conflict. In 1754 the Coachmakers had a go at Wheelwright John Miles for six offences against their rights of monopoly – 'a very avaritious Person' who 'took it into his head' to set up business as a Coachmaker 'without any the least knowledge ... for his own Lucre and Benefit'. Mr Miles carried on.

The year before that, the Company looked askance at its own journeymen too: 'the best hands ... have risen to such an intollerable, insufferable, insupportable height of self-sufficiency and disobedience' that many refused to work by the day, and demanded 'unusual and unwarrantable wages'. They wasted their Masters' time in 'Rioting, Drunkenness, and Debauchery', so that prices must rise.

It was in 1763 that the Carmen's Court laid down a dress code; anyone who came wearing a coloured handkerchief or an apron was fined 2s 6d. Every Assistant either produced his freedom on Court days, or paid 1s.

In the 1760s the City made headway paving the streets, and removing hazardous shop signs. Sewers and drains were improved, the markets flourished and London was the nation's greatest consumer. A gentleman could live for £200 a year in 1762, which is what James Boswell received from his father. His London lodgings cost £50, food, fuel (coal £7), cleaning and clothes £107, so that 'by this calculation, I have just £43 left for coach-hire, diversion and the tavern'.

Fish and coal came to Billingsgate, fruit and vegetables to Covent Garden, Borough Market and Spitalfields and corn to Bear Quay and Queenhithe. Meat came on the hoof to Smithfield. Covent Garden attracted night trade for carts from 15,000 acres of market gardens within ten miles of the City.

By 1742 Roomland, at the top of Billingsgate Dock, was the 'Place where the Masters of Coal Ships, Coalmongers and Heavers daily meet to transact their Affairs'. This was in 1746 'the great remarkable Coal-Market ... the Coal Brokers are called Crimps ... the Coal Ships they call Hags, Cats, Fly-Boats, and Hagboats ...'.

No sooner had peace settled 'twixt Carmen and merchants, than Thames Street erupted yet again. Thomas Day, Assistant in 1763, Warden in 1768, recorded in 1769 'From the vast increase of the National commerce' after 1757 'a grievance, which then existed in so very small a degree that it was neither felt nor noticed by us' started to emerge. Clearly Thames Street had been quiet long enough. That 'vast increase' was partly due to the development of canals from 1760, linking and improving the existing network of waterways which carried bulky freight.

Many carts had been idle due to the 'total loss of the Coal business' until 1761. However, many City traders had acquired their own carts, so that some Carmen were forced to find business by the waterside. There they faced trade carts fetching their owners' goods, 'and frequently those of others', as well as waiting before their loads were ready. That year Upper Warden, Joseph Springwell, left a carroom to the Fellowship.

'Lower Thames Street was ... grievously pestered' with carts and carriages. Inevitably, residents and Carmen fell out. Matters were not improved by the 'uncontrolled and destructive custom' of 'enormous and unlawful loads'. The dispute flared for three years, costing both sides a great deal of money.

The traders 'instead of acting like men of consideration and candor ... commenced hostilities against us'. They exhibited 'an exalted opinion of their superiority' and claimed the City's laws were on their side. For sixteen months, two paid patrols counted carts in excess of the forty permitted by a century-old regulation 'when the Commerce of the city bore a very small proportion to its present state' now that business was fourfold.

Carmen and traders went before the Lord Mayor. He rebuked the traders 'for their violence' of manner. As Day records 'The interference of the Fellowship' was necessary to protect its weaker members if they were to keep their livings. Master Carman Jno Lane was deputed to enforce the prevailing regulations.

If Carmen denigrated traders, others found Carmen wanting. When Oliver Goldsmith described Gray's *Odes* as 'terribly obscure' Thomas Davies, actor and bookseller, replied 'And why not? He is not writing to porters and carmen. He is writing to men of knowledge'.

In 1767 theft was becoming a major problem. Sir John Fielding warned 'Stage Coachmen, Carriers, Book-keepers, Tradesmen' and others to 'secure [luggage] behind with a small Chain' and ensure they never 'send the Coachman from his Box' and 'have a Man at least to guard' coaches or waggons 'five or ten miles out of town', to stop 'that Gang of unhappy wretches, who live in Idleness and subsist on Plunder' stealing goods 'out of Waggons, from the Baskets of Stage-Coaches, Boots of Hackney Coaches, and out of Carts which carry goods'.

Wheelwrights fell on hard times too – in 1771 Samuel King was in 'extrem low condition' and received a guinea. Ten years later journeymen went on strike for shorter hours and more pay. The Court refused, they struck again, were prosecuted and convicted.

In 1773 the General Turnpike (or Broad Wheels) Act sought to reduce the ruts in roads by heavy vehicles, and defined tolls by vehicle type. The carriage trade was exempted, so the Wheelwrights suffered where the Coachmakers did not. Carmen found the new wheels ruined their horses.

In 1771 Carmen were summoned before the Lord Mayor for leaving horses unattended and feeding them on street. The cases were dismissed after a memorial from the Carmen that 'the grand concourse of Carts to Lower Thames Street was the vast increase of the National Commerce'. The Fellowship had done all it could but the 'Trade of the City must be accomodated'. In 1772 the Thames Street Association was dissolved.

It all cost time and money. Assistant William Murden reckoned he attended Guildhall 72 times during his Wardenships in 1770 and 1771. It also cost energy and ingenuity. Carmen physically blocked wine dealers who rolled their barrels by hand to avoid cartage. Cheesemongers' unlicensed carts were blockaded by Carmen's carts 'across the quays'.

Carmen were summoned to court, challenged the dealers to a higher court, and were dismissed and over a few months 'the practice of Rolling was nearly annihilated'. That was after the King's Bench had ruled against Carmen – 'nothing can be deem'd Cart work where a Cart is not wanted'. As Day observed 'This Evil has since pretty well cured itself'.

In 1772 'a similar attempt was made to hinder the Traders Carts' and that went before King's Bench too. Lord Mansfield found that 'the Carmen's right was incontestable, but not exclusive', allowed nominal damages, and told the Carmen to ask the Aldermen for redress. Hay was now £5 a load, so Carmen also sought higher rates to pay 'Horsekeep'.

If the Carmen nominally failed, they had raised their official profile, improved their reputation, and exposed the problem. Thames Street rumbled, but quietly, for twenty years. Rates were revised in 1772 and regularly thereafter until 1799 – in the Carmen's favour.

The war was not only on the streets and in the courts, but also in print. The merchants and traders advertised meetings at the Swan Tavern, Fish Street Hill in the *Public Advertiser*. The Carmen responded in the same paper that 'the terror of Prosecution will not in the least intimidate them'.

When the traders advertised again, seeking details of obstruction, the Carmen responded in the *Gazeteer*, the *Ledger* and the *Daily Advertiser*.

The Fellowship 'take the liberty once more to address the gentlemen who meet at the Swan tavern' to enquire how 'a numerous Company of opulent Traders' sought to 'crush a little Body of People' who were simply asserting 'their legal Rights and Privileges'.

Dismissing 'many separate actions', they declared that 'the Laws of this Nation will not suffer oppression' and they would stand by the verdicts of the courts and continue to prevent 'infringement of their Rights'. They believed that as 'a Body of Freemen, incorporated from time immemorial' who paid their dues, they were 'not obliged to stand by and see themselves robbed of their Labour'.

That was despite the fact they carried customers' goods without knowing their names, destinations or what they might be paid. They would hinder 'any unlicensed Carriage'. Any Carman faced with prosecution was invited to tell the Lord Mayor's office. As a parting shot, the Carmen noted that any unlicensed carrier would be prosecuted 'without Farther Notice'.

The Carmen also asked Christ's Hospital for help. The Governors were unhelpful. After keeping the Carmen waiting, they disappeared, leaving the Treasurer to tell them 'everyone had a right to fetch their Goods from the Waterside'. Carmen were no different from Hackney Coachmen.

The Carmen promptly withdrew their quit-rent and refused to send carts for sealing until the Hospital relented. They pointed out the Hospital had received 'upwards of Forty thousand pounds' from Carmen.

While this new dispute warmed up, Day became Master in 1774. Three years earlier 'a Person at Guildhall removing an old Chest from the Irish Chamber' where the Carmen's Court once met, found a Carmen's document. Day examined the contents, found many more, and copied them out.

In 1774 John Lloyd was apprenticed, a carter whose family produced generation upon generation of Carmen for two centuries.

In 1777 the fine for working an unlicensed cart was set to rise from 13s 4d to £10 and admission reduced from £50 to £25 – both to encourage compliance. It died the death because Aldermen friendly to the Carmen fell out over 'that Contest' – the American War of Independence.

In the seventies, the Fellowship sold £400 of South Sea Annuities to settle debts. The War was affecting trade. Those working the Fellowship's carrooms were given notice, and their brasses stored in the Fellowship's chest. Three years later, 'such a number of Carts stood daily unemploy'd in Thames Street as grievously incommoded the residents'.

At a general meeting, Carmen agreed to voluntarily remove thirty carts, at least until Michaelmas 1782, to require operators who 'sometimes resorted thither' to waive their rights, and that the rents lost should be paid by those working the quays. Their carts should be stamped 'with the letter C'. It worked. Clearly the Carmen were no longer disorderly.

In 1780 the annual Sealing Day celebrations were scrubbed, dinners were abandoned, and only the Wardens and Committee were excepted. Meanwhile, the Watermen had built a new Hall at St Mary-at-Hill. In 1783 it was decided 'no Money be hereafter allowed out of the Fellowship Stock on account of a Dinner in the Country as formerly' as the Treaty of Versailles recognised America. £100m had been added to the National Debt.

That same year a small balloon went up from Cheapside, after the French breakthrough, and in 1784 Lunardi thrilled 200,000 including the Prince Regent, as they watched him rise from the grounds of the Honourable Artillery Company at Moorfields. Man was airborne.

The first mail-coach left London in 1784 and by 1791, daily mileage was 6,896 – one coach leaving London every four and a half minutes. John Palmer's innovation replaced the post-boys on horseback. Stage passengers boarded and alighted to choice, booked in advance, and could travel cheaper outside. Hired post-chaises were faster. Mails were more regulated and reliable. Poorer people used the stage waggons or simply travelled by cart.

In the aftermath of war, crime increased. Once the scapegoats for 'imbeaslement' from carts, the well-ordered Carmen now faced street thieves. In 1784 they advertised a three guinea reward, payable to anyone who caught a thief. In 1794 street-keepers Thomas Merriman and Joseph Talbot detected and caught one such, 'stealing a Cask of Pork out of a Cart on London Bridge, surrounded by a desperate Gang of Villains'.

If it was not footpads and street thieves, it was recalcitrant carters. When 'a large quantity of Malt' was landed at Brook's Wharf in Queenhithe, Mr Winkworth claimed it out of turn. The Fellowship took him to Court, where he was convicted, but rejected the decision, producing 'an Opinion of the Recorder in his favour'.

The Committee involved turned to 'Mr Whitbread's Brewhouse' but the response was a long time coming, so they took matters in hand, attended the wharf, and directed 'Carts entitled to the Labour to be set at the Warehouse in such a manner as to hinder Mr. Winkworth's Carts from loading'. Mr Winkworth gave in.

If American independence affected trade, the 1789 French Revolution echoed earlier City radicalism, expressed by Wilkes and others in Common Council, just as public protest was chanelled through riots. In 1793 the French incited revolution elsewhere and England went to war.

In 1791 the Fellowship tried to vary non-feeding and attendance, saying 'the innocent Owner ... is liable to be fined 500 times in a week' because they often had perforce to leave their charges. Thames Street traders objected, and it was dropped.

In 1792 Coachmaker freemen numbered 'upwards of nine hundred'. In 1798 their dinners discontinued and they paid £100 'into the Bank yearly for the Defence of the Country against Invasion'.

When the Treasury was asked to let tobacco imports be landed south of Blackfriars Bridge, Carmen, wharfingers and porters all protested at the potential loss of trade. William Pitt was among those who ruled in the protesters' favour. The City Solicitor's bill for representing the Carmen was £102 19s 10d.

In 1793 rates were raised. The war with France and bad weather combined to push up the price of hay. Clover was £7 and hay £5 12s a load. When Army Packers Hodgson and Hayter complained there were not enough carts, the Carmen explained that many 'Horses have been maimed and wounded and universally strained and damaged' and also 'half of their Journeymen laid up with Colds and other disorders'.

Wharfingers came back to haunt the Carmen when Thomas Wilson, who rented a wharf, and was also a farrier, applied for admission. He was turned down. He petitioned the Aldermen, alleging the fine for admission had been raised, he would not stand for hire, and he could not even handle a quarter of his own workload.

The Fellowship suggested 'he has not alledged any sufficient reason', he was no different from other wharfingers, he had served no apprenticeship, and no Carmen should have their living 'torn from them by the irresistable hands of opulence and avarice united'. The Aldermen thought it 'highly improper to admit any Public Wharfinger' and they turned him down too.

When William Adams applied before finishing his indentures in 1799, he was turned down too. He petitioned the Aldermen, and this time they agreed. Despite Aldermanic threats, the Carmen were steadfast. He was never admitted, even though in 1801 he tried again and then 'went into Thames Street with a blue ribbon in his Hat' to ridicule the Carmen.

In 1799 the Parcel Act 'to regulate the delivery of all Parcels and other Goods Brought from any part of Great-Britain by any Waggon, Stage, or Carrier, to London, Westminster, Southwark etc' was on sale at 'all the booksellers'.

It was enacted 'to prevent the Exactions and Abuses practised' in porterage and delivery of goods under 56 lbs weight. The delivery charge from the receiving houses – mostly taverns – was 3d under a quarter mile, 4d up to half a mile, 6d a mile, 8d one and a half miles, 10d two miles and 3d a half mile thereafter. Overcharging attracted fines from 5s to 20s.

Every parcel must have a ticket, with destination and price of carriage and delivery, with the porter's name on it. Penalties for non-compliance ranged up to 40s. Delivery times were maximum six hours, between 7 am and 4 pm. Stage waggon deliveries could be taken on up to 24 hours later. Storage charges were also limited – 2d a time, plus 1d a week if uncollected.

Refusal to pay, neglect, misbehaviour or misconduct were all subject to court action, but complaints had to be registered within fourteen days. For the Carmen, the saving grace was Clause 12 'in favor of the Immunities of the Citizens of London' which 'states that nothing in the Act shall extend to authorize the Employment of any Porter in the City, contrary to its Laws and Usages'. Fines were split between the Informer and the Poor of the Parish.

By 1755 Roomland had become the Exchange for coal, a market unregulated by the City until 1803, and around 1769 the coal buyers and factors built a Coal Exchange on land at Thames Street, opposite Smart's Key.

The coal factors had formed a Society of Coal-Buyers by the 1770s. Their profits came from discounts, lighterage, carriage charges, premiums, 'abatements' from the bought-in price, special gratuities and carriage charges. With capital of some £7,000, profits were between 4 and 5s a chauldron.

By 1796 'Colliers and Coasting Traders form the greatest proportion of Shipping and Tonnage of the Port of London ... [with] 900,000 Chadrons per annum ... [worth] £1,800,000. In 1795 4,395 Sail arrived in London'. 'The Banks of the River are lined with Timber and Coal Barges ... floating Store Craft, in order to save the Expense of Wharfage.'

Now the coalmen were the successors to the Woodmongers and Lightermen. In 1800 a Select Committee concluded that the Coal Exchange 'is of late years become a close Market'. In 1803 the first of several Acts decreed a free market in coals, and the City bought the Exchange.

In 1800 the Carmen faced revolt and revolution. At last Common Council had agreed to bring unlicensed carts under the Carmen's regulations. 'They behav'd very generously and genteely' and the Fellowship 'dined with them ... without any expence on our part.' To no avail.

The unlicensed carters were not about to be put 'on a level with Common Carmen' and 'declined to meet the Question fairly'. They resisted the Bill, procured its postponement, and 'Its death warrant was thereby as completely signed as if it had been totally rejected'. Thomas Day recorded 'Some of them manifested a great deal of asperity towards us in the Lobby of the House of Commons'.

He added that 'the Docks at the Isle of Dogs have almost cured the evil with respect to the Grocers Waggons' and concluded 'what consequences may follow the opening of those at Wapping, is not I believe in the power of the wisest man now existing to foretel'.

The merchants had backed another Bill – for a wet dock, the first in the Isle of Dogs and another at Wapping. The Carmen petitioned the House, pointing out 'the Trade and business of the City and Port of London would in a great degree be removed' outside the City, where anyone could operate without licence or controls.

They petitioned Christ's Hospital, and Common Council. The former was distant, but sought a clause protecting its rights over Carmen. The Carmen lost. The West India Docks opened in 1802. Carrooms fell to £30 and the Fellowship stopped paying its staff. In 1800 Thomas Day closed his neat minute books, tracing the Fellowship since 1679 – from the old records in that half forgotten chest to the minutes of his own Court.

He left this epitaph on Christ's Hospital: 'I am sorry to have occasion to record' that the petition for assistance against the wet dock scheme 'met a similar fate with all the Petitions ... within my memory, being very coldly and reluctantly received'. There was 'very little regard paid either to Petitioners or Petition'.

Change was in the air, on the water and in the streets. London was fast growing beyond the City bounds. Napoleon cast his shadow over the Channel: Fleet Street prints forecast a French invasion – by balloon and raft. Docks were draining business. Carmen were concerned.

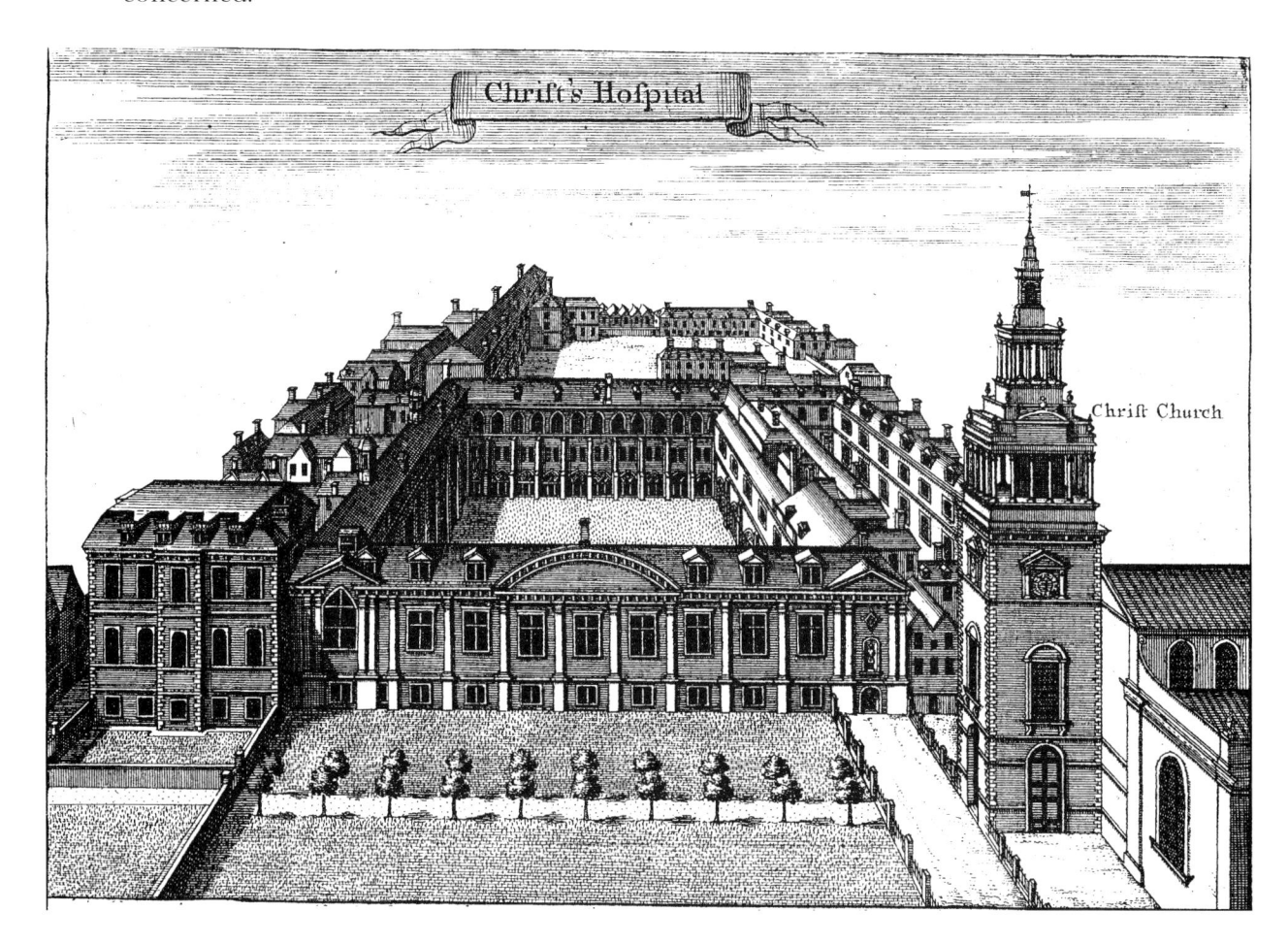

Christ's Hospital in 1725 – where there were 820 boys and 80 girls 'provided with Lodging, Diet, Clothing & Learning' and then made apprentice, though 'some of the Boys ... are sent to University'. (CH)

ABOVE: In 1683 the Thames froze over, and the Frost Fair came to town. A later Fair on 28 January 1739 was recorded, showing a man-powered hackney coach and becalmed wherries. (GL) BELOW: Philip Fruchard's trade card of 1730 suggested sweetness and light as a coal heaver moved between Lightermen and Carman. (GL)

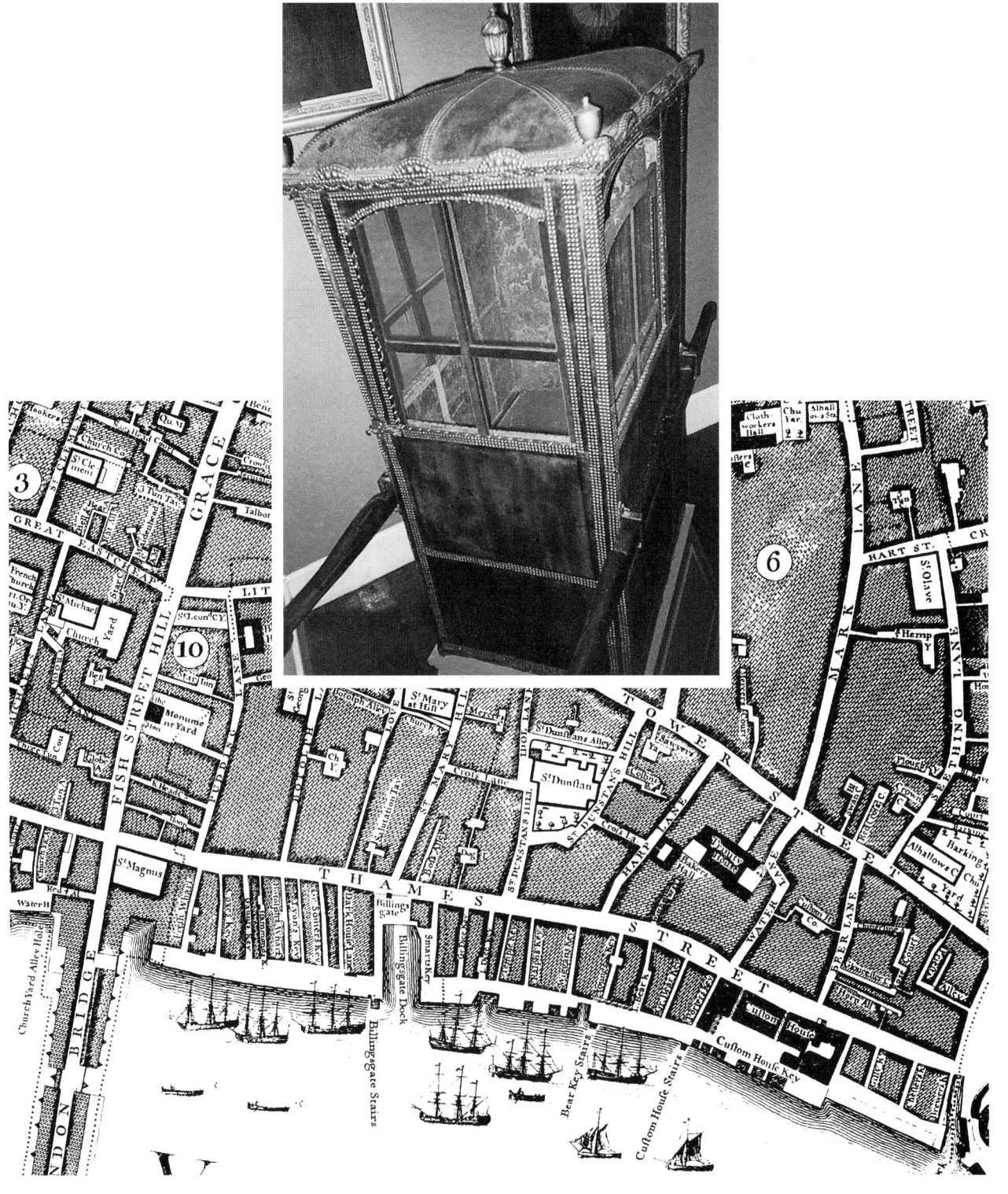

East of London Bridge ran the legal quays – Coxes, Gaunts, Hammonds, Lyons, Gt Somers, and after Billings Gate, Smarts, Gr Dice, Lt Dice, Temple, Ralphs, Wiggans, Youngs, Little Bear, Porters and Custom House, Gilly, Chesters and Brewers. Roomland is behind Billings Gate in Rocque's 1746 map. (GL) INSET: Sedans were labour-intensive – two manpower to carry one. This fine example at Shalstone Manor belongs to Geoffrey Purefoy, whose ancestress ordered it in the 1740s. (CB)

LEFT: Coachmakers were at loggerheads with RIGHT: Wheelwrights over rights to work, and standards. (CM) BELOW: Coach, dray and cart traverse Cheapside outside St Mary-le-Bow, in Maitland's 1739 *History*. (ML)

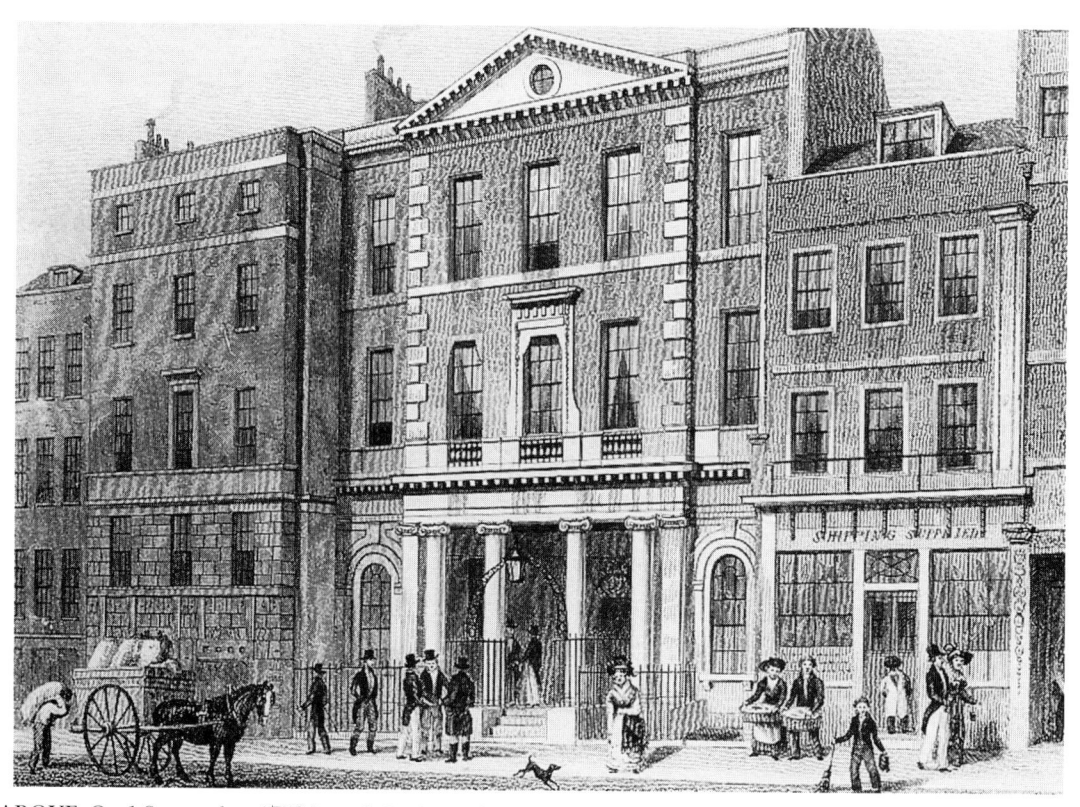

ABOVE: On 1 September 1750 Joseph Springwell was admitted to the Carroom of the late executor of Mary Paulding, widow of Carman Richard. (GL) BELOW: In 1769 the coal factors built their Exchange in Thames Street, opposite Smart's Key, here in Thomas Shepherd's drawing of 1830. (GL)

ABOVE: The Broad Wheels Act created waggons like this one in St Martin Outwich, at the corner of Threadneedle Street – in this later 1830 print; two hackney-coaches stand on the right. (CB) BELOW: Passengers join the stage coaches at the Bull and Mouth. (CB)

𝔇𝔥𝔞𝔱 No CARMAN shall come with his CART or CARTS to any of the Wharfs or places of keeping Turn between *London Bridge* and the *Tower Wharf* or to any of the Streets or Lanes within this City or the Liberties thereof, or to *London Bridge* before FIVE of the Clock in the Morning in the Summer time, or before SEVEN of the Clock in the Morning in the Winter time, unless a Merchant or any other Person having extraordinary occasion shall require his coming sooner, under the penalty of TWENTY Shillings, the Months of *November, December, January* and *February* being accounted Winter, and all the other Months Summer for the purposes of this Order.

𝔇𝔥𝔞𝔱 No CARMAN shall be allowed to Carry in his Cart at one time a greater Quantity of the Following Goods than as hereafter specified, and which Quantity shall be accounted a Load, upon the penalty of paying for the first Offence FIVE *Shillings*, for the second Offence TEN *Shillings*, and for the third and every other Offence TWENTY *Shillings*, that is to say.

Four Packs of Irish Cloth.	Three Hundred Scale Boards.	Two Large Hogsheads of Hams or Three Tierces.
Eight Bundles or Boxes of ditto.	Six Barrels of Smalts or Blue.	Ten Bags of Pepper.
Ten Bales of Irish Yarn.	Three Casks of Bristles.	Two Pipes of Wine
One Pack of Brown Cloth.	Six Bags of Rotterdam Flax.	Two Puncheons of Rum
Two Packs of Hessians or Hastings.	Ten Casks of Cochineal.	One Piece and One Puncheon of Brandy.
One Drum Vatt.	Three Casks of Antimony.	Ten Quarters of Malt.
One Large Chest of Hamburgh Dowlas.	Three Casks of Madder.	Two Hogsheads of Sugar.
Two Small ditto.	Fifty Firkins of Butter	Eight Chests of Tea.
Six Small Chests Silesia's.	Nine Bags of Gauls.	Sixteen Half Chests of ditto.
Six Small Bales Russia Linen.	Nine Bags of Spunge.	Thirty-two Quarter Chests ditto.
Four Large ditto.	Twelve Fangots or Sacks of Mohair, Yarn, or Silk.	Four Bales of Furs and Skins
Thirty Matts Duck.	Ten Bales of Cotton Yarn.	Eight Barrels of Provisions.
Two Dantzick Packs.	Three Bales of Carpets	Three Hogsheads of Tobacco.
Six Rotterdam Cases.	Three Bales of Safflour.	Ten Barrels of Oil.
Sixteen Bales Turkey or Leghorn Silk.		

N. B. All Casks of Sugar weighing Eight Hundred and upwards are Hogsheads, and Ginger and Pimento are to be carried only by Weight.

And Lastly, it is ordered by this Court that these Rules, Orders, and Ordinances shall with the space of Thirty Days from this time be Printed and Published in one of the Daily News Papers, and also Printed and affixed up at some Convenient and Conspicuous Place at or near the *Royal Exchange*, and upon or near the several Public Gates of this CITY, and upon the KEYS of *London*, and also upon some Convenient and Conspicuous Place at or near the several Places appointed for the standing of CARTS in and about the said CITY and Liberties thereof.

By the Court,

ABOVE: For the early mail coaches travel was still hazardous. (CB) BELOW: In 1787 the Lord Mayor, Recorder and fellow Justices laid down new 'Rules, Orders and Ordinances' to govern 'Licensed Carts, Carrs and Carr-Roons (sic)'. (GL)

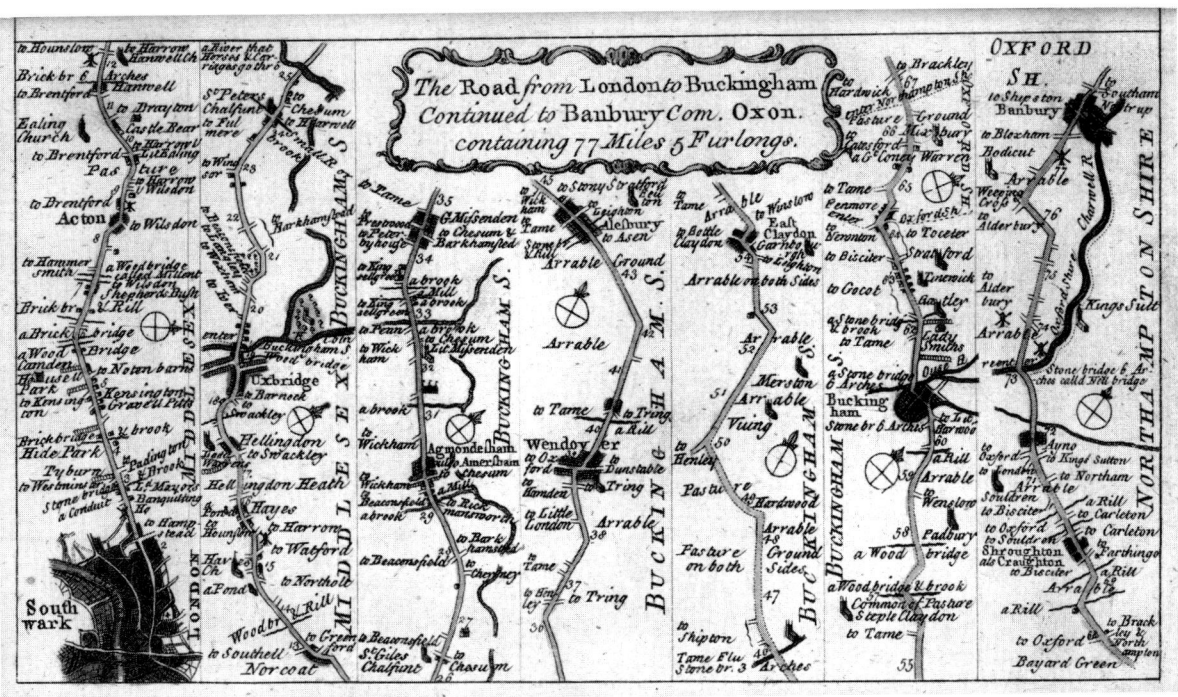

ABOVE: The fast post-chaise used the best roads available – here through the turnpike at Hyde Park; a waggon lumbers out on the right in B. Longmate's drawing in the *Gentleman's Magazine* supplement of 1792. (CB) BELOW: How they got there: the road from London to Banbury *via* Buckingham – a typical 18th century strip map, after John Senex, 1719. (CB)

The *price* of Cartage from the Public Wharfs (high and burdenſome as it is ſometimes repreſented) in reſpect of the *average value* of the Merchandize imported, does not exceed ONE HALFPENNY IN THE POUND STERLING: a very trifling conſideration for our labour, riſque, and reſponſibility for damage and loſs!—It is, therefore, greatly diſproportionate to the Penny received by the Fellowſhip Porters for ſhoring a Baſket of Oyſters, or other Fiſh; which for the ſake of that regularity and diſpatch neceſſary for public accommodation, is cheerfully ſubmitted to by perſons, to whom that Penny is a far greater object than the Halfpenny is to any of the Traders: and as we are compellable under ſevere penalties to do our buſineſs at the requiſition of *any perſon whatever*, at a price not optional, with reſpect to individuals, be the times and circumſtances what they may, and have paid ſince our laſt incorporation near Fifty Thouſand Pounds to Chriſt's-Hoſpital, for Licenſes to carry Goods, beſides a much larger ſum in the purchaſe or hire of Car-rooms, ſurely *then* we ought to be authoriſed, in common with the other fraternities at the Water-Side, to DEMAND OUR LABOUR ONCE out of all Goods landed at the Quays and Public Wharfs of this City.

It is neceſſary to mention that the enormous ſize of ſome of the Traders Carts and Waggons, and the immoderate Loads carried by them (ſometimes to the amount of Five Tons) from the Quays and Wharfs (many of which Loads would ſubject them on Turnpike Roads to very heavy Penalties) are not only injurious to us by depriving us of a great quantity of labour, but are really terrifying and dangerous—and (independent of damage to the pavement) the room occupied in the Public Streets and Lanes by thoſe Carriages, is the cauſe of much danger, inconvenience, and damage to the Carmen, Inhabitants, and Paſſengers—of all theſe circumſtances we can bring authentic teſtimony. In ſhort, the miſchief done in and about London, by overloaded Carriages, is beyond general conception; and we therefore apprehend theſe facts demand the ſerious attention of the Legiſlature of this City.

ABOVE: Carmen sought redress in 1798. (GL) BELOW: The 'old' Horse Ferry was a quiet enough spot in 1800, when Carman and Lighterman transacted business. (CB)

8

FLOREAT CARMEN

For now I see the true old times are dead...
The old order changeth, yielding place to new.

Things do not change; we change.

Alfred, Lord Tennyson; *Idylls of the King* 1878
& Thoreau, Henry David 1817–1862

Carmen continued to combat crime and tried to gain cartage rights over dockland. Despite their trials, and despite centuries of enforced conveyance for the Crown, they united against the Corsican corporal.

On 12 August 1803 the Court resolved

'That as an infernal Fiend ycleped Bonaparte has in his tender mercies threatened to murder us our Families and Friends and to lay waste and dispoil this happy land it is the bounden duty of every Englishman manfully to resist this Enemy of the human Race and his numerous slaves the devil's Judges and the very refuse of mankind.'

The resolution continued in like vein:

'That should this vile and abominable miscreant with his hungry Legions of dishonour "armed" with fury and Hell flames dare to set their cloven feet on this Land of Freedom we will supply the Government of this Country with 420 Carts and 1000 Horses...' to carry stores, ammunition and weaponry 'at an hour's notice' on the Lord Mayor's request anywhere in the kingdom.

The Lord Mayor responded within three days, enclosing Lord Hobart's note of the King's acceptance and uttering such words of praise and contentment as must have amazed the 'rude' Carmen: 'I embrace this opportunity...great compliment you have been pleased to bestow...high station I have been entrusted with' and signed as 'Your ever faithful and Obt humble St'.

The Carmen were so gratified they wanted to publish offer and response, but alas! it appears nowhere in the public prints.

At the first census in 1801, the City was still home to 64,615 but London's population was 958,865 overall. Population was linked to transport; the 40 feet wide New Road was created in 1756 as a by-pass into the City on the north but simply served to expand the population as, first Somers Town, then Pentonville, and finally Camden and Kentish Towns developed between 1786 and 1791.

The Thames separated the south until Waterloo (1817) and Southwark (1819) Bridges breached that barrier. The 1770 Blackfriars Road led southwards. In 1817 John McAdam's process brought new surfaces to all these roads.

As London grew, so did petty crime. Street-keepers were augmented with cart watchers, and even the police received rewards. In 1802 Carman Samuel Day prosecuted Joseph Perkins. He had worked for Day, and was accused of following carts, then presenting 'his' bill after delivery. He had defrauded numerous Carmen.

To protect their backs, they also decided to print 1,000 handbills and advertise that they were not liable for goods stolen in transit. The traders objected but a general meeting of the Fellowship agreed that 'on Account of Carts robbed by gangs of desperate villains' anyone hiring cartage 'that cannot be delivered before sunset' must provide a guard, since Carmen could not protect goods and manage horses at the same time.

Pilferage also bedevilled the Legal Quays. The 1801 River Police were powerless to stop the rising tide of crime. There were too many ships for too few wharves. The 1802 West India Docks were merely the start of a waterside, City and trading revolution – and the inevitable decline of civic power and Carmen's trade.

Lighters carried cargoes from docks to City. The City raised £400,000 to build the London Docks at Wapping in 1805. St Katharine's Dock came in 1828 in Stepney, just outside the City walls. Across the river in 1804 the Surrey and Commercial Docks sprawled into being.

Coastal carriage far eclipsed road freight. Adam Smith observed that 'Six or eight men, therefore, by the help of water-carriage, can carry and bring back in the same time the same quantity of goods between London and Edinburgh, as fifty broad-wheeled waggons, attended by a hundred men, and drawn by four hundred horses'. It took six weeks for an eight-horsed broad-wheeled waggon to haul four tons. A small coaster could carry two hundred tons in the same time.

In 1805 the cab began to replace the hackney-coach. Nine were licensed, without much impact. In 1823 'coffin-cabs' emerged, for two passengers – by 1830 there were 150. A popular song ran

'In days of old when folks got tired,
A hackney-coach or a chariot was hired;
But now along the streets they roll ye
In a shay with a cover called a cabrioly'.

In 1814 Boney fell. There followed heavy taxation, trade recession, poor harvests, mechanisation and riots. Reform was in waiting, but not here yet. In 1824 employment was deregulated, and in 1825 there were a run on the banks, widespread insolvencies, and poverty.

In 1815 the first paddle steamer – George Dodds' *Thames* – left the Pool. The river was the capital's highway. By 1841 the service to Greenwich was half-hourly. Boats connected with coaches and, later, railways. Steamboats brought southern commuters across the water to the City and they also plied for pleasure – until an 1878 disaster drowned 600, and the paddlers lost their popularity.

Faced with the new docks, the Carmen tried to secure the cartage rights. They drew up rates, petitioned the West India Dock Company, and then sought compensation. The Company refused to intervene between the Fellowship and customers for their warehouses.

The Dock Act covered compensation for losses at the West India, so next the Carmen focused on Wapping Dock, and petitioned Parliament for exclusive rights there. Master Edward Unwin subscribed £20 to the costs, £230 were raised, and 5s levied on each carroom operator. They got nowhere.

Times were hard when John Holmes was re-elected Clerk in 1805. He was unpaid. James Outon, Beadle, received three months' salary so he could 'procure a Situation'.

In 1807 his pay was restored. In 1830 Holmes was given a piece of plate for his 'long and ffaithful services' and in 1839 he retired, after over 48 years in office.

In 1811 the Carmen asked to present a child annually to Christ's Hospital. The Fellowship had produced over £50,000 in annual payments of £400, itself equivalent to the qualifying sum for a Life Governor. Benjamin Harris, one of Carman James Harris's six offspring was, at eight years old, 'a fit and proper object to be admitted' since his father was 'unable to provide for...or afford him suitable education' without help.

Silence. A month later they wrote again. Nothing. Two months after that John Holmes addressed his counterpart, Richard Corp, demanding explanations and a proper response. He said the Carmen 'cannot but consider themselves as treated with neglect bordering on contempt'. They had waited an hour and a half at the Hospital's Court, which had 'departed without calling them in', or telling them the fate of their petition.

Holmes moved up a gear and told Corp 'this is not the only instance of neglect...experienced', particularly from Corp himself, whose conduct was 'the more extraordinary from a Gentleman who has been brot up and Educated in some measure' at Carmen's expense.

Under the circumstances, the Fellowship was considering an application to the Lord Chancellor to be relieved from their annual dues – and why. Corp replied briefly that the petition had been shelved.

The Carmen filed the incident for future reference. They then asked the Hospital to take legal action against unlicensed carters. In 1814 the Hospital sought 13s 4d fines in the Mayor's Court.

This compared badly with the same fine plus 4s 6d costs the Carmen had charged for several years.

In 1815 a Hospital street-keeper seized a cart. The unlicensed carter, one Finch, promptly sued, which cost the Hospital £31 19s 6d in compensation. Clearly irritated, in 1817 it approached Common Council, claiming carts were being worked by unlicensed tradesmen, suburban carters, even Carmen. They were losing income, a hundred carrooms were idle, and something should be done.

The Corporation did little, so the Hospital proposed a £5 fine, half to the informer and half to itself, plus the right to impound unlicensed carts – and their horses. By that time the Carmen had themselves taken legal advice.

City counsel William Bolland told them that, by their 1757 edict, the Magistrates had exceeded their authority. They were not empowered by the Act to fix the Hospital's 17s 4d annual rent for each licence, the 3s 6d fee, the 20s alienation charge or the 40s penalty. Their authority was simply to assess rates and make rules to enforce those rates.

Bolland gave his opinion that 'the Carmen cannot be compelled...to pay all or any of the above sums'. The Act of 1665 was repealed by that of 1667 and that Act by its successor in 1681. The justices had overlooked the sequence of legislation.

'The Hospital is empowered to demand a forfeit of 13s 4d' from anyone who worked a cart without licence, and 10s a day from any who let a cart for hire without authority. 'The fee of 3s 6d...I do not recommend the Carmen to contest, as it seems a very ancient and, I think, reasonable fee' but they should refuse to pay the rest and 'leave the Hospital to any remedy it may be advised to adopt'.

Past Master Isaac Day took up the cudgels. He wrote demanding repayment of £90, reflecting the 17s 4d fee on his carrooms over several years.

He sent his draft to John Holmes with these comments: 'Be pleased to make any alteration, addition, obliteration, or any other ation you may judge proper – even to annihilation, and when convenient return it to me with your observations – and when I have it in my power I will endeavour to make you an enumeration alias remuneration'.

Christ's Hospital ignored him. In 1820 the Clerk warned that the Carmen would go to Court to recover Day's and their money, unless the Governors 'render legal proceedings unnecessary'. The Hospital sent it all to the Lord Mayor so in 1821 Isaac and Samuel Day filed a Bill in Chancery, claiming all their payments for carrooms over six years. William Applebee was Master, 1819–1825, a record.

In 1824 the Lord Mayor, Corporation and Commonalty of London were added as defendants. Then in 1827 Joseph Maberly, the Hospital's lawyer, decided to settle, observing that 'the City were therefore roused from their state of supineness on the subject by finding the attack turned on them'. It had all got out of hand and too expensive.

It was agreed that the City amend the by-laws as suggested in 'the Memorial presented long since', that the Hospital abandon claims to arrears – and everyone paid their own costs.

In May 1829 Common Council fixed the penalty for working an unlicensed cart at £5 and the Fellowship agreed to send their carts for sealing, and pay 17s 4d per carroom each year. Carmen's costs came to £254 12s 6d and the Days gave £100, but the Fellowship repaid them, settled up and raised sufficient surplus to invest £300 in the 'new 4 per cents' that same year.

Christ's Hospital tried hard. They appointed an extra street-keeper, and took legal advice on prosecuting wayward carters. In 1831 they took a carter called Pope to court, and got a conviction. But Maberly could read the runes.

The case rested on unlicensed working of a cart; carriers were only licensed if they were freemen of the Fellowship. Where the owner of a carroom was not a Carman, the licence went to the proprietor's Carman nominee, 'who is then admitted to what is called the "working part" of the carroom'. Mr Pope said he applied and was refused. This was unproved.

Maberly suspected that, had Pope been the proprietor, applied and been refused a licence, 'the Jury would not have convicted'. The cost of admission was 'the great grievance'. The Company wanted licences restricted to their members and, so long as the by-laws supported that, the Hospital was protected. If not, custom might not be enough to refuse a licence.

After the trial there was a flood of applications. Some proprietors 'may still refuse to bring their Cart to be licenced'. Should the Hospital 'grant licence to strangers' carts, giving the go-by to the recusant carroom proprietors' to make up the 420? Maberly added 'If we were to prosecute a man for working an unlicenced cart...having refused him a licence' when there were some to spare, 'I should not have great reliance on obtaining a conviction'.

His Governors called a meeting with the Carmen. They wanted reasons for refusing licences to other freemen, if 420 carts were not sealed. Clerk – and solicitor – John Holmes cited the 1668 rules and the 1825 regulations. These meant only carts licensed by Carmen could stand or ply for hire. Maberly disagreed. He read the documents and suggested that licensing was not 'consequent but an antecedent' to becoming a Carman.

Both sides took legal advice. Joseph Payne agreed with the Carmen. William Earle disagreed. Maberly told the fellowship in 1831 that the Governors would license any freeman, give preference to Carmen, then to carroom proprietors.

The Carmen reacted, expressing 'astonishment at the hasty Resolution' of the Governors, especially since they had not been told about Earle. The Governors suspended their decision for 14 days, so that sixty-plus proprietors might seal their 134 unlicensed carrooms. Otherwise the Fellowship would be given the options and, failing that, any other freemen.

Within a week the Carmen responded at length and with feeling. They thanked the Governors for their expedition and courtesy, and hoped their words would not give offence, but these arose from the Governors' intention 'to licence persons who are not by Law entitled to that privilege'.

Looking back over two centuries of records and half a century of recollection, their privileges 'have been gradually invaded' without redress to the point where they were almost 'non ffreemen'. They had hoped the £5 fine would encourage enforcement, but instead the Governors seemed determined to permit unlicensed operators. This 'will at one stroke virtually annihilate the fellowship'.

The Carmen blamed 'the weakness and inefficiency of the Law' and 'the unwillingness of the Hospital Authorities to prosecute'. And this was despite revenues of over £50,000. Given that many Governors were on Common Council, the Fellowship was 'astonished at the precipitate step' which would 'virtually disfranchise a whole Corporate Body' which was indisputably 'as ancient as any of the other Companies'.

If the law was so feeble it afforded Carmen no protection, then it was also unable to enforce their payment to 'any Public Charity'.

'The ffellowship as ffreemen of London have equal privileges with other ffreemen' and their rights did not depend on Christ's Hospital. Even if they had paid 'a very large amount', demand for that contribution was 'illegally made'. They had honoured it, expecting the Governors to honour their part of the bargain.

The Hospital had acted yet again as it had for two centuries, and now held out the threat to license 'other than ffree Carmen'. There was no obvious benefit to be gained by paying the Hospital and the Fellowship would henceforth operate independently.

The Carmen closed by reminding the Governors theirs was not a petition but a remonstrance. They were now going to ask Common Council to remove the Hospital's authority of 1681.

The Clerk signed Christ's Hospital's reply, but it was drafted by their lawyer. It expressed injured innocence, said the law was hopeless, it had done its best, not all Carmen had cooperated, and it had offered empty carrooms to the Carmen.

In March 1832 Common Council recommended that those licensed by the Hospital should be admitted as Carmen for £25, and carrooms increased from 420 to 600.

This was unacceptable to the Fellowship. There were over 200 unemployed carrooms already, and through market forces, not its monopoly. Nine freedoms had been bought for £100 each, voluntarily paid by unlicensed carters, yet the annual dues from all other Carmen over forty years averaged £61 per annum.

Thomas Pope had started it all. In 1832 he begged the Hospital's pardon. He was a Liveryman of the Bricklayers Company, and entitled to work a cart. He had a wife, two children and a mother of 99. Despite his pleas, the Hospital declined to interfere with the Court's decision. Unfortunately for the Carmen, three years later the Act was passed.

Seven years earlier, 70 year old John Lloyd was made free of the Company; apprenticed in 1774, he had been 'employed for many years as Horseman to the late Joseph Ball'. In 1826 he was listed as a Carman of Whitechapel; his son, David, helped run the family firm and his grandson, also David, was apprenticed to Carman Joseph Press in 1823.

Meanwhile Carmen were working for coal merchants, making an average of 3.5 journeys daily for 300 days a year, carting 8.75 chaldrons a day for 6s $9\frac{1}{25}$d nett. The merchants profited, not so much on sales, as on cartage, barge working, discounts and credit. At 15,750 chaldrons a year, William Horne turned over £3,743 7s at a nett profit of £306 13s. His biggest expense was horse keep at £1,248. His 'wains' cost him 25 gns each to hire. He used nine.

In 1829 the first police or Peelers (after Sir Robert Peel, Home Secretary) paraded – in Bloomsbury. The City had rejected the idea, but formed a Night Watch three years later and its own City Police in 1839. Electoral reform, abolition of slavery, new poor law, revised factory hours, tithe commutation and municipal representation changed the political and social face of the nation in the 1830s.

In 1834 and until the late 1850s, coal factors, coal owners and ship owners collaborated to control the market in coal. In 1836 Parliament investigated in response to public criticism that the colliers held a monopoly, and maintained high prices.

The turn system had worked until now. In 1841 it was abandoned. Thereafter improved production, increased demand and better transport and unloading changed the factors' options. In 1849 a new Coal Exchange was built.

The railways began to erode the coastal trade. Mechanical handling improved unloading. After 1843 the emphasis was on household coals. Over-supply followed a free market. Then steamships replaced sail. Cranes and derricks revolutionised dockside handling. By 1863, one firm, Cory's, handled one million tons of coal, used iron steamers, owned 250 lighters, dockside premises, hydraulic cranes and a floating derrick.

In 1829, 1,500 coaches a day left London. There were some 1,000 turnpikes by the 1830s, responsible for 25,000 road miles. Over 1,000 hackney carriages plied for hire. More than 400 short stage coaches served the suburbs, and William Hazlitt observed 'You will hear more good things on the outside of a stagecoach from London to Oxford than if you were to pass a twelvemonth with the undergraduates or heads of college of that famous city'. Shades of the later 'man on the Clapham omnibus'.

Credit for the first omnibus goes to George Shillibeer, though his was not a commercial success. The first 'bus, three-horsed abreast, took 22 passengers from The Yorkshire Stingo down the New Road to Bank *via* the Angel, Islington. Competition forced Shillibeer out in 1832.

In August 1850 Eliza Meteyard, writing as Silverpen, described how England had 'developed means of transit by the improvement of the roads, the cutting of canals, and the formation of railways' and how 'the metropolis cast aside its sedans, its hackney coaches, and its suburban stages...with the cabriolet and omnibus'.

Silverpen wrote of Shillibeer's heavy 'buses 'enriched by a library of books', and how lighter 'buses brought 'his utter ruin' and started 'a system of disgraceful competition'. The Courts heard cases of conspiracy between proprietors, 'indescribable ...confusion, furious driving, injury to horses...and the arrest of conductors and drivers'.

This led to the first voluntary associations of omnibus proprietors, which regulated fares, stages, number and frequency of vehicles and routes. In the 1840s double-deck 'buses emerged.

Silverpen also wrote 'the most singular fact in the history of omnibuses is, that women have been successful speculators'. Mrs Wilson of Holloway had nearly six hundred horses, omnibuses, premises, a job and post-horse business 'valued at from forty to fifty thousand pounds'.

In 1796 William Birch had started a stagecoach service from Exeter to Plymouth; in 1832 his grandson, William Manley Birch, commenced his cab business at Horseferry Road; in 1847 Widow Birch launched the first omnibus service to Mansion House and started the Westminster Omnibus Association. Her son, William Samuel, and later, his son, William Henry, chaired the powerful Atlas & Waterloo Association – it controlled 357 'buses.

Shillibeer had imported a Parisian idea – the first omnibus ran there in 1819 – so it was entirely logical for London to follow Paris again when the Prefect of Police pushed for a city-wide merger. La Compagnie Generale des Omnibus de Londres was registered under French law in 1855, six months after Parisian operators had amalgamated.

The London 'bus business was declining after a peak year in 1851 with the Great Exhibition. The Anglicised London General Omnibus Company was capitalised at 25m francs (£1m) and bought in 586 'buses at £510 each.

In 1850 the omnibus industry consumed corn, hay and straw worth £1,762,000, employed 11,000 with capital invested of some £963,000. Drivers worked a 16 hour day for a 12s weekly wage of which up to half went to horse keepers; extra cash could be earnt by charging outside passengers in fine weather. Accidents were charged to the driver.

Because 'buses started from pubs 'the custom of omnibus servants', faced with long hours, 'exhaustion of body', and 'laborious work', was to spend their earnings 'in stimulating drinks'. In 1845, 'of 1,107 cab-men and coachmen taken into custody, 361 were for furious driving... 29 could neither read nor write, 289 imperfectly'. The enlightened Eliza suggested 'bus termini, shift work and a 12 hour day, higher wages, apprenticeships and a 'bus inspectorate.

As passenger carriage developed in and beyond London, City goods cartage diminished. The wharf trade had left the City. The Fellowship had received £90 for its three charity carrooms in compensation. Christ's Hospital claimed losses of over £500 and was awarded £800 in settlement.

Meanwhile, women made free of the Company included Elizabeth Buckee in 1835, Elizabeth Dorsett and Mary Shoobert in 1836, and Sarah Bingham Court, who joined them in 1872. In 1837, young David Lloyd's sister, Amelia Charlotte, took over the family firm; it became A.C. Lloyd. In 1841 she was a bonded carter and in 1845 she became a Carman. She traded 'opposite the Customs House' in Thames Street, where A.C. Lloyd remained until 1909.

Amelia was helped by her sister Keziah. She died in 1880 and Keziah in 1893. Nephew and Carman George John took over; his sons, George Henry and Charles John joined him. They were succeded by Charles' sons, Charles William and George Cullman.

In 1843 John Paice was Master, and again and again until 1850. Masters come and Masters go, even if, like Paice or Applebee, they served for several years. Clerks sometimes seem to flourish and continue for ever: John Holmes put in just short of half a century, from 1790 to 1839.

In 1837 700 mail coaches carried post worth £2,000,000 compared to revenues of £420,000 in 1784 and £160,000 before the mail coach era.

The growth of London led to new trades in banking, insurance and exchanges. In 1844 the Royal Exchange opened and the Bank Charter Act led the way. Tollgates paid for roads like Telford's Archway Road from Holloway to Finchley; tolls at 6d a horse and 1d a pedestrian. There were over eighty such turnpikes in London overall, and transport was changing.

Felton's four-wheeled carriage was made in Leather Lane as far back as 1803, but it was Walter Hancock's Stratford East factory that produced the first viable steam carriage, and his brother Thomas who first vulcanised rubber for tyres, in Goswell Road. In 1830 Hancock's *Infanta* entered public service between Stratford and the City. At 90 passengers daily, it made little impact, though it used 'modern' omnibus coachwork, where Gurney's 1827 steam coach had followed horsed designs.

Gurney's pioneering led to a Select Committee and suggested State aid but the government was not impressed. The 1840 Turnpike Acts tolled Hancock's Steam Enterprise Omnibus vehicles off the road and anti-motor restricted-speed legislation effectively killed this form of passenger road traction.

The 19th century also saw vast improvements in vehicle design, as the roads improved. The high bodied phaeton was followed by the two-horsed two-wheeled curricle. The Coachmakers hired out small gigs to escape the tax on carriages and, of many carrs and carts, the most popular was the light dog-cart of 1800.

The private drag, a four-in-hand, was joined in 1822 by the convertible landau and the barouche. In 1823 David Davies introduced the hackney cabriolet or 'cab', the brougham emerged in 1838 and in 1842 the wagonette. Hansom invented his two-wheeler in 1834, much modified by John Chapman in 1837 and part of Victorian folk-memory.

The four-wheeled equivalent 'growler' was also known as the clarence, introduced in 1842, though cab operator William Birch claimed it predated the Hansom: 'all our 2-wheeled cabs had in black letters over the windows "Hansoms Patent Safety"'.

Where Coachmakers built for passengers, Wheelwrights made carts for the goods trade. The dog-cart originated as a four-wheeler in 1669, horsed in tandem, became the two-wheeler by 1800, drawn by two horses abreast. The market cart equivalent came in many varieties, but was essentially the tradesman's vehicle, and emerged in 1842.

The London Carmen's trolley had a turntable fore-carriage with single shafts for one horse or a pole for two, four smaller-than-average wheels, low side-rails, a driving seat and a pedal brake. These cost from £30 to £50. The London hay cart was a two-high-wheeled cart with high lateral rails and a canted rake at the back.

The London coal cart was open-sided with vertical iron rods topped by long name-plates and no tailboard. Goods waggons were similar, but with tailboards. These heavy carts were drawn by two or three chain horses. Drays varied, but all had a high driving position. These were the suburban carriers' carts.

Later heavy horsed mails were drawn by four horses, working two abreast – high-sided four-wheeled vans with a high seat, footboard, railed loading roof, brakes and rear access. They replaced the mail coaches, which had carried passengers since 1784, seated outside from 1803.

Mid-century, stage and mail coaches, carts and 'buses competed hard for space. Surtees' Mr Jorrocks described the scene on the road from London to Brighton: 'The streets were werry full, but Sir Wincent wormed his way among the coal waggons, wans, busses, coaches, bottom-over-tops, – in wulgar French, "cow sur tate", as they calls the new patent busses – trucks, cabs etc.' and he stressed the state of the roads:

'errand cart...kept dodging across the road to get the sound ground, for the whole line was werry "woolley" as you calls it'.

London costermongers used a small, low, slant-sided cart with two shafts and two high wheels, drawn by a small horse or donkey. Hand carts were used for local deliveries. Delivery vans were usually two-wheeled, with rectangular body, a small canopy, footboard, and a railed roof for small packages. There was a door or double doors at the back. Railways employed semi-open-sided carts in different sizes, drawn by one to four horses, according to capacity.

In 1831, after years of concern about rotting piers, watermen dead from shooting the rapids, and the danger to shipping, London Bridge was replaced 100 feet further west. The old bridge went the next year. Its houses had been condemned in 1758 and demolished by 1762.

In 1827 the Watermen and Lightermen were incorporated by statute, an Act of 1859 extending its powers, though the Thames Conservancy Act of 1857 restricted operations to the east of Teddington Lock and in 1908 the birth of the Port of London Authority removed its duties and its authority.

The Carmens' authority was radically changed. The 1835 Act of Common Council confirmed the old rights and Christ's Hospital's oversight. It entitled freemen to be admitted for £25, increased carrooms to 600, affirmed the £5 penalty for working unlicensed, and required Assistants to be elected by the whole Fellowship.

Freemen flocked to the Carmen's colours. Carmen made sure of their carrooms. Isaac Day paid £12 for admission to twelve carrooms, most of which had been in the family for forty years. Carmen took 473 carts for sealing, reluctantly paying two fees, due to the Act. The Hospital rebated half. Assistants received 5s for attendance at Court.

Two test actions were taken at law. One action was against Needle, who had served 'in His Majesty's Land or Sea Service' and was therefore entitled as a 'King's Freeman' to exercise any trade in the City. He claimed the right to work a cart without licence. That conflicted with the Carmen's rights. The Court found for Needle, since 'the business of a Carman is a trade within the meaning of the Act'.

As Maberly said, this might well 'operate as a total destruction of the privilege of the licensed carman' but he was not able to advise an appeal.

The other case, against Langton, questioned the penalty if an unlicensed carter picked up in the City and put down outside it, or *vice versa*. The Court ruled that a conviction relied on operation entirely within the City.

Maberly also pointed out the difficulty of proving the hire. Unlicensed Carmen would often pretend they were not hired, or that they worked gratuitously. Without proof, cases fell to the ground.

The Fellowship agreed, and petitioned Common Council, with the Hospital's blessing and active support. Then the Carmen learnt what was happening in Common Council, and gave notice they would pay no more to the Hospital. In 1838 a new Act removed the Hospital's authority.

Now Guildhall would license carts at 5s for life. Annual marking would also cost 5s. The penalty for unlicensed hire was still £5 and, if a car was not marked, the licence was forfeit. The Fellowship remained the same, with one exception – redemption was reduced to £5.

Unlicensed carters persisted. In 1840 William Hilton was summoned for obstruction in Thames Street with an unlicensed cart; the case was dismissed, so the Carmen petitioned the Court of Aldermen, demanding action. There were 190 licensed carts, yet the streets were choked with non-freemen.

Five years on, Richard Owen was successfully charged, joined the Fellowship and paid his dues. Many others followed suit.

In 1836 the first passenger railway served City men, but ran from Southwark to Greenwich – the London and Greenwich Railway Co, capitalised at £1m. In 1841 a cable railway linked the City to the docks, but closed in 1849. In 1843 watermen hung out black flags when the first river tunnel opened, linking Wapping with the Surrey side.

In 1841 the London and Birmingham Railway linked City and Midlands, *via* Euston Station. Within twenty years London was the hub of a nationwide network. Railway timetables were a nightmare, until 1880 British Time was adopted, using the Greenwich meridian.

In 1838 the pneumatic tube postal railway opened at St Pancras and in 1849 the penny post was inaugurated, replacing recipient payment – when the postman found you – with prepaid, one price payment for a standard half-ounce letter. At St Martin's-le-Grand GPO, 112,000 letters left on the first day.

By 1846 the Fellowship had been meeting in Guildhall, when Master John Paice was entertained by the Lord Mayor; in 1848 the Clerk reported the Aldermen might grant, and in 1849 the Carmen sought, a Livery.

They claimed 'several Members...are of considerable substance', they would assist 'the honour, dignity and service of the City', and this would put the Fellowship 'on a respectable footing equal with the rest of their Fellow Citizens'. The Livery was granted on 29 September 1848 for 100 with admission not less than £20.

The first Liverymen were admitted that December – John Paice, Master John Scholes, Samuel and Thomas Bateman, John Eyke, Joseph Bingham, Thomas Priestley, George Grinslade, and Richard Johnson. In 1857 the Court gave a special dinner to Paice, Scholes and Wright 'as an honourable testimony to their efforts'.

It was 1849 when Past Master Richard Back appealed for help. He had gone bankrupt in 1834, owing arrears. In 1840 the Court gave him £5 when he was 'in difficulties'. He resigned in 1849, and the Court voted a pension of 5s a week. When he died, the Master paid for his funeral, and the Court repaid him for 'his Christian and praiseworthy conduct'.

Less fortunate was Thomas Breden, Master in 1859. He owed £55. It emerged that he was in prison for debt. He wrote from Horsemonger Lane Gaol explaining his predicament – 'not finding friends...disposed to relieve me of my confinement...I fear must remain till the time expires' and he would pay up 'Immediately I am at liberty'.

He was dismissed as an Assistant, twice appealed for help, twice refused. By 1854 the Company was in funds – £2,025. Nothing was paid to the Great Exhibition, but £20 went to the Patriotic Fund for the Crimean War. The Albert Memorial Fund in 1863 was refused. In Paris, trams were launched in 1851 and the LGOC tried to import them to London, but Commissioner of Works Sir Benjamin Hall (after whom, Big Ben), hated them. His carriage had twice fallen foul of Welsh horsed railways. The proposed legislation failed.

In 1863 the City of London Traffic Regulation Act tried to regulate 'buses and the 1867 Metropolitan Street Act forced them to stop on the left, and not on the side the passenger wanted. One-way operation was imposed at Liverpool Street. 1858 attempts to lay tram tracks from Notting Hill Gate to Bank were successfully opposed, but the first two-horsed tramway opened in 1861, single deckers carrying 18 seated and 12 standing.

Most single deck 'buses were 14-seaters. Double-deckers seated 40. Gentlemen sat upstairs – ladies inside, for the sake of decorum. But the larger 'buses could not handle gradients such as Ludgate Hill, so double-deckers settled down as two-horsed 26-seaters. They cost £150 to build. Each would use ten horses a day and cover 60 miles, each pair working 4.5 hours.

The first pillar box replacing the itinerant collector was opened in 1855 on the corner of Fleet and Farringdon Streets. Carmen were now concerned with trivia – in 1852 only tea and coffee were served at Court, and then no refreshments at all. William Wright was appalled; tea and coffee returned in 1853. The Court met at the Blue Anchor in Coleman Street, debated a move to Finsbury, but decided to stay put.

In 1863 the underground railway opened – the Metropolitan Railway linked Paddington, Euston and King's Cross Stations with the City at Farringdon Street. 26,500 used it daily in the first six months. By 1866 four railway bridges crossed the river to Victoria, Charing Cross, Farringdon and Cannon Streets. By 1874 there were 432,000 road carriages in use nationwide.

In 1865 government restricted steam 'buses and any other mechanised transport to 4 mph on the open road and 2 mph in towns. The man with the red flag walked ahead to warn the populace of these modern monsters. The Southwark Bridge tollgate was abolished in 1866 when the City bought the bridge. In 1869 Holborn Viaduct eliminated the grinding haul for horses up Holborn or 'Heavy' Hill, easing road traffic into the City.

Yet the Corporation faced criticism. Its powers spilled over into Southwark and Middlesex, it ran the main markets, it culled coal duties, and it controlled the river. It ignored the suburbs and was accused of being 'complacent' and 'antiquated'. An 1854 Royal Commission report called for abolition of Aldermen, Common Hall and City police. Nothing transpired.

The Liveries did not escape censure either. In 1872 Froude wrote of 'certain ancient societies' who floated about in 'quaint gilt barges' processing downriver for 'civic feastings'. He added: 'But for what purpose they were called into being…few people now care to think or enquire'.

The plain fact was that technology had overtaken traditional trades. London had burst its City bounds. The fights for rights had become protective and introspective. The City and its ancient guilds had been overtaken by events.

In 1865 only three Assistants attended Court. Fines were imposed. By 1868 only Master Thomas Priestley and Past Master George Grinslade were present. By the '70s most meetings comprised Priestley, Thomas Fardell and George Johnson and there were no Courts at all between November 1871 and August 1872.

The attendance fee went up to a guinea. Since no Master had been elected, Priestley just carried on. In 1873 his son Thomas Potter Priestley was admitted, clothed, elected and attended the Court. Then Johnson's son and two sons of Fardell followed suit. For thirty years these seven elected each other – and kept the Carmen going.

Priestley was Master in 1853, 1854 and then for nine years from 1866 to 1874, again in 1876, 1879, 1883, 1888, 1892 and 1895. That was an absolute record, though Fardell did his bit to keep things going, as Master in 1861, '2 & '3, 1875, 1877, 1880 and 1885. James Fardell made his Masterly contribution in 1881 and J.R. Fardell in 1886 and 1890. C.E. Fardell took his turns in 1882, 1887, 1891, 1894 and 1898.

The Clerkship became hereditary too. Alexander Baylis served from 1850 to 1874. His son took over until 1898. Business was hardly onerous. In 1869 the Court gave £10 to

London Hospital. In 1883 accounts were audited for the first time for five years. Arrears were uncovered, and some quarterage recovered. In 1879 seven subscribers used the first London telephone exchange, in Coleman Street.

The Court met twice a year in the Clerk's office, and dined after Christmas and Midsummer meetings only. The attendance fee was halved until 1896. Dividend income in 1885 was £35 but £3 went to James Heartzell, a Carman for 26 years in distress – 'I do not think the poor old man will live long'. Other claims were refused.

Life at the lower end of the cartage scale was rough. Henry Mayhew described 'one of the narrow streets which branch off like the side-bones of a fish's spine', where costermongers' carts stood outside the doors. A paved 'cartway' in the middle was 'just wide enough for a truck to wheel down it'.

Young boys and girls swept the crossings so that pedestrians might avoid the filth: 'When I sees the buses and carriages coming I stands on the side, for I'm afeard of being run over'. Thus 'a little girl, who worked by herself at her own crossing' was recorded by Mayhew. From nine to four, she took up to eightpence and 'My broom costs me twopence ha'penny and in wet weather lasts me a week'. Such rates put Carmen's fines in perspective.

In 1893 Charles Boutland paid £1, then wrote in disgust 'as there are no benefits or privileges accruing...I wish to resign'. Although he stayed on, he paid nothing in 1901 and left in 1909. Yet in 1892 there was a glimmer of the old pride in Fellowship. For 10 guineas a Master's badge was made in gold and enamel, with the motto 'Scite, Citissime, Certe'. In 1894 Tower Bridge opened, its bascules operated by steam.

Matters came to a head that year when only Thomas Priestley and Henry Johnson attended Court. Two Fardells had died and in 1895 H.A. Jacobs was invited to join; he was clothed and became Master in 1897. That was the year when the Daimler 4 hp van pioneered the 'motor car' in Britain.

The Light Railways Act facilitated tramways, but gave local government a right of veto. The City refused permission for lines to be laid in its heartland by the North Metropolitan Tramways Company. Yet by 1875 three London companies between them ran 251 cars over 50 miles and carried 20 million passengers in six months. In 1901 electrification began.

In the 1880s the hobby-horse of the 1820s had graduated to the Safety Bicycle, with its pneumatic tyres – themselves a precursor of the motoring revolution – and cycling had become a major means of individual transport, primarily for pleasure. This popular pastime revived many inns, congested urban streets, and generated a lasting desire for freedom of movement.

Also in the 1880s a group of City men formed the London Road Car Company, introducing a major force into London's road passenger transport, with increased 'bus capacity, and new ticket systems.

By 1880, the railways had a monopoly of parcel traffic when the Post Office decided to handle parcels too. Miffed, the railmen jacked up the tariff. The Post Office did its sums, and decided it could cut costs with horsed mails. In 1887 the first mailvan set off for Oxford. John Manley Birch got the contract – and for Brighton. Arthur Russen drove the Oxford coach – 67 miles and four changes of four horses, from Royal Mail Yard, Kentish Town *via* Paddington PO.

Throughout the century, cart horses had been variously treated; by 1885 their lot was still variable, often with poor stables, ill-fitting harness, foul air and uneven roads; feeding and watering were irregular for many, and grooming often non-existent. Then coachman's son and national vintner Walter Gilbey founded the English Cart Horse Society in 1878, renamed it the 'Shire' in 1884, and organised a London Cart Horse Parade in 1886.

Of 20,000 horses within seven miles of Charing Cross, 383 with 278 vehicles appeared the following year. Standards improved as a Home of Rest for Horses was founded, then the Horse Accident Prevention Society. By 1902 the *Telegraph* reported the Parade had 'raised the standard of heavy draught horses throughout London'.

Meanwhile, the Ward Electrical Car Co Ltd had produced battery-powered omnibuses in 1887, and in 1897 a 10-seat 10 hp version appeared under the auspices of the London Electric Omnibus Co Ltd. It carried no fares. The London Steam Omnibus Co of 1898 ran out of steam without operating anything, became the Motor Traction Co Ltd, and operated a 26-seat petrol 'bus, but for only one year.

That was the year when C.E. Fardell proposed himself as Master, and so served and Charles Scholes joined Company and Court. Charles Scrivener joined too, and succeeded him.

The fine for Freedom went up to 10 guineas, despite the 1838 Act; the Livery fine went up too, to 25 guineas, and Court entry was set at 50 guineas. New members were sought and recruited, and the first Livery Dinner was held in 1899.

Revitalised, the Carmen plunged into battle once more. That year the City decided to abolish licensed stands. The Company petitioned. By 1900 a new list of both Licensed and Temporary Stands was agreed. Two stands for licensed Carmen, plying for hire, were reserved at Aldermanbury, Camomile Street and Dowgate Hill; at Milk Street and Queenhithe and at Watling Street by the church.

Three stands were located on Lawrence Pountney Hill and at St James' Place, and four on the south side of Knightrider Street. There were sixteen Temporary Stands for vans and trade vehicles, under police control.

Educational reform, trade union recognition and a wider franchise reflected the later 19th century concerns for social improvement, while conflicts continued worldwide, culminating in the Boer War. In 1899 the Company gave 10 guineas to the Lord Mayor's Fund to equip volunteers and received a medal 'in commemoration of the spontaneous and patriotic liberality shown'.

Theft remained a problem in London's streets. Mayhew observed: 'Thousands of our felons are trained from their infancy in the bosom of crime'.

Some robbed carters when their backs were turned. One burglar, the son of a coach and harness-maker, told Mayhew that at 11, in 1836, he had worked for a binder, and left 'a truck loaded with books...I came out I found the books were gone'. His brother had taken them, he was fired, and he himself soon turned to crime.

The end of the century saw coal dues abolished, most household coals brought in by rail, while sea-coal still fuelled industry and supplied the gas industry. In 1896 the biggest London coal business was Wm Cory & Son, comprising merchants, factors, shippers and lightermen. It handled seven million tons.

The Wheelwrights approached the new century with support for the City and Guilds of London Institute, and in 1894 started classes for wheelwrights at the Carpenters' School; in 1904 lectures were initiated 'on the elementary work of the motor-car'.

Christ's Hospital, meanwhile, started expanding its educational scope through a Charity Commission scheme of 1890. In 1902 it moved to West Horsham. Moving out of town for excursions was also popular – horse brakes catered for community travel, the precursors of the modern coach.

The Coachmakers, described in 1867 as a 'worn out and effete Guild' boasted Royal and Prime Ministerial members two years later, and in 1883 Thrupp, Hooper and Maberly, coachbuilders and all called George, started the Institute of British Carriage Manufacturers. Masters included two Hoopers and a Birch: 'Omnibuses built on the most modern principles Guaranteed to use best seasoned Timber only'; telegrams to 'Coaching, London'.

In 1895 their Master, John Philipson, said of the 'automobile' – 'the new development will assuredly grow to extraordinary proportions', while two years later Coachmaker Alexander Henderson took a different view: 'most people will still prefer...the animated appearance of well-appointed horse traction to any dead mechanism'.

Dead mechanisms had meanwhile revolutionised travel, for the railways had shortened journey time, opened up markets, and changed public perceptions of both time and distance. 'Railway speed' had changed society. Samuel Smiles in 1862 observed 'by saving time...the railway proved a great benefactor to men of industry in all classes'.

Far from eliminating road transport, rail moved more goods and people, requiring more local distribution, especially in London. Horses were the staple of short-haul goods carriage. In 1891 1.3 million of them consumed 1.4 tons of corn and 2.4 tons of hay a year. That food had to be moved – by horse. Horses had to be stabled, and their waste shifted. The streets of London were congested, polluted and approaching critical mass. New mechanisms were needed, dead or alive.

In 1900 there were some 8,500 Liverymen in the City and in 1901 Carmen reverted to rule, electing James Mumford to replace the late Henry Johnson. Twenty-eight Carmen attended the poll. Also in 1900 George Lloyd joined the Company, maintaining the longest-lived family link. In 1904 the Court was increased and again in 1906.

The Carmen were on the march again, their causes just, their Court enhanced, their Company increased. They looked beyond the City but they guarded their rights, and relished their role as providers, innovators and standard bearers for a major growth industry.

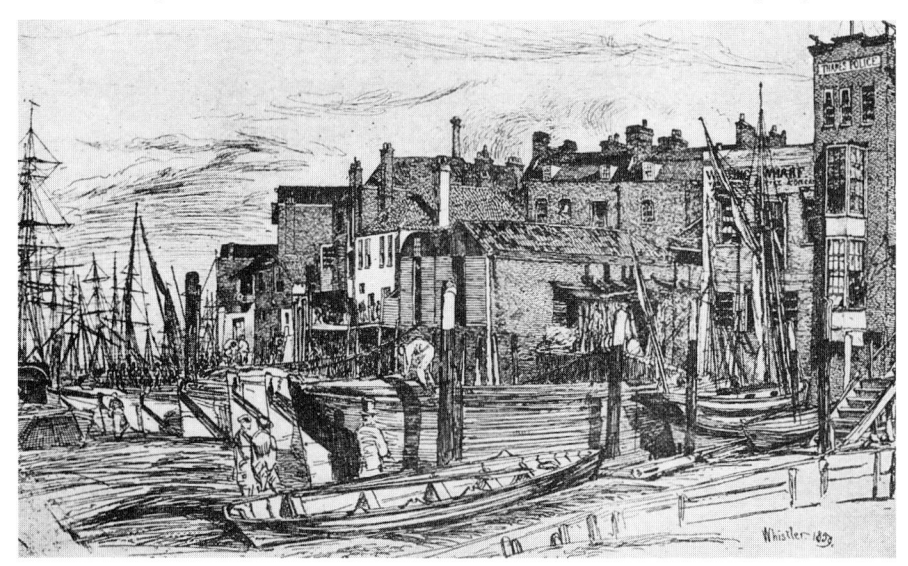

The River Police faced problems with the crime wave on London's teeming wharves, as J. McNeill Whistler graphically illustrated in 1859. (CB)

ABOVE: Southwark Bridge linked the City and 'the Surrey side', in A. Shepherd's 19th century painting. (CB) CENTRE: In 1823 the coffin cab emerged, drawn here by Cruikshank. (RS) BELOW: In 1815 the first paddle steamer left the Pool of London, like this; the Batavier Line warehouse (left) boasted 'London, Rotterdam & the Rhine – Daily Service'. (CB)

ABOVE: When Surrey & Commercial Docks opened at Rotherhithe, Carmen's quayside business leached away. (CB) BELOW: Carmen worked for coal merchants, and those merchants built a new Coal Exchange, recorded by R.S. Groom in 1849. (GL)

ABOVE: The old London Bridge, painted by R.P. Bonington in the 1800s. (CB) BELOW: The 'new' 1831 London Bridge. (CB) RIGHT: Throughout the century, canals carried heavy goods across country, like the Grand Junction at Fenny Stratford. (CB)

103

MEASURED from LONDON BRIDGE.	LONDON TO HYTHE AND FOLKSTONE.		THROUGH MAIDSTO and ASHFORD.
		From London.	
HATCHAM. Mrs. *Hardcastle.*	*From the Surrey Side of* London Bridge *to* The Bricklayers' Arms	1	HATCHAM. W. Holcom Esq.; and *Tim. Stanfield*, Es
LEWISHAM, before, *D. W. Harvey*, Esq.; at the Lime Kilns, *John Lee*, Esq.; beyond the Church, a White House, *Abraham Constable*, Esq.; and a little farther, — *Tanner*, Esq.	Green Man Turnpike Cross the Surrey canal Turk's Head, *or* Halfway House Hatcham,	1½ 2¼	LEWISHAM, beyond Church, The Priory, *John Th eray*, Esq. LEWISHAM, a very po lous village, extending near mile on the road to Brom contains a church of mod erection, in which there several monuments deserv notice. Many of the house this parish are situated in chapelry of Sydenham, on S. W. side of Lewisham, joining Surrey, and on the o of Sydenham common, from upper part of which is a v beautiful and extensive prosp At this place are some min springs of a cathartic qua and nearly resembling thos Epsom; they were discovere 1640, and have all been dive to the same well.
LEE. Lee Place, *unoccupied.*	New Cross T. G. Cross the Croydon canal New Cross, *Marquis of Granby* Enter Kent.	3½ 3¾	
ELTHAM. Well Hall, *Robt. Sutton*, Esq.; The Eagle House, *J. H. Latham*, Esq.; and Park Farm Place, Lady *Mordaunt.*	Forward to Dartford 11¼ m. *To* Lewisham, *Bridge* Cross the riv. Ravensbourn *To* Bromley 5 m.	5	
FOOT'S CRAY. Foot's Cray Place, Lord *Bexley.* This elegant mansion was built by Bouchier Cleve, Esq., after a design of Palladio's: Sir George Yonge, Bart. obtained it in marriage with Mr. Cleve's daughter, and afterwards sold it to the late Benjamin Harence, Esq., who was high sheriff of Kent in 1777. The house is built of stone, has a beautiful octangular hall, surrounded by a gallery conducting to the bed-chambers, enlightened from the top: it is situated on rising ground, with a gradual descent to an artificial branch of the river Cray, which is here made to represent a small river flowing through the grounds; and opposite to the house is a pleasing cascade. —— Near Foot's Cray, North Cray Place, *Thomas Wm. Coventry*, Esq.; Dowager Marchioness of *Londonderry*; Mount Mascal, Captain *Cator*; and Lamienby, Mrs. *Malcolm*; a little farther, Blendon Hall, *John Smith*, Esq.	* Lee, *entrance of* At the 7 Mile-stone, *To* Mottingham 1 m. thence *To* Chislehurst Ch. 2¾ m. * Eltham to Shooter's Hill 1½ m. *Through Eltham,* to Dartford 8½ m. *To* South End *To* Chislehurst 2¼ m. Sidcup * Foot's Cray Cross the river Cray Birchwood Corner	5¾ 8 9 11½ 12¼ 14	LEE. Lee Lodge, *J Sladden*, Esq.; The M. House, *F. Perkins*, Esq.; Grove, *Thomas Brandram*, Capt. *Smith*; and Ivy Cott Mrs. *Morland.* ELTHAM. Eltham Lo Lady *Crewe*; and the ruin Eltham Palace. SOUTH END, near, at Ch hurst, Camden Place, *un pied.* SIDCUP, 1 m. before, Ke Farm, Sir *W. Leighton*; I sant Grove, Sir *W. Draper B* and Frognall, Lord *Sidney.*

ABOVE: In 1826 *Paterson's Roads* guided travellers 'from the side of London Bridge' or Southwark, Westminster, Blackfriars or Waterloo Bridges. (CB) LEFT: William Birch pioneered the hansom, after he started his business in 1832. (CB) RIGHT: It had not changed much by the 1880s. (CB)

No. 341—1.

NOTE.—This Licence must be delivered up when a Supplementary Licence is required.

No. of Licence.
1321

METROPOLITAN STAGE CARRIAGE ORIGINAL LICENCE.

WHEREAS a Certificate, granted by the Commissioners of Police of the Metropolis, dated the *30* day of *Novr* 186*7*, in pursuance of the Act 16 & 17 Vic., cap. 33, has been produced to me, the undersigned Collector of Excise, certifying that a Carriage, known by the following marks or description, viz.*— *34204 O* is in a fit and proper condition for public use as a METROPOLITAN STAGE CARRIAGE, and that the number of Persons to be carried in and by such Carriage, exclusive of the Driver and Conductor, is specified in the said Certificate relating to the same: NOW THEREFORE, I, the said COLLECTOR OF EXCISE, being hereunto duly authorized by the COMMISSIONERS OF INLAND REVENUE, and in pursuance of the Statutes in this behalf made, DO hereby grant LICENCE to *Frederick Clark* of *34 Artillery Road, Brewers Green, Westminster* to keep, use, and employ the said Carriage as a METROPOLITAN STAGE CARRIAGE, with Plates, to be numbered *6599* for the purpose of conveying Passengers for hire between *Victoria Railway Station Pimlico* and *Royal Oak Bayswater* by the following Route or line of Road, (that is to say;) *Grosvenor Place Park Lane Edgeware Road & Praed St* being a distance of *three* Miles, and with the said Carriage, to perform to and from the said extreme Places on the days hereinafter mentioned, in each and every Week during the continuance of this Licence, the following number of Journeys, viz.—

70 on Monday,
70 on Tuesday,
70 on Wednesday,
70 on Thursday,
70 on Friday,
70 on Saturday,
and *70* on Sunday,

making a Total of *Four Hundred & Twenty* Miles in each and every *Week*.

And this Licence is to continue in force from the *Second* day of *Decr* One Thousand Eight Hundred and Sixty *Seven* inclusive, until and exclusive of the first Monday in November, One Thousand Eight Hundred and Sixty *eight* the Sum of *£3 - 3/-* having been paid to the said Collector of Excise for the same.

DATED the *2nd* day of *Decr* One Thousand Eight Hundred and Sixty *Seven*

M Hargreaves Collector of Excise

Countersigned *[signature]* Assessor.

of London *West* Collection.

In 1867 Frederick Clark obtained his stage carriage licence number 6599, sanctioning 420 journeys a week between Victoria and Bayswater. In 1868 he assigned it to John Edwards. (CB)

ABOVE: George Stephenson wanted to join London to Birmingham *via* Amersham; landlords objected. In 1853 the LNWR proposal was opposed. In 1860 London-Aylesbury was newly mapped – rejected. In 1881 Parliament's scheme failed. It was 3 October 1891 before the *Henry Appleby* took the Metropolitan Railway Co through Amersham. (CB) BELOW: The railways brought a need for station omnibuses like this LNWR two-horsed version, serving the successful London–Birmingham line. (CB)

ABOVE: Public service design evolved; by 1860 de Tivoli's patent omnibus served the GWR from London Bridge to Paddington. (CB) RIGHT: 94: *The Conductor*, no 123 on the Bank route. (CB) BELOW: Steam brought early success to Walter Hancock, whose 1836 *Automaton* was one of several advanced designs. (CB)

107

LEFT: Watermen put out black flags when the Wapping Tunnel linked London and Rotherhithe; road ran under river with the 1897 Blackwall Tunnel. (CB) RIGHT: The 1849 penny post saw 112,000 letters leave the GPO at St Martins-le-Grand. (CB) BELOW: The underground Metropolitan Railway was inaugurated on 24 May 1862 by the builders, with Prime Minister Gladstone on board. (LT)

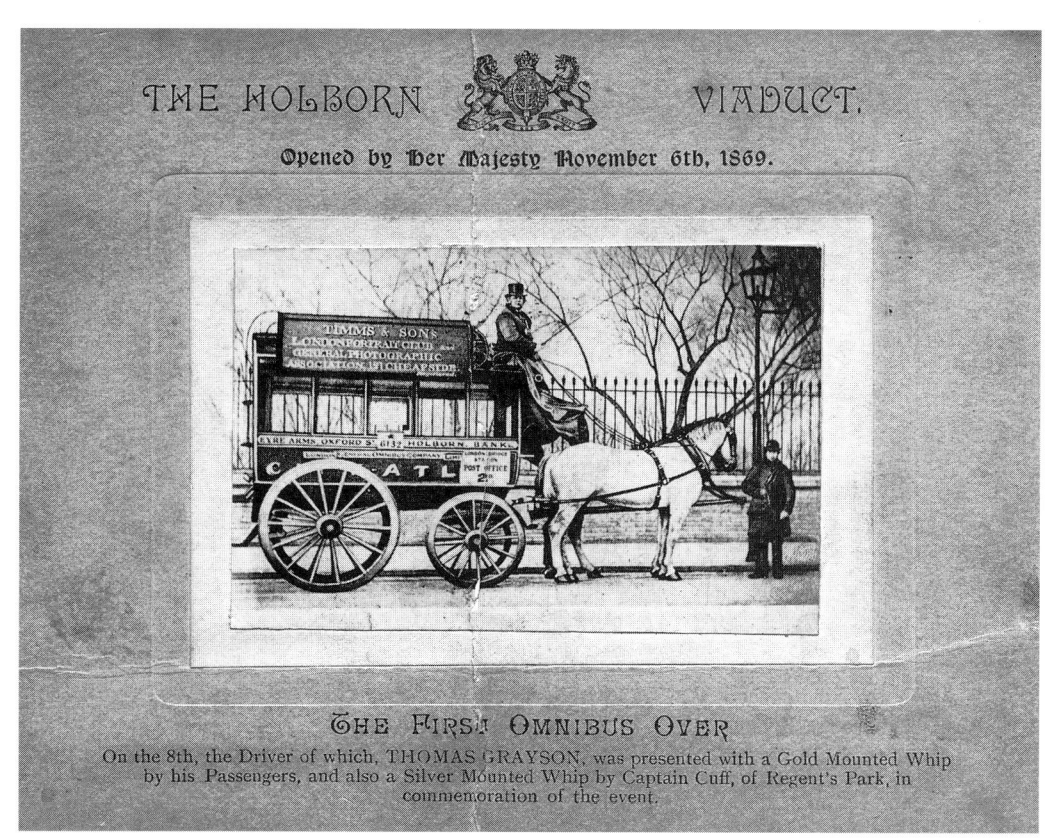

THE HOLBORN VIADUCT.
Opened by Her Majesty November 6th, 1869.

THE FIRST OMNIBUS OVER

On the 8th, the Driver of which, THOMAS GRAYSON, was presented with a Gold Mounted Whip by his Passengers, and also a Silver Mounted Whip by Captain Cuff, of Regent's Park, in commemoration of the event.

ABOVE: Holborn Viaduct eased the horse 'bus up Holborn Hill in 1869. London General's Thomas Grayson was the first man across. (CB)
BELOW: Congestion at Ludgate Circus was reasonable, after the Viaduct was built. (CB)

ABOVE: Traffic by the Royal Exchange was terrible, with carts, waggons, 'buses, cabs and handcarts vying for space. (CB) BELOW: The Underground tried to take the strain – with the 'twopenny tube' of the Central London Railway. (CB)

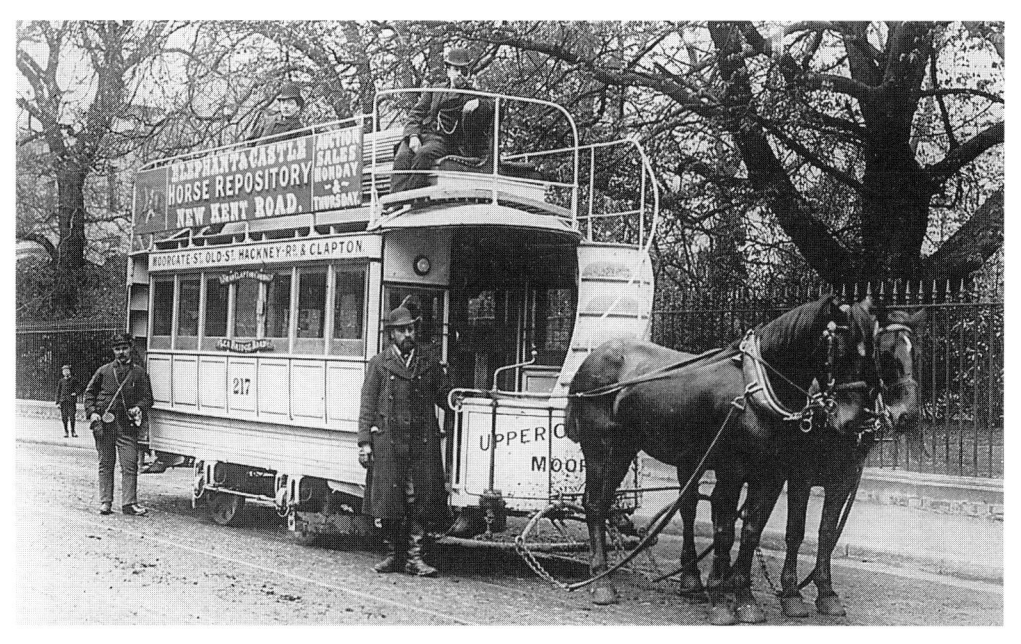

ABOVE: Trams, or 'light railways' came to town, with the horsed tram of the North Metropolitan Tramways Co of 1879 linking Moorgate and Clapton Common *via* Old Street. (LT) BELOW: The first horsed mailvans stole the railway's trade in 1887 – they finished in 1909. (CB)

ABOVE: By the end of the century, 'bus design had moved on, with more seats on top, rear entrance and easier access. (CB) BELOW: The advent of the 'safety bicycle' brought universal mobility – the precursor of the motorcar. Clubs were formed, outings planned, and pubs and cafés prospered: Chesham's cyclists outside the Coffee Tavern in 1890. (CB)

ABOVE: Wheelwrights and coachmakers together built cabs, 'buses and mailvans at Royal Mail Yard, Kentish Town. (CB) BELOW: In 1893 Evan Cook set up in business at 72 Queens Road, Peckham – this was his first hand cart. (EC)

ABOVE: Carmen and suburban carters did business at Smithfield, London's meat market. (CB) BELOW: Cheapside was thick with traffic as the century turned – with parcel vans, drays, hansoms and clarences, and the ubiquitous horsed omnibus. (CB)

9

INTO ACTION

We can forgive a man for making a useful thing as long as he does not admire it.

Oscar Wilde: *The Picture of Dorian Gray* 1891

With the old Queen gone, and a new century, reforms gathered pace and Empire was consolidated. Planning, pensions and protection of children were among the measures of that first decade. Successive Acts had reformed local government, but left the City alone. Carmen had faltered, recovered, kept their heads, their licensed stands, and their noses clean. But there were only nine Liverymen in 1900.

With the new century came a desire to expand. The Carmen offered a prize to the Cart Horse Parade Society, and wondered how to 'advertise the Company and bring it to the notice of those who would be interested'.

In 1901 London's first electric tram clattered down the tracks – outside the City, from Hammersmith to Kew. Four years later the first electric Underground ran from Ealing to Whitechapel on the District Line. Kingsway was opened in 1905.

The Company was also looking beyond cartage when, in 1902, a Carman suggested help for the London independents, opposed to a London County Council attempt to gain powers to run 'buses. The Court regretted it had no right to intervene, but wanted to 'identify the Company with the trade'.

When the LCC proposed trams across Blackfriars Bridge, the Company did act, using its favourite tool of dissent – a petition – 'representing the Licensed Carmen of the City of London'. The trams would 'still further aggravate traffic congestion'. If electricity was thwarted, steam was not and the internal combustion engine was commercially imminent.

Thomas Clarkson's single-deck steamer entered service for the London Road Car Company in 1905 but, the year before that, the first motor-buses were on the London streets: one Milnes-Daimler from Thomas Tilling Ltd and two from Birch Bros – all bodied by Birch. They were followed by London General with 20, the London Road Car Company's 65, and then Tilling again with 20 and Birch with another 14 – all within the year. By 1906 there were almost 800 motorbuses on London's streets.

Cartage, though still dominated by the horse, saw a limited number of petrol-driven light goods vehicles used by businesses on their 'own account', while steam traction made serious inroads into rail traffic and horsed haulage. Freight steamers carried long distance freight, like frozen meat, by road in that first decade.

In Parliament, the Trades Disputes Act conferred collective rights and the Workmens' Compensation Act covered employee injury.

In 1907 46 Clarkson steamers were withdrawn as dangerous on police demand. Birch Bros withdrew their motor-buses due to breakdowns, police harassment – and heavy losses. New rules held speeds to 12 mph and capacity to 34 for a double-decker 'bus.

The next year Carmen revived an ancient practice. Edward Maybury was bound apprentice to his father; 'the Master then offered the right hand of Fellowship' to young Maybury and, 'after a few well-chosen words' gave him a Bible. He was clothed in 1914, the year after the records were disinterred from Guildhall vaults.

Looking back stimulated renewed interest in cartage and Carmen found that many stands were used by railway vans and haulage contractors. The Clerk promptly wrote to these companies, inviting their management to take up the freedom. Gradually, horsed lurries and trolleys were giving way to mechanised lorries and trucks, as the Fellowship reasserted its leadership and traditions. In 1914 the LGOC alone had some 3,100 'buses on London's streets. Yet firms like Wells carried 1,000 horses on their books.

In 1909 Bleriot flew the Channel, and in 1913 Herbert Austin joined the Coachmakers, one of the first motorcar manufacturers to join a Livery. The first trolleybus never ran on the highway, but was demonstrated by the Metropolitan Electric Tramway in 1909 and within three years the LCC conducted trials over an existing tram route. Nothing immediate transpired. That same year on 31 March, the last horsed mailvan left Paddington Post Office, high-loaded and tarpaulined, for Oxford. The motorvan took over.

Next year the Road Board was empowered to buy land, widen roads, and classify them. Soon concrete was to emerge as a roadmaking material. In 1911 State insurance was launched; workers on the railways and in the docks went on strike. In 1911 the Unic taxi was challenging the horse-drawn cab. Then came war.

By 1915 John Charrington might say 'The old Society of coal factors is practically extinct' but in 1919 coal was still forwarded from colliery through factor to coal merchant, though some dealt direct. The dealer bought from the merchant, while some factors sold direct too. George Rose, Chairman of the National Council of Coal Traders, wrote that 'a coal factor is a man who distributes coal wholesale in truck-load or barge-load or ship-load...a coal merchant delivers...by van'.

He also distributed coke, and so did many a carter, for this by-product of the gas industry heated homes and factories alike. Those homes and manufactories needed local haulage.

War almost stopped play, but the Carmen contributed to the City of London Artillery and warned the Reserved Occupation Committee that carters, lorrymen and draymen were being called up when they were needed in dockland. The Committee confirmed that they were exempt from military service, and the Company told its members. During the war, of LGOC's 3,071 'buses, 1,319 were requisitioned for overseas use.

In 1917 there were 868,931 horses on active service, as against 2,079,122 'civilians'. In London, 101,185 were employed.

When the war was over, the now mechanised Army had 66,000 surplus trucks on its hands and Carmen faced an uncertain future. In 1919 the Ministry of Transport was established, and took over the Road Board. Then, in 1920, the retiring Master Carman, Alderman James Roll, became Lord Mayor.

At long last, the turbulent carters of four centuries had scaled the civic heights. A Carman was Chief Magistrate of the City of London. That same year, Ernest Coxhead enrolled. The Roads Act introduced vehicle licensing and national funding for roads.

In 1921 the Court was enlarged by one, and again by two more in 1924, although Livery numbers were not that high. Post-war slump brought unemployment and widespread unrest. The General Strike of '26 cancelled the May Court. By 1931 nearly three million were out of work.

In 1925 the LCC proposed banning horses from the streets – because they held up motors; Fred Hunt of E. Wells & Sons objected, as did W.H. Smith & Son. It was decided to experiment with a one-way system in Long Acre. In 1921 Aaron John Wells and his brother, Arthur Edward, joined the Carmen; in 1923, his son John Aaron came too.

And in 1922 George H. Lloyd became a Carman – another of the ubiquitous A.C. Lloyd cartage company. Three brothers, Charles in 1931, Richard in 1953 and another George, became Carmen, plus cousin Eric in 1954.

Firms like Wells, 'Coal, Coke and Cartage Contractors' of Rotherhithe, ran fleets of steam-powered trucks, in their case hauling Canadian paper for the *Daily Mail* from docks to Fleet Street, meat to out of town coldstores and tea from Wapping Docks to Birmingham. In the '20s, design and production rapidly evolved, churning out lorries, vans and cars.

Charabancs – a relatively short lived single-decker, often with doors to each row of seats, and with a canvas hood – emerged for outings and excursions: the *Daily Mail* in 1920 observed: 'motor charabancs were becoming very popular'. Motorbuses proliferated. Birch Bros started 'See Britain Tours', with charabancs on ex-Army lorry chassis.

Solid tyred charas and ex-Army 'jitneys' were soon ripping the tar off the roads; pneumatic tyre and bitumen brought welcome relief. The roads improved. By the thirties road haulage was overhauling the railways in long distance goods carriage. There were 257,123 goods vehicles in 1927, doubled to 513,147 by 1938.

By 1918 there were 1,758 'buses on London's streets and in 1922 independent operators started to challenge the London General monolith. With the Admiral racing the General to the 'bus stops, competition was fierce. The City Motor Omnibus Co emerged in 1923 and over 60 other independents appeared.

In 1924 the London Traffic Act attempted to regularise matters. A year later Restricted Street orders eliminated newcomers from some 800 'bussed streets. By now there were 174 independents.

The Local Government Act of 1929 made counties responsible for roads and the Road Traffic Act of 1930 removed speed limits for cars and motorbikes, limited lorry drivers' working hours and introduced compulsory third party insurance; PSVs were regulated and Traffic Commissioners appointed. The licensing system for commercial vehicles was born in 1933.

By 1929 between five and six hundred merchants, agents and factors met and dealt at the Coal Exchange. Prices quoted were ex-pit, and deals were struck verbally. Russell & McIver, vintners, had their offices at the Exchange and Ernest Coxhead was in charge.

During the twenties, Coxhead set about recruiting Carmen – discreetly but with determination. He was instrumental in introducing over 100 new Liverymen from his Coal Exchange contacts, many of them coalmen. In 1931 he was Master. His new recruits introduced their friends and colleagues.

In the right place at the right time, Coxhead effectively built the modern Company and, by a strange irony, ignited the fires of new fellowship from the long cold ashes of past fuellers. The coalmen Carmen were the woodmongers' heirs. The Court showed its appreciation with a special presentation.

In 1928 a sketch was submitted for a coat of arms and in 1929 these were granted. They comprised a silver sword, with a red pommel and hilt, point uppermost between two cart wheels, on a gold background, with a crest on a twisted band of gold and red, surmounted by a silver cart horse with a black collar, resting its left hoof on a wheel.

That same year Past Masters' badges were first worn. By then numbers were up, so the Company asked for a larger Livery: 150 was the new ceiling. A tradition founded in the 17th century but stillborn, was also revived.

Robert Tough, Master, gave the Carmen a Queen Anne style two-handled cup. Two years later he bequeathed a silver lamp and in 1930 Assistant Austin Balls made the first of a series of gifts to the Carmen. The precedent had been set in 1675, when Benjamin Preston presented a tankard, partly funded by the gifts of Joseph Springwell and William Holyland.

Austin Balls gave a trophy surmounted by a woodmonger's horse and cart; in 1933 as retiring Master he gave three goblets for Master and Wardens. In 1930 George Henry Lloyd, Master, presented silver gilt Warden's Badges. In London's transport, change was imminent. The first trolleybuses went into service in 1931.

The General bought independents, others merged, then in 1933 the London Passenger Transport Board was incorporated by statute, and the independents were absorbed. Some held out, Birch Bros extracting a concession: to use fare stages on out-of-town routes within London Transport's domain.

Voluntary associations emerged to represent commercial road users. Carmen were involved. Honorary Solicitor Norman Letts proposed the naming of a new body, the Road Haulage Association; John Pye was chairman of the metropolitan area.

In 1933 the Road and Rail Traffic Act introduced nationwide carriers' licensing. Two years prior, the Highway Code had appeared. In 1935 the driving test emerged; a year later legislation took 4,500 miles of 'trunk' roads back into government control. Minister of Transport Hore-Belisha said horses should be banned. In 1937 the first bans were effected by the London (Slow-Moving) Traffic Regulations.

When the Court expanded by five and the attendance fee went down to half a guinea, dinner was served at Innholders, and Assistants could take two guests apiece. The next year the Company invoked the 1668 Act and pushed the Court up to twenty.

With all this harmony and happy growth, the Carmen's 'stout bodyes' were genteely clothed, but just now and then the old bloody-mindedness surfaced – especially when someone took them for granted. In the thirties, the Company was a broad transport church. When one business assumed rights because its manager had joined, the Company pounced.

The freedom was a personal matter, there was no 'business benefit', and no 'hereditary freedom' on his death.

H.V. Rawles was the new Beadle – salary five guineas, plus a gown – and in 1934 Rev Charles Clark became Honorary Chaplain. He was Rector of St Stephen's, Walbrook, and this splendid Wren building became the guild church on his death in 1939. Rector Rev Canon Frank Hay Gillingham succeeded him.

Master and coalman Sir Charles McRea gave the Company a Loving Cup after his year in office, and an oak charity box in 1939. It was inscribed 'Alms for the Poor Carmen, who have fallen by the roadside, and their families'. That started something.

Past Master E.A. Shadrack took up the cause, and the Benevolent Fund was created. Ten Court members gave £100 each in memory of a late Assistant, J.H. Turner of

Thomas Allen, forerunner of P & O Road Services. Shadrack had joined the Company ten years before, a coal merchant of Coal Exchange.

His Livery Banquet menu suggests Carmen laid a good table. Caviar followed the traditional Hors d'oeuvres; Clear Turtle consommé followed that. Then came Salmon with Hollandaise sauce, quickly pursued by Mousse of Foie Gras and Tongue. This paved the way for Navarins of Mutton Jardinière, before the serious eating began, with Roast Ducklings – yes, Ducklings plural – and Orange Salad.

Curacoa Iced Soufflé helped it all down, with some Gaufrettes, and then there were Dessert and coffee. Wines rolled across thirsty tongues with remorseless momentum – six of them. It started as usual with Birch's Punch, followed by sherry, a five year old hock and then some Bollinger bubbly and a little Mumm Cordon Rouge. A fine 17-year-old port led the 40-year-old Rouyer Guillet brandy, before everyone settled down to the 'benedictine, whisky etc'.

To see fair play Mr Norman Birkett KC was one of seven speakers, who included the Minister of Transport, Lord Mayor, Frank Pick of LPTB and the Viscount Suirdale. Pass the Beechams Powders and the Eno's Fruit Salts, please....

The '30s saw some notable freemen join the ranks – Frank Pick in 1934, Frank Coxhead that same year, and Gordon Sunderland two years before that. Frank Coxhead was appointed an Honorary Liveryman as a tribute to his father Ernest's successful revival of the Company's strength.

In 1938 Ernie Murray was apprenticed to his father, a lighterman: 'Day and night the sounds of that age were the tooting of river tugs, hooting of ships...iron wheels and iron hooves skidding, scraping, showering sparks off cobblestones and the shouts of carters, loaders, dockers and stevies'. The Thames was still a highway, as Lightermen rode the river, their barges steered by muscle, and powered by tide.

In 1935 the Livery went up again – to 250 – and to 350 in 1944. Admission cost 25 guineas. Then in 1935, the Carmen did it again: another Lord Mayor emerged from their ranks, this time Sir Percy Vincent, Master in 1929 and Past Master Austin Balls gave another piece of silver to mark it – the Beadle's Mace.

The Company literally went to town, with a major pageant in the Lord Mayor's Show. A pack horse preceded a genuine 1780s stage waggon, a 19th century railed two-wheeled cart, and a contemporary commercial vehicle. The officers rode in two carriages.

Two years later, the horses rode to arms: the College of Heralds granted supporters to the Company's shield – dray horses on either side, harnessed and bridled, with collars of leaved roses. As Eric Bennett remarked 'It seems a pity that St Katherine did not get in somewhere'.

The rather grand arms required a rather grand badge, so Archibald Russell, Lancaster Herald, designed one. The new Master's jewel cost £95 in gold and enamel in 1938.

Perhaps more important than baubles and blazons, a new Clerk was elected in 1935, the first of a family of Carmen to leave an enduring mark on the twentieth century Company. (Oliver) Gordon Sunderland drove a determined Clerkship, specs on forehead, gown billowing. His brother Arthur Grahame Sunderland was Assistant Clerk by 1938. In 1936 Lord Broadbridge was Lord Mayor; he was a Carman too.

The new Clerk soon found the Company was not incorporated by Royal decree – the last charter was that of 1605, and that technically died with the Woodmongers. Work began on a petition in 1937 and it was presented to Privy Council in 1939. Sir William Coxon was Lord Mayor – he numbered the Carmen among his seven companies.

In those days, maximum speed for lorries was 20 mph, and the long distance drivers were rightly known as Knights of the Road. Sometimes the Court took a lofty view too. When a certain Cabinet Minister was in the running for office, his attendance record was a matter for concern. Perhaps senior Carmen felt he faced a conflict of interest.

Assistant Norman Letts flatly refused to countenance the Minister as Junior Warden. If he was elected, Letts would resign, and with that he walked out of Court. In the ensuing ballot, another was chosen. Letts stayed. The Minister left.

Then came war. Horses were once more free to work on London's streets, but the Company's plate was bombed, the badge damaged by fire and alas! the Charter slipped off the table, as battle plans pushed civic ambitions aside. That year quarterage could be compounded by a single payment, and the older the member, the cheaper it got: under 40, £5; 41–50, £4; 51–60, £3 and 61 or over, £2.

Families were once more a feature. There were two Berrymans, both the Coxheads, George and Henry Dutfield, two Elliotts and two Gilberts. Three Gracies – Christopher, William and William Duncan – and three Lakers were outnumbered by four Lloyds – Charles John, Charles William, George Cullman and George Henry.

There were pairs of Mayburys, Mosses and Rossiters plus Alderman Sir Frank and Joe Pollitzer, three Shadracks, two Youngs and the Sunderlands, Grahame and Gordon. There were four Smiths, including Alderman Bracewell and MP Ben, and four Turners – the Rt Hon James Thomas PC, Frederick, Bernard and Joe, but it was the Wells who scored most, with five contemporary members – Arthur, Aaron (John), Ernest, Frederick and Willie – albeit from different families.

The Company's silver all went to Mansion House for safekeeping, and the archives to the Bank of England. Preparations started for the Company's first 'history'. Carmen were at risk too as they prepared for luncheon at Tallow Chandlers' Hall. It was July 1944.

A flying bomb fell at the corner of Budge Row, the host surveyor said the ceiling was unsafe, but the Carmen simply shrugged it off. Everyone signed an indemnity, absolving both Companies. The guest of honour signed too – Herbert Morrison, Home Secretary. The service was at St Mary Woolnoth – St Stephen's, Walbrook had been bombed.

In December 1944 a newly formed Road Haulage Association was formally incorporated as a company limited by guarantee. Its first Chairman was a Carman, Henry T. Dutfield. There were 15,000 members on 1 January 1945. One of its progenitors was Carman G.W. Quick-Smith. The ban on slow-moving traffic returned and rapidly expanded. The horse's day was done, and the knackers' yards prospered.

In 1944 E.E. Coxhead was Master again, and then, in October 1945 an emergency Court was held – Master-Elect Sir Arthur Holmes was ill. The Court elected Coxhead one more time – a modern hat-trick. At a Livery dinner, his guests were NCOs from Australia, New Zealand, South Africa and Canada – he had invited them to express thanks for Empire's contribution to Britain's war.

'Red sky at night, lighterman's delight' greeted demobbed Lighterman Ernie, back on the Thames: 'unchained the paddles...let *Rosie* drift...' until she 'rolled in the wake of hurry-up merchants, a banana boat for Fresh Wharf, the weekly egg and bacon boat from Denmark...oilers, tugs, tows of lighters gunn'al deep with coal...making for London's wharves...coals to power stations, logs to sawmills' just as the Lightermen of two centuries before.

In the post-war period, the Company met, and ate, at Tallow Chandlers Hall, Dowgate. There was only one nomination to Court in '45: Alderman Sir Frederick Wells – elected. In 1946 the Court gave a shield painted with the Carmen's arms to HMS *Anson* – it was hung in the ship's chapel.

In 1948 the price of a 10cwt Bedford van was £305, a 5 ton long dropside lorry £571 and a 29-seater 'luxury' coach £1,483. British vehicle production saw 287,000 cars and 158,000 commercial vehicles reach the roads. Altogether those roads handled the same number of units as before the war, though now there were more trucks and less cars. A Ford Prefect cost £290.

Uniquely, within two years of Coxhead's last Mastership, his son Frank took office. Frank Coxhead's year saw petrol in short supply, and nationalisation. At the Livery Banquet he pressed the government on fuel, and asked Carmen to cooperate with their Labour masters. Fuel shortage became fuel tax in later Masters' speeches, but the Livery Banquet had become a forum for Master and Minister to cross courteous swords.

At his Installation lunch, the main speaker was Lord Hyndley, Chairman of the National Coal Board, sounding echoes of the Coxhead-Carmen Coal Exchange connection.

In those early post-war days, the Company's all-male luncheons were dominated by uniforms; food was short, and at Mansion House, Carmen stood in white tie, consuming a modest buffet.

The 1948 reception included Sandwiches, Savouries, Lobster Bouchées, Sausage rolls, Reception pastries, Gateaux and Ice cream, followed by coffee and orange squash. To warm the innards, there was 'Consommé on departure'. There were three wines – sherry, claret and champagne, plus some whisky, a claret cup and minerals.

The first post-war Ladies' Festival was held at Grosvenor House in '48; the orchestra played 'the latest selections of popular Light Operas etc' and music for dancing. Entertainment was provided by Miss Phyllis Adrian, light soprano, Petulengro and Pattie, 'Original Romany Gipsies in costume' and, at the piano, Victor Marmont.

The Installation service involved one hymn and Court agendas were printed on four folded pages of blue paper.

Before the war ended, Carmen had presented a 'mobile First Aid Unit' to the City. That ambulance was transferred to the Services Club in Vauxhall Bridge Road.

Came 1946 and peace, and the Charter was once more laid before the King. On 26 June 1946 George VI granted this, the Carmen's dearest wish, without fuss, complaint or difficulty.

Four hundred and twenty nine years after the Carmen first drove down the civic path, they had reached their destination. Sir Bracewell Smith was Lord Mayor within a year; the Carmen were among his six companies. He had joined the Court with Sir Ben Smith – the only candidates. After the charter, eight Carmen sought to serve in Court – Henry Dutfield and Joe Pollitzer were elected.

With peace came new government, and the promised redistribution of ways and means. Nationalisation loomed. Education, national insurance and planning dominated the post-war political agenda and in 1946 the National Health Service was established. Industry turned from battle innovation to commercial advantage. Carmen faced the century's second half with a newly minted Company and major transport change.

ABOVE: Today the car is ubiquitous – in 1902 it was a relative rarity; this Horbick in Broad Street, Teddington, was one of the better-known makes from 1900–1909. (CB) BELOW: Trams crossed Blackfriars Bridge, despite Carmen's objections. (CB) RIGHT: Fleet Street is thronged with horsed 'buses, cabs and vans in the early 1900s. (CB)

ABOVE: Traffic control is haphazard in Holborn as waggons, vans and both horsed and motor 'buses negotiate for space. (CB) BELOW: Twelve dockers and their foreman handle a consignment of Ceylon tea in the 1900s Dock Transit Shed, Port of London, whose manager, J.H. Estell, was available on Royal 2000. (CB) RIGHT: A cabfest on the Embankment in the 1900s – 29 ranked hansoms, 10 *en route*, three carts – and a hearse. (CB)

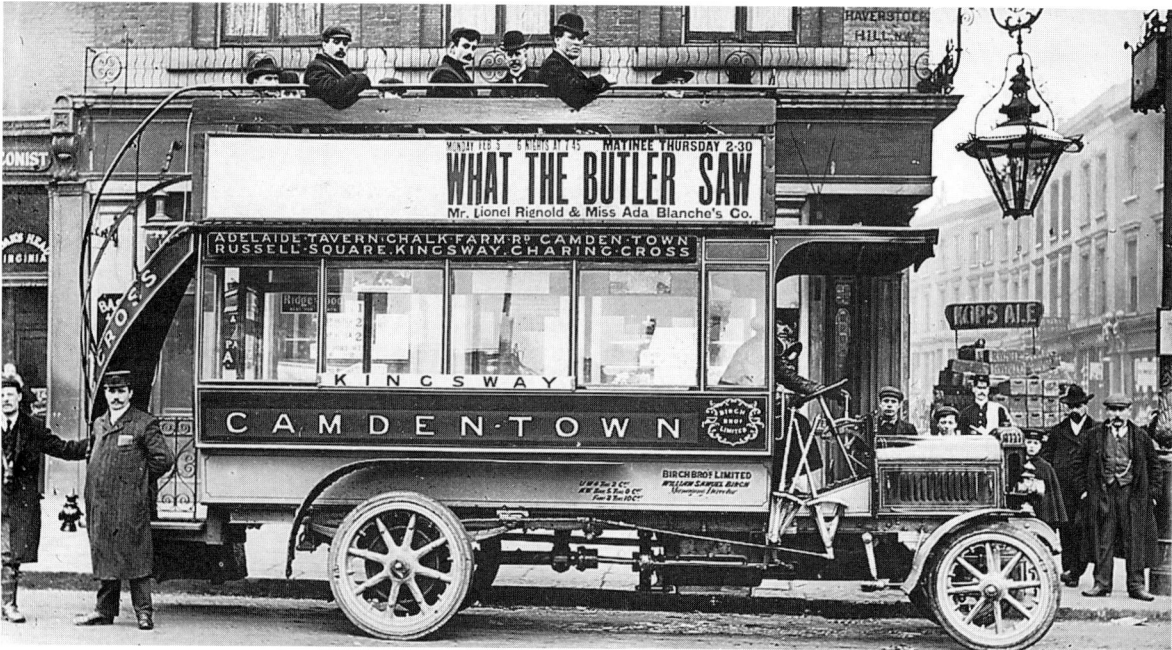

ABOVE: London General tried to put this petrol–electric Fischer omnibus on the streets in 1903; the police turned it down – it was too wide. (CB) BELOW: By 1906 there were nearly 800 motor omnibuses in town: this Leyland Crossley was one of them. (CB)

ABOVE: In 1911 the Unic taxi challenged the hansom's monopoly. (CB) BELOW: A.C. Lloyd carts were a familiar City sight. (LL)

ABOVE: The Carmen's original civic 'deal' to keep the streets clean was still horse-powered in 1915, with this 'automatic road sweeper'. (JD)
BELOW: Brewers' drays were a familiar sight: two horses drawing a London Carman's trolley. (JD)

ABOVE: A Bethnal Green costermonger's cart was pressed into service as an election float that same year. (JD) BELOW: Handcarts survived – 'knives and scissors to grind' – and behind, for shop deliveries. (CB)

LEFT: Carmen scaled the civic heights in 1920: retiring Master, Sir James Roll, became Lord Mayor. (GL) ABOVE: Char-a-bancs pioneered post-World War I excursions, like this ladies' outing with Albert Ewer of 150 Curtain Road, EC2 outside Goswell Restaurant run by C. Cavallini. (JD) BELOW: Eric Taylor's 1929 Model A Ford was used on short-haul: hired out by the hour or day in traditional Carman style from Manor Park, E12. (MT)

ABOVE: Steam dominated long-haul cartage in the 1920s: E. Wells and Son of Rotherhithe carried frozen meat, tea and paper. (JW) BELOW: In 1930 Evan Cook of Peckham delivered £14m of Italian art treasures to Burlington House, with this solid-tyred, 'containerised' Leyland. (EC)

ABOVE: London double-deckers still had outside staircases, but a closed top deck, and ran on pneumatic tyres – a 1930 Leyland Titan. (CB) LEFT: Ernest Coxhead became a Carman in 1920, and Master in 1931, 1944 and 1945. (FC) BELOW: By the thirties the horses' days were numbered: the Rothschild's Hertfordshire station carriage – 'the conceited blacksmith let it fall to pieces'. (SHF)

ABOVE: Long-distance lorry drivers were the 1930s Knights of the Road, like this Wells Atkinson rigid eight-wheeler, taking tea-chests to the Midlands. (JW) BELOW: The first act of nationalisation, when the London Passenger Transport Board was formed in 1933: three Birch generations hand over some of their London fleet – Raymond and John, father William Henry and grandfather, Chairman William Samuel, the founder's son. (CB)

ABOVE: The last pre-war Carmen's Ladies' Festival was held at the Mayfair in 1938. (FC) BELOW: E.A. Shadrack (centre) Master-minded the start of the Carmen's charities in 1939; Gordon Sunderland (left) and W. McAuley Gracie; (right) Col E.W. Crawford and Beadle Rawles. (FC) LEFT: The new Master's badge of 1938. (CC)

ABOVE: Otway & Golder's Albion powered a custom-made low-loader with removeable rear wheels – made by R.A. Dyson in 1938. It was used to move anti-aircraft guns, and for the Mulberry Harbour on D-Day 1944. (GG) BELOW: Docks developed mechanical handling, but Lightermen still rode the river, steering by muscle, powered by tide, and surrounded by barge, tug and steamer, here off Rotherhithe. (CB)

ABOVE: American 'lease-lend' brought vehicles to London like this International run by Eric R. Taylor in 1940. (MT) BELOW: Carmen meet at Tallow Chandlers' Hall in 1943: left to right – Letts, Berryman, Crawford, MacRae, Easton, Coxhead snr, Master Bristow, Holmes, Balls, Parker, Mancroft, Sharman, G.H. Lloyd, B.G. Turner, Laker and Rumsey; Clerks Oliver and Grahame Sunderland before them. (FC)
RIGHT: In 1946 Lt Col Frank Coxhead became Master, here with his wife, Dorothy. (FC)

10

WINNING WAYS

A driver should not say that he would follow a congested route because he had done so all his life.

Alderman Sir George Wilkinson Bt
speech to Carmen 1948

In 1947 the new Labour Government set up the British Transport Commission. The Transport Act intended 'an efficient, adequate, economical and properly integrated system of public inland transport and port facilities'. Carmen knew a thing or two about that.

That same year Sir Frederick Wells became Lord Mayor – his mother company was the Carmen. He was the sixth Carman Lord Mayor in 27 years. 1934's Master, Sir Charles McRea – a coalman – presented the Carmen's banner, and Austin Balls gave its pole. When he died, he left money with which the Company bought a loving cup.

London's 'buses moved smoothly from LPTB to LTE – the London Transport Executive. The Commission acquired other 'bus enterprises. In 1946 the National Coal Board was established; the Coal Exchange had been damaged in the blitz. Revived briefly in 1950, it failed to find a role. In 1948 the railways were nationalised.

'Bus operators were worried, but at least they had a sense of humour:

'I do not understand the fuss
To nationalise the country 'bus…
From some I've asked the reason why,
I've had this curious reply:

The Government must own, you see.
Each public service Q.E.D.!
For it has schemes in contemplation
For functional coordination…'

By 1949 the BTC had acquired 35,000 road haulage vehicles. Britain's transport was fast becoming a State enterprise – and the Commission lost £40 million in 1949. Giving Britain what the new thinking prescribed was expensive.

Real giving began in churches, whose mediaeval guilds cared for sick, maimed, blind, afflicted, widowed or orphaned. That tradition was maintained by their successor trade guilds, like the Carmen. In 1950 they agreed to handle provident funds. The 1864 London Cartage and Haulage Contractors' Provident Institution transferred over £30,000 to the Company. Six Carmen Trustees were appointed, most of them already members of the Institution.

The surplus, after obligatory payments, went to the Carmen's charitable coffers. The Carmen were looking to their very roots. At the same time, on the national stage, the old order was fading. The first steps towards European union saw the Council of Europe convened in 1949. NATO was established.

Early in the '50s the Court also reviewed admission method and cost. New procedures still saw candidates vetted by the Court but the fee rose to 75 guineas and a voluntary subscription was introduced – five guineas. In April '54 the Court was increased to a maximum of 34. Six new Assistants were sworn in 1954.

The year before that the Chaplain died, and Rev William Dormor was appointed, joining the Court in 1955; that same year unrest returned to dockland. The Chaplain became Master in 1970 – the first cleric known to head the Carmen.

One Member of Parliament succeeded where his pre-war counterpart had failed. John Lewis MP did become Junior Warden. Perhaps Carmen had become more pragmatic. Sadly, John Lewis died before the year was out.

By 1952 a change of government brought some de-nationalisation on the roads, but regulation was entrenched in the system, controlling licences, weights and size. British Road Services now comprised the BTC road haulage interest. Carmen found themselves on all sides of the system: Assistant Quick-Smith was prominent in BTC, John Pye in the private sector; Raymond Birch ran the British Electric Traction 'bus interests as well as the family firm, and Carmen drew on other callings too.

In 1953 the Court celebrated the Coronation with two silver loving cups, and the Livery presented three silver gilt dishes. Other silver included a packhorse and a 1911 soldier. Then the Transport Act paved the way for de-nationalisation.

In 1957 an admission by patrimony jolted the Court into setting modern fines – four guineas the freedom, 65 guineas the Livery. Redemption was adjusted to 10 and 85 guineas.

That year the *City Press* welcomed the Company's decision to bind apprentices. Eighteen young men came to be bound, including today's Honorary Assistant Chaplain Duncan and his brother Peter, sons of Past Master and late Chaplain Bill Dormor. Each received a Bible.

Then Carmen, no longer arbiters of cartage skills, decided to reward transport achievement. Reginald Bezzant, the 1956 Master, inaugurated the Viva Shield. Early awards recognised oil research, the Comet airliner, the first motorway, hovercraft and Ro-Ro ferries. Carmen had adopted an extrovert view, well beyond the Square Mile, or the business of hauling freight.

When apprentices were once more bound, again receiving a Bible, the Master told them not to leave it on the shelf; 'It should be a pal...is a great educational force...tells you what a good woman should be'. His grandson Richard replied for all the others when he looked forward 'to carrying on the traditions of the Company'. Three of those apprentices and four of their 'masters' remained forty years on.

Perhaps most significantly, that year saw revival of cart-standings and cart-hiring. Carman T.C. Jacobs of A. Jacobs & Sons (previously Tingle & Jacobs), brought a 'marked' vehicle to the licensed stand on Dowgate Hill. He drove it himself and the Master 'hired' it.

A year on, the Clerk notched up 25 years, and was made an Honorary Assistant; his son, Oliver, became Assistant Clerk. Past Master Frank Coxhead had succeeded his late father as Honorary Almoner – a post he was to hold for over forty years and, with his father, sixty. The E.E. Coxhead Memorial Fund attracted charitable donations to the growing Benevolent Fund.

That same year the City and Guilds Institute needed cash, the Carmen obliged, and a Past Master sat on its Committee. Throughout the fifties and sixties, Past Master Frank Coxhead, John Peters Wells and others discreetly encouraged hauliers and those directly associated with road transport to join the Carmen. Numbers steadily rose.

Closer and closer drew the Carmen's civic ties. In 1958 a Carman, whose packing, storage and export business started in the 1880s, was elected lay Sheriff. Yet Jack Evan Cook's father and grandfather were Paviors, both Masters of that Company, and two of his brothers Paviors too. In 1959 the M1 Motorway opened – the first of its kind. Birch's 203M non-stop London–Bedford service was the first fare-paying user.

In 1960, the European Free Trade Association was born. Sadly, that same year, Junior Warden Herbert Crow died, but he remembered the Carmen in his will, and his widow Annie gave a further £1,000 and a George III silver loving cup. That money endowed the Herbert Crow Memorial Prize, awarded annually to a transport student. In 1983 another (passenger) prize was awarded in memory of Raymond Birch.

Master Ray Birch, who chaired the RSA's Transport Education body and a London polytechnic, in 1961 introduced William Byrd's 1612 *The whislinge Carman* as the Carmen's Musick. Assistant G.W. Quick-Smith had heard it at Lambeth Palace. This was the 444th year of Carmen.

A contemporary ballad is called *The Courteous Carman, And the Amorous Maid, or, The Carman's Whistle*. A predictably 'naughty' song sung by Carmen of old, it went unremarked, not quite acknowledged as the modern Carmen's Song. The last verse echoed the end of Birch taxis in London in 1963 – 'Now fare thee well brave Carman, I wish thee well to fare, For thou didst use me kindly As I can well declare'. Birch cabs had been collecting London fares for 131 years.

Birch was followed by Victor Parker, Master once before – in 1936 – and a founder member of the Farmers' Company. In 1969 Joe Pollitzer took office for the second time; he had served in 1954, his father before him in 1933; his son Richard joined the Livery in 1968.

The sixties saw the final decline of London's heavy horsepower and the end of trolley traction. In 1962 the last London trolleybus was withdrawn. In 1965 one horse still 'carted odds and ends' for the RASC at Regents Park Barracks, but Joe Fountain retired as carman for coal merchants Rickett, Cockerell and Co, after 53 years – his horse, Storm, retired too. That year saw the last of the London Cart Horse Parades. The draught horse's day was almost done, though promotional drays and equestrian events keep the memory alive.

As tastes changed and pockets shortened, the Company dropped the annual dinner dance at Grosvenor House in 1966, one of two ladies' events – the Livery Banquet stayed at Mansion House, a continuing privilege; Carmen, guests and Court sat down to four quarterly meals, and the Fraternity worshipped on Installation Day. The Court and its ladies dined the year out each September and both there and at Mansion House, white tie was the absolute rule.

In that decade Past Masters Norman Letts, Percy Sharman and Frank Coxhead formed a special committee to sort out the bye-laws. Since that meant going to Privy Council, standing orders were created instead. These dealt with Honorary Assistants, removal from office, finding a Master if one died in office and elections to Court.

Candidates needed ten per cent of the Livery to vote them in, but this proved unworkable, so the rule was changed – to 25 per cent of those voting. In 1963 one new rule was invoked. Assistants absent without leave for a year could be dismissed, and two were guilty. One pleaded business problems and ill health – he stayed. The other resigned.

Then in 1965, old troubles erupted again. With double yellow lines restricting City parking, the police wanted the remaining 18 standings abolished as well. Worse, someone 'upon the radio' made fun of the cart marking ceremony at Guildhall. For the Town Clerk this tainted the City's image: 'Perhaps marking as well might be allowed to fall into disuse'. Not if Carmen had their way.

Past Master Letts, the Company's legal eagle, drily pecked: 'There is a modern tendency among the ignorant to discredit those things which at least have the virtue of antiquity'. The Carmen persuaded the Corporation 'to retain marking and to permit standing on one day a year at one point'.

The annual standing and 'hire' continued, and cart marking at Guildhall Yard was maintained, albeit with token vehicles. Nonetheless, parking restrictions finally closed the carrooms. With them died the Carmen's rights and privileges to stand and ply for hire. No longer could the Company stand and fight for cartage rights.

Instead, powerful lobbies and voluntary bodies spoke for transport interests – principally, the Public Transport and Passenger Vehicle Operators' Associations for the 'bus interest, the Freight Transport and Road Haulage Associations for hauliers. Learned Institutions spoke of technology and education. Pressure groups came and went.

Transport developments gathered pace with one-way systems, motorways, ring roads, 'bus lanes; 'buses began to move to one-man operation, road freight accelerated at the expense of railways, as Dr Beeching took the scalpel to branch lines, and hauliers faced ever more complex regulations.

In 1966 the Carmen suffered a grievous loss – Gordon Sunderland, Clerk for 31 years, died. He had been a Common Councilman for 22, Deputy for Billingsgate Ward for nine years. Also Clerk to the Farmers, he had served as Master of the Bakers. Frank Coxhead told the Court 'his was the driving force, his the ability to organise...he was a truly great Carman'. His son, Oliver, was appointed in his stead; that year the Livery ceiling rose to 450.

In dockland, Jackie Dash was leading the work force in a series of strikes, in 1961, again in 1966, '67, '70 and in 1972 and 1974. In 1965 the Company recognised the new roll-on roll-off ferries with the Viva Shield. Ro-ro and containers were to capitalise on dockland's disorder. In 1973 Britain joined the European Economic Community.

'The worst type of strike was that which involved a small group, such as the tally clerks' – because that paralysed the whole work force, as Mr Jeffrys of Scruttons Ltd observed. In 1972 dockers were insisting on doing work in hauliers' premises. RHA Chairman and Carman John Wells was in a cleft stick, when he spoke for the haulage interest. By 1975 the Port of London was paralysed. Wells' vehicles were blacked and he was closed down.

By the eighties, the work had drifted to Tilbury, and then east coast ferry ports reaped the benefit of the demise of that dockland which had decimated cartage profits a century before. Carmen hauliers took up the slack, as European and UK logistics demanded. The 1967 Transport Bill saw the creation of the National Freight Corporation, to fulfil the Labour government's vision of transport integration.

The trouble was not only onshore. The barge owners felt the wrath of Red Mick from 'Ruskin College on a Union grant' and 'hollering for work-to-rule, instant stoppage or...if he had his way, all-out revolution'. No one wanted to 'black-leg' so they went along with it.

It was 'the Age of Slump' for Lightermen like Ernie Murray, 'putting out of action umpteen miles of docks, wharves, and warehouses, two hundred years of trade and commerce'. By then 'timber trade in London was done, dead as the whaling trade...two hundred year ago'.

'Whopping great coffins...ready-loaded boxes...without a stevedore, docker or lightermen in sight or on pay' and so 'we came out on strike in the late eighties' and then 'opted for severance'. It was another end of another era. 'The Royals – Albert, King George and Vic Docks, closed their...gates for good. Union Lighterage, Mercantile, General – all the firms we thought were forever – they all went, strangled by containerisation'. The Lightermen mourned their past as the docks which had once crippled the Carmen closed their gates.

Then on 28 April 1968 Carmen remembered their past as they filed into their pews at St Paul's Cathedral. It was three centuries since Common Council set the Carmen free, three hundred years of Fellowship. With a reception at Innholders' Hall, the Company launched the Tercentenary Appeal. Chairman was Assistant Sir John 'Jack' Cohen, the Tesco supermarket pioneer.

An Aims and Objects Committee was formed to establish an endowment fund, build a Hall, support more charities, help civic education and the CIT, encourage road safety and high standards. A year later, Carmen contributed, with other Companies, to a new oriel window at Tallow Chandlers' Hall, depicting their arms.

The Benevolent Fund profited from the Appeal, the Hall project was shelved, schools were helped. On 24 July the Anniversary Banquet was held at Guildhall, Master Quick-Smith in the chair, and HRH the Prince Philip guest of honour. The Minister of Transport, Institute President, Chairmen of RHA, PTA, PVOA, CBI, British Rail, the President of MIRA, General Secretary of the Transport and General Workers Union and the top soldier in the Royal Corps of Transport were all there.

That year highlighted a recurrent problem – the division of effort, cost and funding between the Company itself, and its charitable concerns. The Benevolent Fund was buoyant. The general funds were not. Bye-laws limited quarterage to a shilling – or five decimal pence. The Company petitioned for the right to 'levy, collect and receive...a competent sum...agreed on from time to time'.

The City agreed. From 1970 quarterage went up to £15 – and no compounding. Existing compounders were asked for a voluntary sub of £10 a year. Eleven Carmen resigned rather than pay up. Fifty per cent took on the voluntary cost. Altogether 178 Liverymen had paid little or nothing towards annual costs, year on year. It had to change.

In 1975, a new capital fund was launched as the Gundry-White Livery Fund – Carmen were invited to pay a once-only lifetime sum.

Treasurer Arnold saw this as an appreciating and uncommitted asset. Its essence was War Loan investment bought by compounded fees, generating interest for re-investment. The beauty of the scheme lay in its posthumous growth and Carmen's savings against fee inflation.

It was Frank Coxhead who proposed the Court sit in order of seniority, to show who had passed the Chair, and who approached it. Attendances immediately improved.

By the seventies the National Bus Co had absorbed most of the independent 'bus firms, including the large BET and Tilling operations. With London Transport and the municipal undertakings, Britain's 'buses were effectively public property. Besieged by National Bus, Birch Bros punched its last tickets.

The Benevolent Fund made its presence felt. From 1973 it gave £1,250 a year for three years to the City University to research tyres and suspension. By now it had established an annual habit of grants to the City of London's Freeman's School.

In 1973 Middle East crisis forced up fuel costs and the miners forced a three day week; coal was scarce, the government fell. Then in 1973 another Carman joined the Shrievalty when Tony Hart, later Master, was elected lay Sheriff. Unusually, the new Carman Sheriff did not drive, but his light Rolls with its dark driver was a familiar sight at Carmen's events.

After 135 years' separation from Christ's Hospital, the Carmen revived that link with prizes, then in 1974 paid £2,000 for a Donation Governorship – the right to present a child and pay for its upkeep. Alderman Assistant Christopher Leaver was the first such Governor. Owen, grandson of Past Master Edward Dutfield, was the first pupil.

That same year Carmen made good their civic ties with a stained glass window in Guildhall crypt – the window was designed by Glazier Brian Thomas and reflects transport in all its forms. The Court also noted that Past Master Henry Dutfield had joined in 1919, was in his 90th year, and made him 'Father of the Company'.

Napoleonic ghosts must have trembled in 1974 when Past Master Pye and Assistant Tony Hart proposed a relationship with the Royal Corps of Transport. The very next year, articles of association were signed by Master Charles Lloyd and Major Generals William Bate and Peter Blunt.

The arrangements envisaged the Master's presence at HQ Mess, the London barracks and Corps Week, a visit to a Corps unit, and the General at Mansion House. The Master would become an Honorary Member of the Institution of the Corps, and the General an Honorary Carman and Assistant. Officers would be welcomed as Freemen at Company events, and as Liverymen.

The association flourished. Generals served the Court well, officers joined, and RCT Bicester's 25 Freight Squadron became 'The Carmen's' in 1982 – the only Army unit to have such a Livery 'title' and later, to display Livery insignia on its vehicles, when the Company approved the use of its crest. Annually, a sword was presented to the RCT cadet top of his year. A senior liaison officer joined the General Purposes Committee.

Then the London Cartage Fund merged monies with the Carmen's own charitable resources. Now there were £100,000 to invest. Within five years, the Fund, chaired by Past Master Quick-Smith, amassed £163,000. Giving was increased, and the scope for donation was also widened, with a heritage fund and *in memoriam* options. 1974 also saw Labour's return to power, and re-nationalisation.

Clerk Murray Donald went to Scotland in 1976 and returned to a small crisis. Company silver was stored in Cheapside with Hicklenton & Phillips. While the Clerk was away, the firm closed. The silver had to move. Frantic phone calls ensued.

Two metal trunks were bought by phone; the National Safe Deposit Company refused them; two other firms pleaded lack of space. NatWest in Eastcheap refused too, then had a change of heart, despite the fact the consignment comprised two locked chests, three sealed wooden ones, a padlocked wooden box and a locked one too. In due course, it all went to the RCT barracks at Regents Park.

Then one fine day, the Court convened, and one chair remained empty – the Master's chair. After some time, Assistants began to ask 'Where is he?' After a longer time, they asked 'Is he coming?' and eventually they realised the answer was 'No'. It transpired that Master McPhail had a pressing commitment, and no one knew. The Court was aghast but coped. Business continued as usual.

1976 saw the formation of the masonic Lodge of Paul's Wharf no 8731, primarily for Liverymen and Freemen of the Carmen's Company. Every year it gives tangible support to Carmen's charity.

In the '70s, fines were reviewed, raised and subscriptions increased; subs became £15, admission cost £10 for freedom, £280 for Livery. Assistants paid £300 to join the Court. For several years past, that year's Master, Edward Arnold, had served as Treasurer – now he saw the fruits of his considerable labours.

The Chaplain resigned that same year. Rev Chad Varah, Samaritans founder, and Rector of St Stephen's, Walbrook, became an Honorary Carman, when his church had to close its doors – it was unsafe and needed restoration. Carmen moved to another Wren masterpiece, St Michael Paternoster Royal and Rev Bill Down became Chaplain. A Masters' board was put up in the church's Whittington Hall. That was in 1981.

The 1979 'winter of discontent' hit hauliers hard with strikes in dockland, steel and engineering. It also hit government; Labour left. With the 1980s came de-nationalisation, de-regulation and legislation to curb Union powers. With de-regulation, the National Bus Company fragmented, new 'bus companies mushroomed, and new groupings formed, melted and reformed. The railways prepared for privatisation.

Transport development was moving fast in size, capacity, speed and safety. Containers, 'just in time' national distribution, faster hovercraft and catamaran ferries; airline services, charters and package tours would move goods and people in ever increasing numbers. Urban congestion was a major and growing problem. 1985 was the year the miners struck – all year – the beginning of the end of King Coal.

With the political unpicking of decades of State intervention, and the birth of new transport entrepeneurs, Carmen had their own problems. Geoffrey Clarkson was Master when the Clerkship went awry. Already an Assistant had had to take minutes at Apothecaries' Hall. Once more the Court was in session, the Master turned to the Clerk and asked a question. Three times he asked, but answers came there none.

It soon dawned on some Assistants that all was not well; in fact Clerk Michael Hinton was not well. Indeed, he was clearly not at all well. Assistant Birch proposed adjournment *sine die* and uniquely, the Court rose. Happily, the Clerk recovered, to become Master of his mother Company, the Farmers and later, the Arbitrators.

A Committee was set up under the Master to find a new Clerk, and the Company realised it was time for change, yet some continuity. Clerks had come and gone with monotonous regularity. Offices were temporary and the Company was at risk. Most alarming, there were shades of past troubles – the accounts were incomplete, records were missing, others muddled, and the Company apparently in debt.

Oliver Sunderland had resigned the Clerkship in 1969, for he found some Assistants autocratic. He and his father before him had given the Carmen virtually free office support.

Francis Barragan served, but very much part-time, for two years. Then Ulick Burke took over for a further two years, his dedicated service inhibited by distance, for he worked from home. His son, Michael, later became Deputy Clerk.

As Assistant Willie McPhail neared office, he offered the services of his right hand man, Murray Donald, and his West End office. That arrangement ended with the end of McPhail's Mastership.

Carman Donald was replaced by David Reid, who acted for several Companies, collected his post from the porch of a City church, and conducted business with an ubiquitous recording device.

Reid lasted two years too. Then came Michael Hinton, a Sunderland in-law, with the same office apparat and a wealth of experience of City and Livery. Two years later his tenure came to a dramatic end. The Clerkship was vacant yet again, with no one in sight and much to be done.

A committee was formed and, through the Corps connection, found its man – Lt Col Geoffrey Pearce as Administrator, and two months later, Clerk. For the first time since 1969, when the family tradition of Clerkly service stopped, a Clerk had been selected on a considered basis, and not as a hasty stop-gap. The new Clerk was also a Carman, and from a transport background. His grandfather ran horsed transport for John Mowlem's construction company.

Offices had also to be found. Initially these were at the Clerk's home, then St James, Garlickhythe – in the vestry, and subsequently St Olave's Rectory – in the basement, until the rector moved and the space was reclaimed. Later, a temporary home was offered by BP at Britannic Tower, then a lease signed on premises in Ludgate Hill. At last the Carmen came to rest.

With silver safe, soldiers on board, worship with Wren, a new Clerk and a change of office, the Carmen were quietly content. Past Master Woodroffe Benton, Hon Solicitor, gave and later left shares in Wanstead Golf Club, an exciting prospect for the future.

Then in 1980 came the ghosts of conflicts past. The Woodmongers returned.

The Society of Coal Merchants had decided to ask the Aldermen for a Livery as the Worshipful Company of Woodmongers and Coal Sellers. The Court erupted. To put it mildly, Assistants were not amused. The Company regarded itself as rightful successors and, given the conflicts of the past, was 'not happy with the title of Woodmonger', much less its use by anyone else.

Master Geoffrey Clarkson told the Coal Merchants the Court thought it 'most unfortunate and undesirable for two Livery Companies to lay claim in succession of the old Woodmongers Company and we reserve our rights'.

What started ominously quickly died. The Company extended the hand of fellowship to the coalmen, and helped them progress – as the Worshipful Company of Fuellers. The last spark from the embers of the past flickered, and died.

> **George the Sixth** by the Grace of God of Great Britain, Ireland and the British Dominions beyond the Seas King, Defender of the Faith, Emperor of India.
>
> To all to whom these Presents shall come, Greeting !
>
> **Whereas** the Master, Ernest Albert Shadrack, the Senior Warden, William McAuley Gracie, M.B.E., the Junior Warden, Colonel Edward William Crawford, C.B.E., D.S.O., and Charles Edward Scholes, Henry Alexander Jager, George Henry Lloyd, Herbert Augustus Easton, C.C., George Tullidge Hedge, O.B.E., Alderman Sir Percy Vincent, Ernest Edward Coxhead, William Austin Balls, O.B.E., Alderman Sir Frank Joseph Coleman Pollitzer, Alderman Sir Charles James Hugh McRea, Henry Wilfred Carter, Victor Harold Parker, and Arthur John Laker, being members of the Court of Assistants of the Worshipful Company of Carmen did by their Petition humbly represent unto Us that the said Company is an ancient Fellowship of the City of London and was constituted a Company of the same City by the Court of Aldermen in the year 1517, but has never been separately incorporated, wherefore they did petition Us on behalf of themselves and all other members of the Court of Assistants, Liverymen and Freemen of the said Company for a Charter of Incorporation for the better management of their common concerns:

The opening lines of the 1946 Royal Charter. (CC)

ABOVE: Carman Sir Frederick Wells became Lord Mayor in 1947. (GL) LEFT: Sir Charles MacRea gave the Company's banner. (CC) RIGHT: In 1956 Master Reginald Bezzant inaugurated the Viva Shield for Transport Improvement. (CC) BELOW: London's wharves were still home to City Carmen – Baker Britt's Commer loads up at Empire Wharf. (EB)

LEFT: In 1957 cart hiring was revived by T.C. Jacobs. In 1960 Master Raymond Birch held the horse. (CB) RIGHT: Carman Jack Evan Cook was elected Lay Sheriff in 1958. (JG) BELOW: Court meets in 1959: R. Bezzant, J. Pollitzer, H. Dutfield, N. Letts, B.G. Turner, P. Sharman, V. Parker, G. Lloyd, R. Cheeseman, R.W. Birch, Master J. Pye, H. Crow, J. Evan Cook, J. Fuerst, H.E. Randall, A.E. Drain, Mr Norman, ?, Beadle, with below, Gordon and Grahame Sunderland, with J.S. Crawford, F. Coxhead and W. Dormor in front. (FC)

LEFT: The Tercentenary Appeal of 1968 was run by Sir Jack Cohen, Master in 1976 (right) with Hon Solicitor and 1965 Master Woodroofe Benton. (CC) CENTRE: 1971 Master Gundry White lent his name to the Livery Fund. (FC) RIGHT: Carman Tony Hart became Lay Sheriff in 1973, and Master in 1982. (AH) BELOW: Henry Dutfield was made Father of the Company in his 90th year. (FC) RIGHT: In 1975 Master Charles Lloyd signed Articles of Association with the Royal Corps of Transport, General Bate doing the honours. (CC)

From those who have never thus guerdoned before,
And have given much travail to get it.
Comes your own honoured sword, in your moment of awe,
With a whole lot of chaps round to wet it.

In a room of military memories vast –
What legend and tale must there be here –
Do the souls of the Waggoners out of the past
Rejoice in the youth that they see here?

LEFT: The Carmen's Window, in the West Crypt at Guildhall. (CC) RIGHT: Master Edward Arnold presented the first Sword of Honour in 1979. (CC) BELOW: As the seventies closed, so did the Carmen's Church at St Stephen's, Walbrook – here at the 1960 service. (CB)

11

FELLOWSHIP

Corps and Carmen, dolls and scholars,
Ward Clubs, docklands, US dollars,
Brokers, brewers, Lords and showmen,
Number crunchers, right Royal yeomen;
Came they one and came they all
To London Wall, to London Wall.

CB: *The Lord Mayor's Show* 1998

Transport was the theme of the Lord Mayor's Show in 1981. That was no surprise to Carmen, for the youngest Lord Mayor this century was a Carman. Sir Christopher Leaver took his family to Mansion House, and the Carmen celebrated. The surprise was different.

As usual, Aldermen who had served the shrievalty came forward for consideration. As usual, Liverymen filed into Guildhall to signify approval. The order of march saw Leaver as 'Next'. It was not the Carman's turn.

At the eleventh hour, the intended candidate dropped out. The Aldermen proposed Leaver, the Livery made clear their wishes; they voted him in.

At the Lord Mayor's Show, over thirty floats reflected transport, including Corps band, British Airways, British Rail, Ellerman Lines, Ford, Raleigh, AA, RAC, NFC, RHA and the Department of Transport. There were bicycles; there was a model Concorde; a stage coach; racing cars.

After the Lord Mayor's Banquet, the Carmen's lunch: in 1981 Assistant Long persuaded the Court to offer simple meals at low cost without formality, at Whittington Hall – to encourage more Carmen to meet one another. With the new administrative order, the Court asked Ken Parry to be Honorary Treasurer, and Sir Kenneth Selby to chair the Viva Shield Committee.

That same year the Company discovered some of its silver was missing. The Clerk recovered it all, save the Boer War medal and an ivory scroll. Next year a Past Master helped to buy a silver Model T Ford for the Lord Mayor, on loan to the Company. Junior Warden Birch was amazed that Carmen signed the roll in ballpoint, so he gave a silver Court Pen. In 1984 he added a silver model of an 1884 Birch horsed omnibus in his father's memory and in 1985 a silver Carman's Whistle with a 'Fare thee well, brave Carmen' at the end of his Master's year. He gave a miniature silver whistle to the Clerk too, for all his good works.

The eighties saw transport emerge from State domination and labour relations mature as government changed the rules. Sex discrimination was outlawed and the City welcomed its first lady Lord Mayor.

New brooms were sweeping clean when John Wells became Master in '81 and proposed new Court procedures, to assist discussion and enhance ceremonial and at the same Court Sir Kenneth Selby declined to stand for office – his wife was unwell. The Master's six measures formed the Court's procedures henceforth.

For six months Clerk, Master, Treasurer and auditors wrestled with the accounts. The Company faced serious difficulties. When the audit was at last approved, the Treasurer produced a financial report, the Livery Scheme was suspended, and quarterage and subscriptions increased for 1982. As Treasurer Parry recorded: 'proper records do not seem to have existed' for subs and quarterage; accounts were incomplete for 1979, '80 and '81.

Then a matter of fees popped up. It seemed the ex-Clerk's firm might claim some thousands of pounds, for he had been on secondment. The Master and his predecessor went a-calling on the senior partner, a past Lord Mayor. Dues were discussed, reconsidered – and decently buried.

By this time, the dress code had relaxed, and black tie was permitted, if not encouraged, at Mansion House, but morning dress was still expected on Installation Day. Less formal events enhanced the programme – Master's Special Event and Carol Service. The new company office opened at St James Garlickhythe and a second edition of the 1952 history appeared.

It was John Wells who persuaded HRH Princess Anne to meet the Carmen, and in 1982 at Guildhall Old Library, she was made free, and clothed with the livery at a special ceremonial Court. Then Wells stepped down, and presented a Clerk's Badge to commemorate a year of change.

During the year, 70% of outstanding quarterage and 50% of overdue subs were recovered, the Company moved into the black, paid taxes due, and cleared its debts. The Clerk was congratulated.

To many, 1982 was a watershed in national as well as transport lives: that February the 10,000 shareholder employees, families and pensioners of the National Freight Consortium plc paid £53.3 million for the National Freight Corporation. State road transport was dying though State imposition thrived – in 1983 vehicle excise duty went up 28.5%. In 1982 38-tonne artics were approved.

When Britain went to war in the Falklands, the RCT was the main supply link. Carmen responded with the '82 Viva Award. The Company also redefined its craft association as 'all aspects of the transport function' with the emphasis on roads and distribution. At the Court Awards dinner, 10 Corps recipients of Falklands awards were the Company's guests. Sir Denis Thatcher was also there, somewhat surprised when Senior Warden Freddie Bird suggested he replied for the guests, instead of General Bate. The soldier won.

Lt Ferrier, RCT sword winner, was appointed the Company's first standard bearer, after the long-lost Company banner was recovered – from Innholders' Hall. Thereafter, standard bearers were drawn from sword-winners.

In 1983 the Benevolent and London Cartage Funds were worth £140,771 and £52,999. Past Master Quick-Smith retired as Secretary and the Clerk took over. The charity box had disappeared, so Assistant Sir Ken Selby gave a new one to honour Almoner Frank Coxhead's 50 years as a Carman. When Quick-Smith retired, Sir Christopher Leaver took the Chairs.

The first 34 Liverymen retired voluntarily in 1983, to make way for new blood and, after some lively correspondence about rights and privileges, Past Master John Pye took Emeritus status – the first to step back from the Court. That year Lady Donaldson was elected Lord Mayor and the Viva became the Awards Committee.

From time to time the Court got excited about a forthcoming Master; would he have the time, or the skills, or the ability to speak? Would he curb his spirits, wear the right clothes, respect tradition? At least three prospective Masters were seen by some as maverick, brash or unpredictable.

When Freddie Bird took office, a self-made haulier who loved nothing better than to work on his trucks, there were mumbled misgivings from more sophisticated souls, who remembered the Bate/Thatcher incident.

Where other Masters gave gifts, championed change, or steered stars to the table, Master Bird was simply himself. He lifted Court and Company with his fond and straightforward approach – for he was a Carman like Carmen of old, 'who says what he thinks and does what he says'.

That year Carmen gave a Land Rover to Princess Anne for the Save the Children Fund, and a Chaplain's cope, embroidered by Assistant Gotch's daughter Jenny. And in October '83 the Court held a special session to consider the state of the Company. Reports deluged them – from Clerk, Treasurer, Assistant Clerk Michael Burke and Assistant Long's Aims & Objects Committee, plus one from the Special Committee.

With a clash between the Clerk's and Special Committee's reports, both were deferred and the latter fell to the ground. The Burke paper was intriguing; it proposed narrowing but deepening the Company's field of transport, looking to customers as well as to operators, and addressing freight security – it was also rejected. The A & O report pressed academic and professional spheres, and visualised a doctorate in transport studies. It came to naught too. Carmen's thinking minds were perhaps enervated by all this administrative action.

Still, the Clerk's paper was largely adopted. It meant 150 new Liverymen, voluntary retirements, 440 as a lower threshold of membership, and minimum funding levels of £100,000 general fund investment, £10,000 on deposit and £30,000 revenue. It also suggested a new Livery ceiling – 500. That was achieved in 1986 and the other targets met too.

It also recorded the *status quo* – 430 Liverymen, of whom 175 paid quarterage, 221 were annual subscribers, 25 paid into the Livery Fund, and nine were Honorary. Recovery of arrears involved over a thousand letters. Another forty Carmen contemplated retirement.

The next year the Company had to move – again. This time the offices were in the basement at St Olave's Rectory. By now, the Court was divided on financial control; the 'cabinet' pushed one way, elder statesmen another. It was a case of Special versus General Purposes Committee, and the latter won the day.

With the adrenalin flowing, the Company told the Bodleian Library it would like its old charter back. The Bodleian refused, so it stayed in Oxford.

Nothing daunted, the Company now decided to make the first RCT Safety Award in 1985, and welcomed a third award with open arms – the Sir Henry Royce Memorial Foundation award for excellence. Liveryman and Foundation chairman Frank Shaw was the prime mover.

Past Master Wells then told the Court he was going to propose some radical change – new rules of engagement for General Purposes, abolition of the Special Committee, and a new Past Masters' Committee. The Court agreed.

The old Special Committee, set up to look at by-laws, had become a fixture. Effectively three wise men guarded the Company's traditions – Coxhead, Pollitzer and Quick-Smith. This was now replaced by the Past Masters' Committee, charged with interviewing candidates for freedom, livery and Court, and watching over ritual and things remembered. The wise men stayed, and Coxhead took the chair.

In 1984 the Royal connection loomed large when the Princess joined the Court and came to dinner at Drapers' Hall. Master Freddie Bird, uniquely faced with two speeches in one evening, started on the first one a second time. His Royal dinner companion stopped him. Without pause, he commented 'I've just been told I'm reading the same speech twice; I'd better read the other one!' The Princess was amused, and the Court applauded.

In 1984 a record number of 23 new Liverymen was clothed at one Court. Mark Pulvermacher joined as Assistant Clerk and Michael Burke was made an Honorary Freeman, Liveryman, and Deputy Clerk. Another 16 Liverymen were clothed at the next Court, making 58 in one year – eight more than the target.

Many families brought their next generation to freedom and Livery, treading the same path as Lloyds, Coxheads, Pollitzers and Wells. Birch Carmen multiplied: Raymond's son Clive, clothed by his father, clothed sons Richard and James in 1984 (in 1998 stepson Jamie was made free). Raymond's brother John and nephew Peter were Carmen too. That same year Birch started a regular Letter to Carmen and rode to church on a 1918 horsed General Service wagon, sign-written 'The Carman's Car'.

He also served as Assistant Master in 1986 and Deputy Master in 1987 by special dispensation, standing in for the Princess when required, and similarly for the past Lord Mayor when *locum tenens*.

A new oath was devised for a Deputy Master, who swore to 'undertake, on behalf of the Master, upon reasonable notice...all such functions and duties...' as the Master is unable to perform...'. Just as well. Sir Christopher was suddenly sick, and his Deputy stepped in for the rest of his year.

In 1985 the January Court luncheon became the Carmen's Charity Lunch and that summer the first Carman's Ball was held at Stowe House, Bucks – it raised over £7,000 for the Benevolent Fund – successive Balls would raise nearly £100,000 by 1999.

Speaker at the lunch was Brian Rix of Mencap and Whitehall farce fame. As Carmen left, they pressed cheques and cash on him in a spontaneous gesture of charitable concern.

March saw the inauguration of the Foundation Day Service and a close-run decision in Court to admit ladies to the Livery – provided they were in transport and 'of merit' – a 'long overdue matter' said Master Birch. The Princess had an HGV licence, and used it to drive a heavy horse box all over the country. With Royal exception, ladies were still barred from Court meals. Girl apprentices were definitely not acceptable.

At the Livery Banquet, the Princess was present. When the Master made way, she demurred 'After you, Master'. As the procession formed up, the Master replied 'No, after you Ma'am' – the Royal prerogative and 'ladies first'. 'No Master, after you! This is your night'. A gracious gesture.

Grace had become a matter of verse for Chaplain Bill Down was a witty man of God:

'God of goodness, bless our food,
Keep us in a pleasant mood.
Bless the cook and all who serve us.
From indigestion, Lord, preserve us.
And if long speeches we endure,
Give us first a good liqueur'

and an official Carmen's Company grace was approved. The Princess agreed to be Senior Warden, with a view to Mastership. The Company acquired a silver College of Arms Quincentenary commemorative goblet for her exclusive use at Company functions.

Mid-'85 Past Master Wells and Assistant Selby suggested all new equipment should be written off the year it was bought, a third of fines become income and the Ben Fund should pay for its own administration.

The Court agreed, keeping Livery and General Funds apart and then turned to the pleasure of giving – a silver horse to Frank Coxhead for outstanding service to the Company – and receiving: Past Master Benton had already given shares in Wanstead Golf Club; now he gave more. Past Master Dormor left £500 to the Carmen's charities. Liveryman F. Adams also left £500 – to the Company itself.

When Corps and Carmen celebrated their first decade together, Maj Gen Derek Braggins hosted a special dinner at Aldershot, and silver gifts were exchanged: an Armada dish for the Carmen and a peppermill for the Corps. New ties and a Company shield were designed. The Corps made all Masters since the '75 accord Honorary Life Members of the RCT Institution; Liaison Officers henceforth became Honorary Freemen.

At regular intervals, usually every decade, Carmen tackled the Great Hall Debate. One scheme at the City of London School for Boys was stillborn; all such schemes foundered on lack of capital, and fear of future costs. The Carmen preferred to move about a bit.

In 1986, the Company planned a Transport Essay competition, believing it a duty to foster transport thinking towards the future. Launched in 1987, it failed to capture pens, minds or many takers.

When the Crow Bequest added an initial £10,000 to the nigh £170,000 Ben Fund, Chairman Leaver proposed an annual £2,000 for sixth form Carmen's Bursaries at King Edward's School, Witley; it shared the same foundation as Christ's Hospital. By now the Company's silver was worth £77,260. St Katherine was adopted as the Carmen's Patron Saint.

With continuing cost pressures, the Court listened with interest to Assistant Selby's study of optimum size. It was agreed to petition for a new Livery ceiling of 500. By April 1986 the Livery was within three of its then 450, even though 105 inactive Carmen had retired. Only two quarterage payers were not coughing up in full, there were eight candidates in the wings and seventy-four other inactive members. The Master said he would write to them all.

Two thirds of the way through the rehab exercise, 85% of new clothings had been achieved, 92% of non-payers retired and Livery strength stood at 99%. General Fund investment was 75% of target, income 92%. Only the deposit account lagged, due to cashflow.

That July Past Master Quick-Smith died. Frank Coxhead voiced the Carmen's tribute. When our past was reviewed, his name would be prominent, because 'he has done so much to further its interests and uphold its dignity and traditions, setting an example of excellence for us all to follow'. The Company paid for refurnishing the foyer of the Motor and Cycle Trades Benevolent Fund Home in his memory – a cause dear to his heart.

Not long afterwards, the missing charity box and ivory gavel turned up – once more at Innholders' Hall – and age weighed heavily upon Court minds, as they failed to agree a retirement threshold for Past Masters.

By now custom had established a special appreciation at year's end for the achievements of each Master. This was Frank Coxhead's idea and the Court empowered him to compose each eulogy. In due course these were formalised in handcrafted scrolls, with the Company's arms. Meanwhile the Clerk's office wrestled with vanishing Carmen – six Liverymen could not be traced and, at long last, the Court decided to revert them to Freemen. They had faded away over five years before.

With three vacancies on the Court, Carmen went to the hustings. There were four candidates. Clearly Carmen were confident in their civic connections; the Court appointed Alderman Levene an Honorary Assistant while Carmen elected the other three. Then they pushed the petition for more Carmen from 500 to 550. Oliver Sunderland proposed the move.

Like Thomas Day before him, Oliver had once been Clerk, and now he was Master. The Court of Aldermen approved 500. Sunderland also set in train a happy tradition: in future, every year the Court would give a bottle of Carman's wine to each member of the Carmen's Squadron.

Echoes of past battles brought a swift response when the Corps asked for Carmen's help to buy the only 'family' VC not in their hands. Assistant Commissary James Langley Dalton earnt his VC at Rorke's Drift Post on 22 January 1879 in the Zulu War. It fetched £62,000; Carmen raised £4,400.

In 1986 the Carmen reached even further than the Mayoralty when Her Royal Highness followed Oliver Sunderland as Master, the first lady to hold that office, and the Carmen's first Royal Master.

Once Court and Company had acclimatised to the Royal presence, they soon realised the Princess was a no-nonsense Master. Court meetings were brisk and decisive, after-dinner speeches short and witty. And woe betide any challenge.

At the Chartered Institute's library, Court members gathered to unveil a plaque that noted the Company's contributions; the Master arrived, badgeless. The Clerk offered the badge to the Master, but the Master declined. The Clerk tried once more time. The Royal Master was wittily adamant – it did not go with the suit! The Clerk wisely gave way, and the Princess got on with the business of the hour.

It was during the Royal rule that Carmen erupted with something of the wrath of ancient times. The Clerk had ordered a computer on General Purposes say-so, within Court-approved funds. Some thought this lacked formal approval, and Past Master Norman Bezzant pressed for disciplinary action, severely and personally criticising the Clerk. Like many minor fracas, this one started to escalate.

The Master was apprised, and the General Purposes Committee heard the Past Master's complaints, which did not spare the Clerk. The place was abuzz as Bezzant mounted his attack. Col Pearce flatly denied all allegations and invited the Court to suspend him, if it felt there was substance in any complaint.

A special meeting was called. Officers were excluded. Sir Christopher Leaver acted as Chairman. Past Master Bezzant had made clear he might feel bound to go beyond the Company but the meeting set this aside. The Committee unanimously rejected all complaints, which it noted were 'couched in unacceptably robust and intemperate language'. The Clerk had served 'with dedication and loyalty', the facts were not as claimed, and the Past Master was invited to withdraw his complaints, without prejudice to his right to further ideas for change.

While all this was going on, another row was building. The Treasurer was unhappy with the accounts, and refused to sign the audit; he claimed his position was redundant, for he did not prepare accounts and had only seen the auditors once. The Clerk stated procedures had been followed – except that Assistant Selby prepared the budgets.

By now it was obvious that the Treasurer was handling investments, Selby budgets and the Clerk accounts. There were too many cooks warming the books, as the Court belatedly realised.

Yet another committee meeting looked again at Bezzant's paper and agreed there was no more to be done – except to abolish the role of Treasurer. Meanwhile, Norman Bezzant defended his right to criticise, when he felt it his duty, and reserved his position. And there it rested. Like old soldiers long gone, this skirmish simply faded away.

Recalling his role in bringing the Corps to the Company, Past Master Tony Hart presented a silver statuette of a Royal Waggon Train field officer c1828. Gifts proliferated. Liveryman Michael Gerson gave a brazier for use at Cart Marking, and the Glovers' Company offered heat-resistant gloves for the same event – presented annually to Lord Mayor, Master and Keeper of Guildhall.

Cart-marking had made its mark – from 1981, when two carrs were marked, to 1987 when 40 came before the Royal Master. Static marking gave way to a slow procession in 1983 and a drive-past after marking in 1985. The Master Glover joined in from 1987 and in 1989 the Lord Mayor came too.

During the Royal year, the artwork for the Guildhall Crypt window was bought and displayed at Regents Park Barracks, where the anteroom to the Mess was now known as the Carmen's Room. And that same year saw the first Carman from an ethnic minority – academic Karra Venkateswara Rao of the City University.

When the Livery reached its ceiling of 450, there were 13 candidates waiting and 16 apprentices, of whom three were shortly to be eligible for clothing, and clothing was much in mind when the Chaplain's vestments were completed with a Priest's Scarf, embroidered with Carmen's arms.

In January, with charity in mind, the Court approved a £2,000 annual sinking fund for tomorrow's children at Christ's Hospital. £1,000 each were also allocated for Master and Chairman to give and it was decided to move towards a new or revised Trust Deed, to merge both the Company's funds and to cover increasing sums saved and spent on good causes.

When Past Lord Mayor Sir Christopher Leaver took office, the Carmen were on a roller-coaster. Livery strength rose to 482, Her Royal Highness sat for a Company portrait and the charitable spend was £42,000. Assistant Norman Collins gave a Master's lady's brooch in memory of his late wife, Glennis, a stalwart Carmen supporter.

Then a Carmen's Award of Merit joined the other three annual awards, and a perpetual Carmen's Company annual Prize was also established at King Edward's School, Witley, in honour of Sir Christopher's year.

It was during the past Lord Mayor's Mastership that he brought Watermen and Carmen together. As Chairman of Thames Line (later Riverbus), he provided three boats to take Carmen to the Thames Barrier. Unfortunately, advanced waterjet technology took against the Carmen, and swiftly steered them towards HMS *Belfast* instead. Skilled pilotage saved the day – Bob Crouch, the Queen's Waterman, was on board. But it was a close naval shave.

In 1988 the Princess's painting by Richard Stone was unveiled, appeared on Company Christmas cards, and leaflets were produced for Cart Marking and for Carmen's Lord Mayors. The Ben Fund exceeded £250,000. Up to £10,000 was authorised for the Lord Mayor's Fund to commemorate the 800th anniversary of the Mayoralty. In the event, £5,000 was given.

After some hesitation, the Court finally came round to the role of the Treasurer – and abolished it. An investment sub-committee was set up instead.

In 1989 the Lord Mayor agreed to participate in the Cart Marking ceremony, and his successors have done so ever since. By 1998 an average of 30 'carrs' were marked annually, there were live commentary, colourful programmes, TV cameras and over 300 witnesses – all for a ceremony once on the brink of Corporate extinction.

A second Carman's Ball raised £14,000 under Master Dennis Baker, who took the Carmen back to Grosvenor House, echoing post-war events. The Carman's Room at Regents Park Barracks was now fully operational and Sir Ken Selby tried to find a permanent office in a city development, but failed. Past Master Benton left more shares in Wanstead Sports Ground, bringing the total to 3,427 and Selby took his seat on its Board.

That year Oliver Sunderland died; his friend, Past Master Leaver, gave a silver cup in his memory – the Sunderland Cup. Like his father, Oliver Sunderland served the City beyond the Carmen. He was a Common Councilman for 16 years, Past Secretary and Master of the Billingsgate Ward Club, a churchwarden at St Mary-at-Hill and Assistant or Deputy Clerk to the Insurers, the Wheelwrights and to the Accountants.

When Chaplain Bill Down retired in 1990, Rev (later Canon) Glyn Jones took over St Michael's, the Missions to Seamen headquartered there, and the Chaplaincy. Bill Down became Bishop of Bermuda, Chaplain Emeritus and later Assistant Bishop of Leicester. The Carmen's Golf Society was resurrected and Past Master Joe Pollitzer became Father of the Company.

Beadle in the late '70s and early '80s was Joe Aldridge – when ill-health intervened, Painter Stainers' Beadle Bob Clarke filled in. Alf Huntleigh-Smith took over in 1994; he died in 1998. Clarke was made free of the Carmen in '97 for sterling service.

The Awards Committee, looking to salvage something from the Transport Essay initiative, lit on the concept of a lecture. As Carmen and Fellows, Wells and Birch approached the Royal Society of Arts, and negotiated a ten year programme of biennial lectures in Adelphi – food for thought, and food afterwards too. The Company sponsored the talks.

The first Carmen's Lecture was a sell-out. Carman Professor Tony Ridley spoke on Transport in Society: Master or Servant? The series continued, every one packed: Secretary of State John Gummer, on Freedom of Movement and Movement in Freedom; European Commission transport chief Jack Short on Urban Thrombosis, and historian Dr Ralph Harrington on Transport Now, Then and Tomorrow. The Carmen looked forward to the final talk in 2000 on Movement in the Millennium.

The nineties dawned with another eponymous threat: London's taxi drivers sought livery status as the Cabmen's Company. Words were exchanged. Fellowship and wisdom combined to drive a better course; the Carmen supported the Company of Hackney Carriage Drivers. Then it was given notice to leave its St Olave's basement and, after decades of domicile at Tallow Chandlers' Hall, table turnouts grew too, moving Carmen to Painter-Stainers' as their 'common' Hall.

Charity was by now concentrated by larger grants on fewer causes: necessitous Carmen, education, City and transport, and those where small sums made a big difference. Major help was extended to Christ's Hospital, where in the '90s a pupil cost £25,000 for up to seven years, and to needy sixth formers at King Edward's School, Witley.

The two schools shared the same charter. One of the Carmen's Christ's Hospital scholars herself became a Carman – Rebecca Gibson went to school at Carmen's expense in 1987; bound apprentice to John Wells, her Governor, in 1994, she graduated with honours from Guildhall School of Music and was made free in 1998. King Edward's Kathryn Tyson, on a Carmen's VIth form Bursary, reached Oxford in 1990.

The Fund had always focused on Carmen in trouble. When one Liveryman fell on hard times, the Company paid his son's way, so he could stay at school. When a truck driver suffered stroke and heart trouble, the Carmen bought him a computer, so he could earn a new living.

The Company was growing, costs were rising, and times were hard when Birch proposed a Funding Committee; the Court agreed, only to change its mind a few months later, passing the buck to the Aims and Objects Committee. Livery strength was holding up at 480 and that year Master Gerry Long repeated the Ball at Grosvenor House, raising £24,899, of which £13,550 went to the Benevolent Fund. He it was who doubled the Carmen's tabled cars – he gave a model Silver Ghost.

The Master also solved the office problem *pro tem*, when his ex-colleagues at BP made space available at Britannic Tower. Carmen nearly went aquatic when Assistant Selby proposed a riverine Carmen's Hall – a Landing Ship Logistic moored near London Bridge. Alas! none was available.

As 1990 got under way, the Court approved a usage that reflected the 'Custom of London' that Past Masters should step back gracefully at an agreed stage and applied the Emeritus scheme more persuasively. Still no one could agree a 'threshold' age for retirement. The Court turned down the Clerk's notion of a Technical Committee to advise the City.

In 1990 Gerry Long's successor, Sir Robert (Bob) Reid (1), British Rail Chairman, tried a touch of 'democracy'. He suggested Past Masters and Assistants sit at random in Court, and not on opposite sides. The Senior Past Master was not happy – he reminded Assistants why the house sat as it did, Assistants ascending, Past Masters descending.

The idea was simple; the execution less so. Carmen stayed in their accustomed places. But they had every sympathy when their Master was burgled, and the Master's Badge disappeared. A replacement was ordered, and the insurers paid up. Then Joe Pollitzer died and Charles Lloyd was appointed Father of the Company – his family could claim the longest Carmanship of all, 165 years, from 1825.

That same year the Carmen had a 125 diesel locomotive named *The Worshipful Company of Carmen*. The Royal Past Master did the honours at Paddington Station, and Carmen entrained to Reading with the Princess on the footplate.

Good ideas sometimes come to nought. Motability was one of them. Since 1988 the Carmen had monitored Government efforts to aid disabled drivers, and hoped to form a Trust with State support. The Carmen's Mobility Scheme was not to be.

Not for the first time, Carmen were exercised about buying guests lunch out of ticket receipts or as a Company expense. Should paying Carmen 'carry' Company guests? In fact, they comprised only 6% overall, but there was a feeling there were too many Masters and Clerks dining at Carmen's expense. Past Master Long suggested a special lunch, just for them.

The Carmen's Masters and Clerks' Luncheon became a fixture – and a desirable meal in the City pantheon. A Carmen's Table was also established at Corps HQ Mess,

Aldershot with ten dining chairs carved with the Corps badge, and bearing an engraved plate – paid from Ball proceeds.

When book keeper Eileen Forde had a heart attack, Company accounts went on computer, to help her cope. As a second attempt at formalising fund raising, Birch suggested a 'think tank' to find ways and means. Most important, the Court agreed to reduce itself to 24 for a trial decade, to speed up succession, put high office within younger reach and balance Assistants to Past Masters.

Then in April '91 the Court approved a move to proper offices, on a nine year lease, in Ludgate Hill. After church porch and Rectory cellar, grace and favour rooms and domestic arrangements, the modern Company at last had a home in sight. Proposals for a new Company history were shelved; a pamphlet was suggested instead, but the Livery fine was increased to cover the cost of the existing book for new Carmen.

The 1991 Ball raised £6,680, the Gundry White Livery Fund reached £70,000 and the Court adopted the Clerk's 'Freemen's Scheme'. This envisaged up to 1,000 new Freemen, to 'enhance the Company's standing and influence' and to increase income.

The scheme encouraged young Carmen who might jib at the cost and commitment of clothing, older entrants who might welcome a limited role, facilitated a 'pause' between freedom and livery, and widened the scope for Company membership beyond the Livery ceiling.

While the Court absorbed all this, it also recognised the voluntary work put in by the Clerk's wife, Jean, and made her an Honorary Freeman – the first lady (after the Princess) made free for more than a century. After some 55 years' service to the Company, Eileen Forde joined her not long after. A second heart attack hastened Eileeen's retirement.

An unusual gift joined the Company's treasures when Liveryman Ellard donated a gavel and block, which he had carved from the war-damaged timbers of the Old Bailey, engraved with the Carmen's arms. Soon after that, Liveryman S.G. Lane gave the Company Flag, to be flown at the Church for services and other occasions, and Master Reid gave a Clerk's Goblet inscribed with his and the Company's arms.

When Eric Britt's wife fell ill, he declined the top office, and Ken Parry stepped up; he commissioned a magnificent statue of HM the Queen on Burmese, which the Livery bought. A year later the Senior Warden again declined office, for his wife had died. Sir Peter Levene offered to serve.

By now recession was biting, numbers were falling and the Livery roll stood at 460. Carmen events featured on Thames Television and in the *Evening Standard*, and a new leaflet was produced. Yet the Court reluctantly decided against advertising its Freemen's Scheme. In Assistant Selby's view this was the bedrock of the Company's financial future.

With cash tight and attendances down, the July Court dinner lost money. For long the Company's awards event, it saw only 78 diners in 1992. Coincidentally, that same year the RCT Safety Award went missing – its previous winner was in liquidation. It turned up again three months later. Awards were moved to April, and the July Court dinner became a domestic Court lunch.

Increasingly worried, the Court decided to crank up quarterage to £200, deferred repairs to its silver, delayed new staff, but backed its decision to launch the first lecture, and amended its forecasts on Selby's advice. It was with some relief that it heard him say that that year's loss would become next year's surplus. The Court gave thanks for all his hard work – in the event, his final contribution. He died suddenly on 9 November 1992.

Somewhat introspectively, the Court continued to contemplate its concerns, when a working party on future operation reported. Assistant Wilmshurst and his colleagues were unanimous. The current cost of running the show could not be sustained and the Company should run only those events it could afford.

Shared Clerk and offices would save money. The Court opted to investigate. The Coachmakers and Fanmakers showed interest, but once again, a good idea faded like mist in the morning sun.

While the attention of Clerk and staff was focused on high matters of finance, the office was robbed – post was thieved containing some £4,000 of Company cheques, and three were fraudulently cashed, even though the Clerk had slammed a stop on them. The bank paid up and Post Office security tightened. The next year's programme was cut back and costs reduced, but losses at Lloyds were biting and the Livery roll was down to 447.

By 1993 it was clear the year had been as bad as predicted. The loss of £11,034 was due to taxation, lower income and higher costs. The Court's depression was slightly cheered by the Benevolent Fund's slight gains – to £315,640.

When government reduced the Armed Forces, the RCT merged with the RAOC, Catering and Pioneer Corps and the postal branch of the Sappers, to form the Royal Logistic Corps and new articles of association replaced the old. The original articles were framed in silver and presented to the new Corps. Past Master Parry gave badges for the Deputy and Assistant Clerks and Chaplain.

The stillborn technical panel was resurrected by Past Master Wells when the Court approved *ad hoc* expertise to advise City and Government on transport. Flushed with enthusiasm, the Court confirmed the lecture series – for at least a decade. Eventually, fifty Liverymen volunteered for the technical panel. In 1994 ten of them formed a Transport Consultative Panel.

Despite hard times, the Court approved a new history pamphlet, produced by Past Master Birch, who also redrafted the Master's and Wardens' Declarations, then the Assistants' and eventually, Freemen's oaths.

In 1992 Carmen held their Installation Service at Bevis Marks Synagogue – Alderman Sir Peter Levene was Master – and that year a third 20th century Carman essayed the shrievalty, when past Sheriff Evan Cook's nephew-in-law, Jeremy Gotch, put up for election.

It was a three horse race, with Alderman John Chalstrey and another layman, Past Master Distiller Michael Broadbent in the running. At Common Hall, Chalstrey and Gotch were declared home, but Broadbent's supporters called for a poll.

A fortnight later Guildhall Yard was seething with rival supporters, as voters appeared, to run the gauntlet of this and that rosetted persuader. Chalstrey was a clear winner. Gotch was ready to concede as the counting went down, and then Broadbent began to look worried. In the Print Room at Guildhall, the result was announced – Gotch home by 16 votes. He took office in 1993.

Meanwhile Carmen were asked what they wanted. 153 responded. They liked the functions, deplored the costs, dismissed free smokes, approved new venues, had enough information and preferred men-only Court meals. The Livery roll continued to decline – to 439. The Livery Fund was left well alone, as a growth capital fund, and rates of compounding were not changed, despite exhaustive discussion.

With equal opportunities legislation on the books, nine years after their first hard-fought gains, ladies were back on the Master's agenda. It was agreed all candidates for the Livery would be considered entirely on merit, gender notwithstanding. This included apprentices. No one could quite explain the hiatus, for women had been Carmen since the 17th century.

Handing over to new Master Britt, Levene gave the Company a silver gilt chain to accompany the new Master's badge. His brother, Carman Colin Levene, produced the 'waggon wheels' in it through the family firm.

In 1994 Frank Coxhead reached the 60th anniversary of his clothing as an Honorary Liveryman and 50th as a member of the Court, which celebrated by presenting him with a scroll, and a framed portrait, to be hung in the Carmen's Room. At the same meeting, the Court delegated screening and admission of freemen not seeking livery to the Clerk – subject to Court approval. By now Carmen's silver was worth £152,315.

In 1994 the Channel Tunnel opened, and the trucking industry used the rail link to speed freight into Europe, while another flag flew for the Carmen when Liveryman S.G. Lane gave one for 25 Squadron RLC (The Carmen's); the Court had agreed this should fly by the Corps flag at Bicester.

It was Master Britt's initiative that moved the Company towards more positive recruitment. He questioned the newsletter, and a PR Committee was formed – the second of its kind; the previous one came and went in the '70s. The newsletter stayed but, for the first time, the Company considered a substantial brochure about itself. The same Committee produced the first ever 'mission statement' for Carmen:

'The Company's objectives are to maintain and enhance its traditional interest in, and service to, the City civic, the transport industry and those in need, through the promotion of excellence, good fellowship and benevolence.' The Court adopted this as the Carmen's message. Liveryman Sherriff retired as the Carmen's press officer – a role he had fulfilled for some years.

It was now thirteen years since the Clerk joined the Carmen. Those in Court with long memories were beginning to worry – what would happen when he left, when would he leave, when should he leave? Such was the Clerk's status, reputation and achievement, that no one was prepared to articulate these concerns in open Court.

Master Britt called a meeting of senior Court members in Guildhall. One after another, Carmen agonised – the Clerk had saved the Company, yet everyone retires some day and there must be a smooth succession. In the end, it was agreed that corporate rules should apply – everyone has to retire, and better to plan it at the peak, than falter in the future.

Whatever their forebodings or reservations, all those there that day were unanimous: the Carmen owed a great debt to Geoffrey Pearce. That October in 1994 the Court formalised his retirement, two years hence.

Like a dog worrying a bone, the Court picked up the Livery Fund again. It was decided to make the buy-in rate £1,000, restrict the annual intake to three, all over 60 and with 15 years' minimum service and an unblemished payment record.

By now all Masters gave silver, and a set of Court goblets were designed, put into reserve, and presented from time to time. Eric Britt started the ball rolling with three to mark his year. Although the Livery had dropped to 421, Master Michael Taylor's Charity Luncheon was fully subscribed – 156 attended – assets were up, and the Company almost broke even. The economy was improving and charitable funds reached £375,256 as Frank Coxhead retired as a Trustee, remained Almoner and was appointed Honorary Life President of the Fund.

Then the Chairman of the Benevolent Fund, Past Master Sir Christopher Leaver, asked the Court to agree a new Deed of Trust. The law had changed, and Assistants faced the option of individual responsibility, or an independent and smaller Trust. The discussion raged over three Courts: should they opt out, and lose control, or accept the risk, and keep it?

Part of the problem was the London Cartage Fund – to merge this with the Carmen's Fund the Charity Commissioners suggested a new Trust. The first draft Deed was replaced. At the next Court a second draft Deed was withdrawn after some dissension. At a third Court, 14 voted in favour of appointing Trustees, and 17 agreed Trustees should appoint replacements. There were no votes against, but several abstentions.

In the end, the two Funds became one Trust, with seven trustees always drawn from Court and Carmen, and the Carmen's charities became independent. Three Past Masters, one Assistant and three Liverymen signed the new Deed in October 1995.

That year the Clerk was elected President of the Fellowship of Clerks, the Court decided to upgrade Assistants' badges from lapel to neck, and incoming Master Golder set up a working party to appoint the next Clerk. Outgoing Master Taylor gave three silver goblets.

Scott, Anderson and Cure would have approved Gerald Golder's move when, as Master, he bound his Wardens to his office as a triumvirate. Once more, three Carmen in concert took the lead. That year committees were questioned when Birch submitted 'Options for Change' in structure, events and management. One 'option' was a fund-raising body; his third attempt.

A good deal of to-ing and fro-ing ensued, not helped by late arrivals at a critical meeting of General Purposes; late trains, appalling weather and a misunderstanding blurred the formal record, a compromise was stitched together and 'Options' were tabled, to trigger a proper inquiry.

Meanwhile another questionnaire had gone to the Carmen – nearly a hundred replied, and 58 offered to serve on working parties. The Carmen's Golf Society was formed, with fifty members but a proposal for a Motor Cycling Club, agreed by the Court, failed to ignite.

Battling costs, the Court decided the sword of honour must be cut, for refurbished weapons were no more to be had. The winner would hold the 'real' sword for a year, and receive a miniature version to keep.

When twelve tea chests of old papers were retrieved from storage, the Court decided it needed a Curator, to handle documentary and photographic archives and other ephemera – three years later it was still looking, though three Liverymen had helped short term. A small step to immortality was taken when the Mormons were permitted to micro-film Carmen's pre-war Guildhall records, to 'bank' in Utah for ancestral baptism.

As '96 dawned, Company strength was well down – at 417 Liverymen, 13 less than 13 years before, though there were now 72 Freemen, and annual dues had risen from a mere £9,440 to £59,480. In July, John Wells celebrated 50 years in Fellowship.

The vogue for political correctness cornered the Carmen when the Master moved that ladies be guests at the Installation Court lunch. Muted murmurs of protest from traditionalists were subdued by vocal support from pro-fair sexists and a bad compromise emerged – Master's, Wardens' and principal guests' wives only. The Court decided to hold the mirror up next time to see who should be fairest in the hall.

Consolation prizes were approved – fifty silver-gilt and enamel brooches for Lady Liverymen and Freemen only to wear. Three months later the Court learnt that General Purposes had solemnly sat on the fence, so it had to decide between those who feared for the ambience and those who felt it was specious and 'Victorian' (a much loved modernism for that which is old and derided) to exclude the ladies from the Carmen's table.

The Court proved its feminist credentials. For the first time, wives could support husbands at the Installation Lunch, and not have to skulk behind smoked salmon sandwiches in Whittington Hall, while Carmen relaxed in Liveried splendour. In the event, not many came, but henceforth they would be welcome at any event.

The brand new Benevolent Trust welcomed £23,167 – the total bequeathed by the late Herbert Crow; his widow had endowed the Herbert Crow Prize with £1,000, to be awarded annually, and gave a silver cup and cover. Then the Court approved the Company brochure.

Mid-year the Court ruled on Options for Change – there would be an inquiry into committees, led by Assistant Hooper. Nature, cost and location of Company administration were deferred for a year. Luncheon Clubs would continue, the Ladies' Court Dinner should be enhanced, and action taken towards raising charitable funds.

In the autumn, Clerk Geoffrey Pearce reached retirement. Cdr Robin Bawtree took his place just as the Company celebrated the 50th anniversary of the '46 charter – and made £6,000-plus in the process, half to the Benevolent Fund. The Anniversary Souvenir was published on cart-marking day and Col Pearce was appointed Secretary to the Benevolent Trust, retiring as a Trustee.

The Court gave their retiring Clerk an antique silver tea service, and his wife a gold necklace and earrings in a moving ceremony after the installation lunch.

The good Colonel had inherited incomplete accounts, empty coffers, missing minutes, no office and a creaking organisation. The moment found the man. Geoffrey Pearce set about bringing order out of chaos, with meticulous efficiency and exemplary dedication. The Company recognised its deep debt when it made him an Assistant, as an Honorary member of the Court. Past Masters recalled his wife Jean's considerable contribution and affectionately recognised 'the real Clerk'.

Publishing was much in mind when the company's brochure appeared; at the same time, Liveryman Shadrack sent his father's 1939 Livery Scrapbook as Master, a perfect microcosm of the Carmen's pre-war year, and the Court approved £2,000 for research towards a new history book.

In 1997 came the findings of the inquiry into Carmen committees. The Hooper Report meant General Purposes and Past Masters stayed, as did Awards. Investments teetered, but survived. PR was dormant, so it did not count – the only committee to voluntarily shut itself down once its work was done. The new panels were Fund Raising, Cart Marking and Events.

Aims and Objects was changed to the Livery and Freemen's Committee. Lectures and Technical Panels stayed the same. In the end there were more bodies, more people, and more results. Significantly, Carmen off-Court joined the new bodies.

Jeremy Gotch became Master in 1996, already chairman of the Technical Panel, which produced a seminal paper on City congestion. He stressed the significance of a new Selection Panel, which would nominate members of all the new bodies. It comprised Master, Wardens and a Past Master. The Hooper provisions were put on one year's trial.

In 1995 several ladies had become free of the Company – first was Janet Reid, daughter of the late Past Master, shortly followed by Major the Countess Attlee, Mrs Ann Deighton, Diane-Elizabeth Napier, and (later Lady) Heather Roche, who was made an honorary freemen when she retired as the Carmen's secretary.

Within two years, the first commoner lady Carmen were liveried. Gillian Sheddick, Denise and Elaine Williams were all clothed at the January Court. Now families brought daughters as well as sons for clothing.

Simon, son of the late Assistant Norman Collins, served the Carmen well. His father left £98,500 in trust for the Benevolent Fund; with his fellow trustees, he ensured this went to the Carmen's new Trust, the largest sum received from a single source. Funds now stood at over £550,000. The Court voted unanimously to confer the Honorary Freedom on the late Assistant's son – in open Court. The very next year the Benevolent Fund launched the annual Coxhead Award at £3,000 for 'young or elderly persons in great need'.

Half a century on, with a naval Clerk, the Company again sought out a suitable ship, and this time adopted HMS *Cardiff*. Then the Court turned to a perennial problem – its own numbers. Five years before, it had agreed to reduce to 24 elected members. This gave Assistants a fast track to office, but in 2002 the Court would have to revert to full strength, or go to Privy Council to rewrite the by-law. The Court stayed at 24.

Then the Selection Panel disbanded itself; henceforth General Purposes would nominate Chairmen and Chairmen would choose members – the Court would have the last word.

The wider world saw the return of Labour to government, but nationalisation was not on the political agenda, the car was perceived as a problem and the railways, an opportunity. The haulage industry held its collective breath.

In 1997 John Ratcliff, a past UK and international Chief Barker of the Variety Club, took office. His freeman wife, Marsha Rae, the first lady Chief Barker, was clothed by him. His year saw record attendances and a Master's reception for all Liverymen.

When the Company mounted a Gala Ball at the InterContinental, it raised £46,000; the world of show business turned out. The Young Set, the Magic Circle, cast, star and musicians of the West End show, *Sweet Charity*, did it all for the Master, for nothing.

At his Charity Lunch, HRH Prince Philip returned. That year the Benevolent Fund exceeded £700,000 and another third generation joined the Livery when Richard Sunderland was clothed.

In 1998 the City decided to extend the Freedom to EU nationals, and the Carmen were the first to take this up when Renault supremo and Frenchman Louis, nephew of Albert Schweitzer, was made free of City and Carmen. Then another moving force drove up. When logisticians contemplated a company, Carmen suggested they had one, and the idea was dropped.

With office lease renewal looming, a working party found that to stay in the City would cost little more than to move to the suburbs. A home in the country was cheaper, but undesirable. The Company should stay City-based – provided numbers increased.

At St Michael's, Carmen swore their oaths again at their Foundation Service, in a new re-dedication ceremony created by Birch, and a *Carmen's Fanfare* composed and played by Christ's Hospitallers. The Master's lady painted the cover for the order of service. In 1999 Liveryman Paul Sutherland contributed a new *Carmen's Hymn*, dedicated to St Katherine. This time, Dulwich College lads played the fanfare.

Master-Elect now was Basil Hooper, but ill-health made him withdraw. He was appointed Past Senior Warden as a mark of respect. When the new Senior Warden also declined early office, Junior Warden Telfer Saywell stepped in. Senior Assistant David Bluett declined to put up for Warden and Assistant George Cognet retired, both to the Court's regret. It decided to hold an election, and declared four vacancies.

Cognet explained: his great, great, great grandma lived to 110, until she fell out of a tree, protecting her honour in the Franco-Prussian War. At 84 he would not impose the risk of ill-health on future office, for he was neither a lady nor as exceptional as she.

In July '98 thieves struck again. Fraudsters siphoned £7,200 from the bank account with a forged transfer. The bank put it back and the police took an interest.

In 1999 the Court realised that its Livery Fund – started in 1975 – was attracting no new recruits. Carmen were not compounding their quarterage, and the capital was lying relatively idle. It was decided to review matters. One idea was a Perpetual Fund, absorbing all fines, its income going to revenue. When Eddie Price reviewed his Carmen's half century, he decided to give ten more silver goblets to the Company.

By then many more families supported the Fellowship: four Adams, four Britts and four Eltons; the Levenes, father, brother, and sons; three Sparshatts, -Worley, -Potter and plain Sparshatt; four Williams, three of them ladies; three Glyn Thomases, Golders, Cognets and Lemmers, thirteen fathers and sons, two husband and wife teams, an uncle and nephew, brother and sister and one father and daughter.

The count-down to millennium also saw ladies first one more time, when Lieutenant Gemma Claire Lowth RLC won the Sword of Honour; she electrified the Carmen with her forthright yet diplomatic words at Plaisterers' Hall. 'Authoritative leadership' said the citation. This international lacrosse player became an honorary Carman.

In 1998 Carmen went to Common Hall to support a fellow Carman in his bid for the Mayoralty for 1998–1999. The Lord Levene of Portsoken was elected, the eighth Carman Lord Mayor, and Past Master of this, his mother Company.

In the '80s Levene had put right a long wrong for Carmen when, with military precision, he set the Docklands Light Railway on the right tracks, thus returning to dockland that which dockland once took from Carmen – viable transport.

The Lord Mayor's Show cast a wide net and within it the Carmen rode high, wide and handsome, with the 1893 original Evan Cook handcart, Michael Gerson's immaculate 1902 horsed pantechnicon, Jack Henley's 1952 Bluebird coach and an Isuzu 21st century urban shuttle, plus the Master's carriage, Corps band, floats and four-in-hand equipage. Carmen bought the Lord Mayor a silver model Alvis Stewart amphibious carrier.

In 1999 the City itself was reviewing its franchise, while government continued to wrestle with too many cars, too late trains, road pollution and urban congestion, plus continuous regulation from a discredited Eurocentre in Brussels.

Fuel tax, bane of post-war Masters, went up a punitive 11.6% and vehicle duty to ten times that of Continental competitors. Carmen scoffed at Euro 'harmonisation', and talked seriously about flags of convenience.

With their eighth Lord Mayor in Mansion House, charitable money moving towards a million, 430 Liverymen, some ladies, and 110 freemen, the Carmen approached the year of our Lord 2000 free of past conflict, at ease with themselves, and in high City regard.

The Carmen of the millennium stand at the heart of the City and of their industry, strong in ancient and in modern fellowship, and flourish root and branch. May they continue so to do, now and forever.

ABOVE: Alderman Sir Christopher and Lady Helen Leaver brought youth, vigour – and a smile – to their Mayoral year. (CL) BELOW: Master John Wells headed a Court seeking change: left to right – Past Masters Paige, Quick-Smith, Benton, Pye, J. Pollitzer, F. Coxhead, Hodkinson and Clarkson; Warden Hart, the Master and Warden Bird; Past Master Bezzant and Assistants Selby, C. Birch, B. Evan Cook, Collins, Johnson, Leaver, Parry and J. Evan Cook. New Clerk Pearce sits (left) opposite Deputy Clerk Burke. (CC)

LEFT: Sir Kenneth Selby reads out a citation, in 1982. (CC) RIGHT: Carman of Carmen Master Freddie Bird shares a joke with Chaplain Bill Down. (CC) BELOW: Carmen bought this special Land Rover for the Princess's Save the Children Fund. (CC)

LEFT: In 1982 at Guildhall, HRH (then) Princess Anne joined the Carmen. On her way from the ceremony with Master John Wells, she glances at the Junior Leaders of the Royal Corps of Transport. (CC) RIGHT: Past Master Quick-Smith with Past Master Joe Pollitzer. (CC) BELOW: In 1984 the Master rode to church, in a 1918 General Service waggon, marked The Carmen's Car. (CB)

ABOVE LEFT: Carmen and their guests watch the Corps band Beat Retreat at Stowe during the first Carmen's Ball, 1985. (CB) RIGHT: Master Birch presents the Senior Past Master and Honorary Almoner, Lt Col Frank Coxhead, with a silver horse – the Company's gift for outstanding service. (CC) BELOW: On the tenth anniversary of the Corps-Carmen concord, RCT bandsmen march past on Corps Day at Aldershot. (CB) RIGHT: Master Dennis Baker and Keeper of the Guildhall John Lucioni watch Lord Mayor Christopher Collett mark a carr in 1989. Ever since, Lord Mayors have joined the Carmen for this event. (CC)

166

ABOVE: Cart marking became the Carmen's public event – here Coach No 2 of the Institution of the Royal Corps of Transport arrives in Guildhall Yard from the Royal Mews. (CC) BELOW: The Royal Past Master names *The Worshipful Company of Carmen* at Paddington, with Master Sir Robert Reid, acting Wardens, Chaplain and Clerks. (CB)

ABOVE: Beadle Bob Clarke leads Carmen to lunch from St Michael Paternoster Royal on Master Britt's Installation Day, 1993. (CC) LEFT: Outside Court, Carmen do business without undue formality – Sir Colin Cole chairs cross-Livery support for Carman Gotch's Shrievalty bid. (CB) RIGHT: Assistant Jeremy Gotch was elected Sheriff in 1992. (JG)

LEFT: HM the Queen on Burmese – one of the Company's pieces of silver. (CC) RIGHT: Reforming Clerk Geoffrey Pearce reversed the roles when he supported his wife, on the day she was made an Honorary Freeman in 1992. (CC) BELOW: Denise and Elaine Williams were the first ladies, after the Princess, to be clothed with the Carmen's Livery, in 1997 – by Master Gotch. (CC)

ABOVE: The 1997 Court that welcomed the eighth Carman Lord Mayor in 1998: left to right – PM Britt, Deputy Clerk Burke, PM Golder, Lord Mayor-Elect Lord Levene, PMs Taylor, Sir Christopher Leaver and Birch, Asst Saywell, PMs Gotch and Wells, Clerk Cdr Bawtree, PM Lloyd, Assts Owen, Cognet, Wilmshurst, Power, Meyer, Cullimore, Barrett, Pullman, Asst Clerk Pulvermacher, Asst Pearce; seated Senior Warden Hooper, Master Ratcliff, Junior Warden Silbermann; Painter Stainers' Hall. (CC) LEFT: In 1998 Christ's Hospitaller Rebecca Gibson, apprenticed to Past Master Wells, was made free of the Company. (CC) RIGHT: Master's wife Marsha Rae Ratcliff recreated past Carmen for the Foundation Day Service in 1998. (CC)

THE WORSHIPFUL COMPANY OF CARMEN of LONDON

PLEDGE FOR RENEWAL and REDEDICATION

Resolution of the Court of Assistants on the Anniversary of the Foundation of The Fraternity of St Katherine the Virgin and Martyr of Carters.

Inasmuch this Fraternity and Mystery of Carmen was founded on the nineteenth day of March in the year of our Lord fifteen hundred and seventeen.

Be it resolved that this Pledge for Renewal and Rededication be granted with the blessing of our Lord and that this Worshipful Company of Carmen Root and Branch, may continue and flourish for ever

Whereto we, the Court of Assistants, Liverymen and Freemen of this Ancient Guild, do renew our fealty to our Sovereign Lady the Queen, and rededicate ourselves and all our fellow Carmen, Freemen and Liverymen alike, to the furtherance of the objectives of this our ancient Guild:

To maintain and enhance its traditional interest in, and service to, the City civic, the transport industry and those in need, through the promotion of excellence, good-fellowship and benevolence

Dated this nineteenth day of March in the year of our Lord 1998

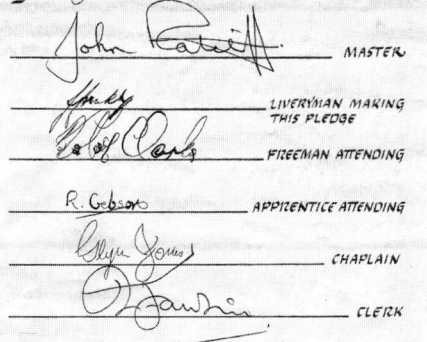

Signed:
- John Ratcliff — MASTER
- [signature] — LIVERYMAN MAKING THIS PLEDGE
- [signature] — FREEMAN ATTENDING
- R. Gibson — APPRENTICE ATTENDING
- Glyn Jones — CHAPLAIN
- [signature] — CLERK

LEFT: A new dedication ceremony saw Carmen pledging their oaths afresh. (CC) RIGHT: Eileen Forde, Carman book keeper for over fifty years. (CC) CENTRE: The first European Carman – Louis Schweitzer. (CC) BELOW: The largest gift to Carmen's charities was bequeathed by Assistant Norman Collins, here with his wife Glennis in 1985. (CB)

The Gala Ball raised £46,000 nett in '98 – ABOVE: Marsha Rae Ratcliff's invitation card. (CC) BELOW: The Young Set entertain Carmen with their carrs. (CC)

LEFT: The Rt Hon the Lord Mayor, 1998–1999, the Lord Levene of Portsoken KBE, Past Master Carman. (PL) RIGHT: Carr and Carmen prepare for the Lord Mayor's Show – Richard Sunderland and Colin Barrett flank Mrs Barrett outside Assistant Jack Henley's Bluebird coach, (CB) with BELOW: Senior Warden Basil Hooper (right) and (behind) Past Masters Britt and (left) Long with Carmen and guests inside. (CB)

ABOVE: Court members gather in 1998 to honour Frank Coxhead on his 90th birthday: hostess Barbara Long, Marsha Rae Ratcliff, Geoffrey and Jean Pearce, Clive Birch, Robin Bawtree, Michael Power, Basil Hooper, John Ratcliff, the guest of honour, host Gerry Long, John Wells, Telfer Saywell and Christopher Leaver. (CB) Modern Masters gather at Plaisterers' Hall to greet the Millennium: left to right standing – Jeremy Gotch, John Ratcliff, Gerald Golder, Michael Taylor and Eric Britt; seated – Sir Christopher Leaver, Gerry Long, John Wells and Clive Birch. (CC)

ABOVE: Mansion House 1999 when the Carmen came home again, to dine with their own Lord Mayor – the fullest house in living memory. (CC) BELOW: Master Telfer Sawyell presents the 1999 Sword of Honour to Lt Gemma Claire Lowth RLC in the presence of HRH and Past Master the Princess Royal; toastmaster Sullivan and Past Master Wells look on at Plaisterers' Hall. (CC)

The Worshipful Company of Carmen

The declaration by a Freeman

I do sincerely and solemnly declare to be true to our Sovereign Lady the Queen and her heirs and successors according to law. In all things lawful, as a Freeman, I will be obedient to the Master and Wardens of the Company and will support the Company to the best of my ability. I will observe the lawful Acts, Charters, Bylaws, rules and regulations, made for the good government of the Company, and I will do no wrong to any fellow Carman but will behave myself in my trade well and honestly.

The Carman's Oath. (CC)

THE MASTERS

or Upper Wardens by year of installation

1668–1676 Wardens
1677 Eldest Warden
1678–1839 Upper Warden or Master

1668	John Hill
1669	William Stanley
1670	John Fox
1671	William Turner
1672	John Earle
1673	James Maw
1674	Edward Benson
1675	John Chitwell
1676	John Sandford
1677	James Ruffhead
1678	Edward Oxladd
1679	Simon Tomlyn
1680	John Earle
1681	John Chitwell
1682	John Matthews
1683	William Pinchbeck
1684	Stephen Sandford
1685	John Miller
1686	Jasper Rawlins
1687	Henry Blunt
1688	Edward Rogers
1689–1691	Edward Jempson
1692	Willl'm Butler
1693	William Rogers
1694	William Haynes
1695	Abraham Palmer
1696–1697	James Bingham
1698	Robert Marshall
1699	Edward Champ
1700	William Franklin
1701	John Mawby
1702	John Warren
1703	Richard Avery
1704–1707	John Bowyer
1708	William Lovell
1709	Richard Harris
1710	John Toone
1711	John Mitchell
1712–1713	Miles Edis (dec'd)
1713–1714	Robert Marshall
1715	Ralph Garrett
1716–1718	John Toone
1719–1720	Richard Slater
1721	John Hart
1722	Francis Titcom
1723	Thomas Ward
1724	Daniel Webb
1725	John Darling
1726	William Grant
1727	Thomas Hedges
1728	William Machin
1729	Daniel Sell
1730	John Falkener
1731	Edward Holden
1732–1733	Joseph Bates
1734	James Crutchfield
1735–1736	William Gibbs
1737	Jeremiah Francis
1738–1739	William Pryor
1740	George Palmer
1741–1742	David Quinton
1743	William Jenkins
1744	Anthony Wright
1745–1746	Thomas Cooper
1747	Edmund Such
1748	John Flexney
1749	Samuel Day
1750	William Drake (dec'd)
1750	Francis Titcom
1751	Abram Owen
1752	James Andrews
1753	Richard Spooner
1754	Joseph Springwell
1755–1756	Edward Mayor
1757–1758	Joseph Buck
1759	James Gentleman
1760	James Turner
1761	William Harris
1762	Joseph Springwell
1763	Samuel Bridgman
1764	John Mott
1765	Joseph Bybee
1766	Henry Smith
1767	Richard Harrap
1768	William Jeffs
1769	Josiah Broadbent
1770	George Spencer
1771–1772	John Miller
1773	William Holyland
1774	Thomas Day
1775	John Barnjum
1776–1777	William Murden
1778	Thomas Cooper
1779	David Davies
1780	John Flexney Jn
1781	Thomas Griffin
1782	William Mott
1783	John Stevens
1784	Richard Butterworth
1785	James Hall
1786	Joseph Buck
1787	Mark Stokes
1788	William Smith
1789	Erasmus Taylor
1790	William Applebee
1791	Richard Harrap
1792	Thomas Jeffs
1793	William Parker
1794	John Unwin
1795	John Holyland
1796	Samuel Day
1797	Josiah Keeves
1798	William Press
1799–1800	Richard Bailey
1801–1802	James Robinson
1803–1804	Richard Unwin
1805–1806	Richard Clark
1807–1808	Thomas Clark
1809–1810	Isaac Day
1811–1812	John Bailey
1813–1814	William Jury
1815	Thomas Ashenden
1816–1818	William Aspin
1819–1825	William Applebee
1826–1829	Thomas Bailey
1830–1833	Richard Back
1834–1835	Thomas Cobley
1836	Henry Smith
1837	John Bailey
1838	James North
1839	William Wright (res)
1839–1842	James North

1843–1849	John Paice	1907	G.R.N. Stollery	1956	Reginald Bezzant
1850–1851	John Scholes	1908	R.A. Kearsey	1957	Maj Gen J.S. Crawford
1852	John Eyke (dec'd)	1909	C.E. Scholes	1958	R.G.L. Cheesman
1853–1854	Thomas Priestley	1910	W.A. Perry	1959	Col John Pye
1855	James Golding	1911	W.W. Allen	1960	Raymond Birch
1856	Thomas Bateman	1912	G.R.N. Stoller	1961	Victor Parker
1857–1858	George Grimslade	1913	R.A. Kearsey	1962	Fred Cumber
1859	Thomas Breden	1914	C.E. Scholes	1963	H.G. Randall
1860	John Bendel	1915	C.T. Scrivener	1964	Col E.G. Dutfield
1861–1863	Thomas Fardell	1916–1917	G.R.N. Stollery	1965	A.W. Benton
1864	George Johnson	1918	W.W. Allen	1966	George Fuerst
1865	John Paice (dec'd)	1919	Ald James Roll	1967	G.W. Quick-Smith
1866–1874	Thomas Priestley	1920	H.A. Jager	1968	Norman Bezzant
1875	Thomas Fardell	1921	Charles Webster	1969	Joe Pollitzer
1876	Thomas Priestley	1922	G.H. Lloyd	1970	Rev Bill Dormor
1877	Thomas S. Fardell	1923–1924	George Lavington	1971	Col L.A. Gundry-White
1878	Henry Johnson	1925	F.H. Brundle	1972	A.E. Drain
1879	Thomas Priestley Jn	1926	H.A. Easton	1973	Stanley Paige
1880	Thomas S. Fardell	1927	R.N. Tough	1974	Charles Lloyd
1881	James Fardell	1928	G.T. Hedge	1975	M.W. Harris
1882	C.E. Fardell	1929	Sir Percy Vincent	1976	Sir John Cohen
1883	Thomas Priestley Jn	1930	G.H. Lloyd	1977	Willie McPhail
1884	Henry Johnson	1931	E.E. Coxhead	1978	J.E.O. Arnold
1885	Thomas S. Fardell	1932	W. Austin Balls	1979	W.A. Hodkinson
1886	J.R. Fardell	1933	Ald F.J.C. Pollitzer	1980	Lt Col Geoffrey Clarkson
1887	C.E. Fardell	1934	C.J.H. McRea	1981	John Wells
1888	Thomas Priestley Jn	1935	H.W. Carter	1982	Tony Hart
1889	Henry Johnson	1936	Victor Parker	1983	Freddie Bird
1890	J.R. Fardell	1937	A.J. Laker	1984	Clive Birch
1891	C.E. Fardell	1938	E.A. Shadrack	1985	Oliver Sunderland
1892	Thomas Priestley Jn	1939–1940	W. McAuley Gracie	1986	HRH the Princess Royal
1893	Henry Johnson	1941	Col E.W. Crawford	1987	Ald Sir Christopher Leaver
1894	C.E. Fardell	1942	W.A.G. Mitson	1988	Maj Dennis Baker
1895	Thomas Priestley Jn	1943	F.G. Bristow	1989	Gerry Long
1896	Henry Johnson	1944–1945	E.E. Coxhead	1990	Sir Robert Reid
1897	H.A. Jacobs	1946	Percy Sharman	1991	Ken Parry
1898	C.E. Fardell	1947	Lt Col Frank Coxhead	1992	Ald Sir Peter (later Lord) Levene
1899	C.E. Scholes	1948	B.G. Turner	1993	Eric Britt
1900	C.T. Scrivener	1949	Lt Col Norman Letts	1994	Michael Taylor
1901	C.E. Scholes	1950	W.G. Manthorpe	1995	Gerald Golder
1902	H.A. Jacobs	1951	Maj Gen Sir Leslie H. Williams	1996	Jeremy Gotch
1903	C.T. Srivener	1952	W.H. Walker	1997	John Ratcliff
1904	J. Mumford	1953	Henry Dutfield	1998	Telfer Saywell
1905	R.A. Kearsey	1954	Joe Pollitzer	1999	John Silbermann (Master-Elect)
1906	C.E. Scholes	1955	Lt Col Norman Letts		

The Clerks since 1668

1668–1677	William Parry	1730–1751	John Boden	1929–1935	J. Woodman Smith
1677	Thomas Johnson	1751–1758	Richard Marsh	1935–1966	O. Gordon Sunderland
1678–1686	Nathaniel Wickens	1758–1778	Jonan Colston	1966–1969	Oliver Sunderland
1686–1692	Thomas Johnson	1778–1790	William Holder	1969–1971	Francis A. Barragan
1692–1696	William Newman	1790–1839	John Holmes	1971–1973	Ulick J. Burke
1696	George Minnitt	1839–1845	John Hudson	1973–1977	J. Murray Donald
1697–1706	William Newman	1845	Solomon Jones	1977–1979	David Reid
1706–1708	Mr Purchase	1846–1850	William Jackson	1979–1981	Michael H. Hinton
1708–1726	Thomas Jackson Jn	1850–1874	Alexander Baylis	1981–1996	Lt Col Geoffrey T. Pearce
1726	John Yeo	1874–1898	E.A. Baylis	1996–	Cdr Robin Bawtree
1727–1730	Thomas Jackson Jn	1898–1929	Harry W. Capper		

THE CARMEN'S AWARDS

The Viva Shield

1957	Dr E.M. Dodds	Lubricating oil research
1958	De Havilland Aircraft Company	Comet IV jet airliner
1959	John Laing & Son Ltd	Construction of M1 motorway
1960	Sir Christopher Cockerell	Invention of the hovercraft
1961	Dr Albert Fogg	Work for MIRA
1962	BMC Ltd and Sir Alec Issigonis	Mini cars
1963	O.A. Kerensky, Freeman, Fox & Partners	Design of Medway Bridge
1964	Sir William Glanville	Road safety/traffic research
1965	Lt Col Frank Bustard	Pioneering Roll on-Roll off
1966	Sir Gilbert Roberts	Advancement, suspension bridge design
1967	J.F. Allan Baker	Pioneering UK motorways
1968	Automotive Products Co Ltd	Design/development, automatic transmission gearbox
1969	W.H. Lindsey, Rolls Royce	Marine gas turbine development
1970	no award	
1971	no award	
1972	Professor W. Gisane	
1973	Dunlop Rubber Co	Founding Birmingham Accident Hospital
1974	Shell Co Ltd	Denovo tyre
1975	Transport & Road Research Laboratory	Shellgrip road surfacing material
1976	British Railways	Computerised traffic signals
1977	Motor Industry Research Association	High speed train
1978	Sir Freddie Laker	Crash test development
1979	no award	Skytrain
1980	Tyne & Wear Passenger Transport Executive	
1981	Lucas Industries plc	The Metro
1982	Royal Corps of Transport	Automobile component engineering
1983	West Midlands County Council	Transport support, Falklands
1984	Transport & Road Research Laboratory	MAGLEV transit system
1985	Liveryman Tom Beagley	SCOOT area traffic control system Establishment of European Society of Transport Institutes
1986	GEC – Mowlem Railway Group	Dockland light railway
1987	no award	
1988	Motor Industry Research Assoc	
1989	Rover Group	Electro-magnetic compatibility testing chamber
1990	no award	K series engine
1991	International Automotive Design	
1992	Land Rover Ltd	Cleanair LA 301 hybrid car
1993	Thames Utilities Ltd	Range Rover and Discovery vehicles
1994	Eurotunnel	London water ring main
1995	no award	The Channel Tunnel
1996	no award	
1997	Thrust SSC team	
1998	Royal Mail	Supersonic and land world speed records Railnet scheme

Sir Henry Royce Memorial Foundation Award

1983	Thrust Cars Ltd	World land speed record
1984	Leyland Vehicles Ltd	C44 Road runner
1985	Rolls Royce Motors Ltd	Bentley Turbo-R sports saloon
1986	Sir John Egan	Personal achievement, Jaguar
1987	Ford Motor Co Ltd	2.5 litre direct injection diesel and CTX continuously variable transmission
1988	Sadler Tankers Ltd	First haulier with BS5750
1989	Dr John Prideaux, Intercity	BR Intercity 225 Project
1990	Ricardo Consulting Engineers	75 years' excellence
1991	RCT and REME	Operation Granby
1992	Frank Williams Renault Team and Nigel Mansell	10 Formula I victories and World Championship
1993	Balfour Beatty/AMEC	Limehouse link tunnel
1994	Tracker Network (UK) Ltd	Stolen vehicle tracker
1995	no award	
1996	Rolls Royce plc	The Trent engine
1997	Thrust SSC team	Outstanding vehicle design
1998	Lotus Engineering	Lotus Elise sports car

Carmen's Royal Logistic Corps Safety Award

1984	The Rt Hon the Lord Nugent of Guildford	Seat belt legislation
1985	Ford Motor Co Ltd	Anti-lock brake as standard over complete range of cars
1986	Sheller-Clifford Ltd	Soft safer steering wheel
1987	Steering Development Ltd	Disabled driver tiller
1988	no award	
1989	WDM Ltd	SCRIM sideway force coefficient routine investigation machine
1990	Astatic (Cars) Ltd	Skidmaster training equipment
1991	no award	
1992	no award	
1993	WDM Ltd/Longdin & Browning	High speed monitor & clear cones
1994	LDV Ltd	Improved safety, minibuses
1995	Department of Transport	Puffin pedestrian crossing
1996	Centrex Ltd	Imaginative training programmes
1997	Institute of Advanced Motorists	40 years' training drivers
1998	BRAKE/Mary Williams	Road transport safety

Carmen's Award of Merit

1988	Jaguar Cars Ltd	1988 Le Mans winning car
1989	Miss Ann Frye	MAVIS and transport for disabled
1990	The Royal Mews	Restoration, Irish state coach
1991	David Martell	Trafficmaster
1992	Liveryman Sir James Duncan	Services to transport
1993	no award	
1994	Sir John Fairclough	Engineering leadership
1995	Sir Peter Thompson	Services to transport
1996	Richard Branson	Transport improvements
1997	Sqn Ldr A. Green	World land speed record
1998	Liveryman Graham Westcott	Transport training

PLATE AND POSSESSIONS

1675 Tankard the gift of Benjamin Preston (and Joseph Springwell/William Holyland)
1712 Two handled cup presented by Robert Neal Tough, 1928
Silver lamp bequeathed by Robert Neal Tough 1930
Silver gilt trophy presented by W. Austin Balls 1932
Three Master's & Warden's goblets given by W. Austin Balls 1933
Loving cup given by Alderman Sir Charles J.H. McRea 1935
Beadle's mace presented by W. Austin Balls 1936
Silver cigar box given by Lt Col H.N. Letts 1950
Wardens' badges given by George Henry Lloyd 1930
Master's badge (since stolen, and replaced) from Arthur John Laker 1938
Alms box presented by Alderman McRea 1939 with ivory gavel in case
Carmen's banner presented by Alderman McRea 1947
Banner pole given by W. Austin Balls 1947
Two silver golf cups, the gift of Alderman Sir Frank C. Pollitzer and Sir Arthur E. Morgan
George III silver loving cup bought from bequest of W. Austin Balls
Two silver cigarette boxes, gift of Col J.F.E. Pye
Two silver loving cups, given by the Court to commemorate the Coronation of Elizabeth II
Three silver gilt dishes subscribed by the Livery 1953
Chased and parcel gilt rose water dish and ewer, gift of R.G.L. Cheesman
Silver cigarette box presented by Oliver Cutts
Viva Shield given by R. Bezzant
Four silver cigar and cigarette boxes
One modern cup
Silver medal of the South Africa War 1899–1902, awarded by Edward VII (lost, but officially replaced)
Late 19th century silver tankard
Silver packhorse presented by Pickfords Ltd (G.W. Quick-Smith)
Model Jaguar centrepiece
Silver cup given by Mrs Crow in memory of Herbert Crow
Silver cup given by Victor Parker
Silver cup given by Sir John Cohen
Silver cigar and cigarette boxes given by Charles Lloyd
Silver cigar box given by H. G. Randall
Silver Army service Corps officer, 1911, presented by the RCT 1975
Silver Court pen provided by Clive Birch 1982
Silver Model T Ford presented to Alderman Sir Christopher Leaver and on loan
Silver horsed 1884 omnibus, the gift of Clive Birch 1984
Silver Spirit of Ecstacy Royce trophy, presented by the Sir Henry Royce Memorial Foundation
Silver fruit bowl presented by Sir G. Messervy, Lucas Industries
Silver cigarette box, given by Norman Collins
College of Arms Qincentenary goblet, the Princess Royal's cup
RCT safety trophy
RCT silver Armada dish
Silver Carmen's whistle presented by Clive Birch 1985
Replacement charity box presented by Sir Kenneth Selby
Four silver place cards given by John Wells
Silver Royal Waggon Train officer presented by Tony Hart
Silver plate fruit basket given by Norman Collins
Silver Jubilee centrepiece given by Norman Collins

Jewelled Master's Lady's brooch from Norman Collins
Cream and sugar set the gift of Norman Collins
Oliver Sunderland Memorial Cup presented by Sir Christopher Leaver
Mayoralty silver beaker given by Dennis Baker
Model Rolls Royce Silver Ghost presented by Gerald Long
Two two-branch candelabra presented by Norman Collins
Three five light candelabra, two given by the RCT and one by Sir Kenneth Selby
Two three-light consort candelabra
Four silver plate candelabra
Clerk's silver goblet presented by Sir Robert Reid
Silver statuette of HM Queen on Burmese subscribed by members of the Company to commemorate the 40th year of the Queen's reign
Clerk's badge presented by John Wells
Chaplain's badge presented by Ken Parry
Deputy Chaplain's badge
Assistant Clerk's badge
Silver gilt Master's chain given by Alderman the Lord Levene of Portsoken
Thirty silver Court goblets, including gifts by Geoffrey Pearce, Jeremy Gotch (3), Bob and Janet Reid, John Ratcliff, Gerald Golder (3), Michael Taylor (3), Eric Britt (3), T.J.E. Price (12), George Cognet and the RLC (2) for Major Generals Burden and White
Sword of honour
Alvis Load Carrier Stalwart Mk II subscribed by the Livery in honour of the Mayoralty of Lord Levene
Portrait of HRH the Princess Royal
Portrait of Alderman Sir Christopher Leaver
The Chaplain's embroidered vestments
The Master's, Wardens', Clerks' and Beadle's gowns, two Livery gowns
15 silver-gilt Assistants' badges
Cut glass Georgian sherry decanter presented by Woodroffe Benton

Winners of The Sword of Honour

1979   Maj Adrian Paul Taplin*
1980   Lt Col Patrick Simon Reehal
1981   Maj James McDonald Ferrier*
1982   Lt Col Andrew Malcolm Hood
1983   Maj Malcolm Robert Little*
1984   Capt Stephen Arthur Bruford Hemsley†
1985   Capt Christopher John Theodore Hain†
1986   Capt Anthony James Lewis*†
1987   Maj Rowland Ernest George Judge
1988   Maj Justin Philip Stanhope-White*
1989   Maj Angus Smart James Fay
1990   Maj Jonathan David Vere Martin
1991   Maj Steven John Shirley
1992   Maj Nicholas John Byrne
1993   Capt Christopher John Strathern Rose
1994   Capt Gareth George Wright
1995   Capt David Gerhard Luedicke
1996   Lt Michael Gerard Daly
1997   Lt Crispin Tony Grant Driver-Williams
1998   Lt Patrick Simon Reehal (2)
1999   Lt Gemma Claire Lowth

*Liverymen by Redemption   †Retired

BIBLIOGRAPHY

Anon. *Cavalcade of Enterprise* British Omnibus Companies Public Relations Committee, London 1946
Arnold, James *All Drawn by Horses* David & Charles, Newton Abbot 1979
Barker, Felix & Jackson, Peter *London: 2000 years of a City and its People* Macmillan, London 1974
Bennett, Eric *The Worshipful Company of Carmen of London* WCC/Simpkin Marshall Ltd, London 1952 Barracuda Books Ltd/WCC 1982
Birch, Clive and Harper, Len *On the Move – the Road Haulage Association 1945–1994* Baron, Whittlebury 1995
Blacker, K.C., Lunn, R.S., Westgate, R.G. *London's Buses Vol 1* H.J. Publications, St Albans 1977
Boswell, James *London Journal 1762–1763* Wm Heinemann Ltd, London 1950
Carter, George *Outlines of English History* Ward Lock, London 1962
Chivers, Keith *The London Harness Horse Parade* J.A. Allen, London 1985
Dale, Hylton B. *The Fellowship of Woodmongers* Coal Merchant & Shipper, 1921
De Vries, Leonard *Panorama 1842–1865, Illustrated London News* John Murray, London 1967
Ekwall, Eilert *The Concise Oxford Dictionary of English Place Names* Oxford University Press, Oxford 1936
Gibbs-Smith, C.H. *The Great Exhibition of 1851* HMSO, London 1950
Hazlitt, William *Essays* The Folio Society, London 1964
Hope, Valerie; Birch, Clive; Torry, Gilbert and Birch, Carolyn *The Freedom: The Past and Present of the Livery, Guilds & City of London* Barracuda Books Ltd, Buckingham 1982
Hyde, Ralph *A to Z of Georgian London* Margary, Kent 1981
Klapper, Charles F. *Golden Age of Buses* Routledge & Kegan Paul, London 1978
Latham, R.C. and Matthews, W. *The Diary of Samuel Pepys* Bell & Hyman, London 1970
Mayhew, Henry *London Street Life* ed Raymond O'Malley, Chatto & Windus, St Albans 1966
Murray, Ernest G. *Tales of a Thames Lighterman* Baron, Whittlebury 1992
Nockolds, Harrold ed. *The Coachmakers* J.A. Allen, London 1977
Parker, James *A Glossary of Heraldry* (1894), David & Charles, Newton Abbot 1970
Perry, Don *Dockers in Distress* privately published, London 1998
Prokter, Adrian and Taylor, Robert *A–Z of Elizabethan London* Margary, Kent 1979
PSV Circle, The *Birch Bros Ltd & Luton Corporation* 1970
   London's Trolleybuses The Omnibus Society, London
Scott-Moncrieff, D. *Veteran and Edwardian Motor Cars* Batsford, London 1955
Smith, Raymond *Sea Coal for London* Longmans, London 1961
Sommerfield, Vernon *London's Buses* St Catherine Press, London 1933
Straus, Richard *Carriages & Coaches* Martin Secker, London 1912
Strong, L.A.G. *The Rolling Road* Duckworth, London 1956
London's Trolleybuses The Omnibus Society, London
Times, The 'Royal Mail Coach', 1 April 1959
Torry, Gilbert *The Book of Queenhithe* Barracuda Books, Buckingham 1979

Nineties Carmen move the nation's goods. (PA)

SUBSCRIBERS

Presentation Copies

HRH the Princess Royal
The Rt Hon the Lord Mayor, the Lord Levene of Portsoken
The Corporation of the City of London

Grant A. Simmonds MBE, Assistant Remembrancer
John Lucioni, past Keeper of Guildhall

Associated Livery Companies and Guilds

The Saddlers	The Paviors	The Coachmakers and Coach Harness Makers
The Painter-Stainers	The Loriners	The Watermen and Lightermen
The Stationers and Newspaper Makers	The Glovers	The Fuellers
The Farriers	The Wheelwrights	The Hackney Carriage Drivers

Associated organisations

Chartered Institute of Transport	Freight Transport Association	International Road Union
Institute of Road Transport Engineers	Bus & Coach Council	Timber Trade Federation
Road Haulage Association	Royal Society of Arts	

Affiliated organisations

Royal Logistic Corps   HMS *Cardiff*

Clive Birch	Jeremy M.B. Gotch	Neil Bruce Copp
Lt Col Geoffrey Pearce MBE	David J. Fisher	Lt Col D.J.R. Martin MBE RLC
Alan Percy Walker	Ron Hancock	Graham R. Westcott
Keith Affleck	Lt Col R.J. Stone	R.H. Russett
Ian Johnston Blakey	Robin M. East	John H. Williams
Jeremy Sean Blakey	Brian Wadsworth	Denise A. Williams
Michael A. Bone	Clifford Wilson	Elaine D. Williams
Capt. J.M. Davies RD DL RNR	Peter N. Acton	Jonathan S. Lawton
Derek W. Johnson	Kevin Fitzmaurice	Sir James Duncan
Allan Highfield	St John Hartnell	John Farrant
Harold Lloyd Payne CBE	Col J.C. Lucas OBE	Philip Hall
Edgar Porter	Barry A. Prior FCIT	R. McL. Reid
Robert Rowan	John Older	John Edward Ratcliff
Ronold Ernest Shadrack	Andrew Michael Callaghan	Marsha Rae Ratcliff
Frank Shaw	Raymond Gent	Peter John Ratcliff
Sir Henry Royce Memorial Foundation	Robert Constant	Ralph Holman
Lt Col Roger Charles Smith	Graham H. Smith	J.H. Gabb
Jonathan Wilmshurst	David F. Bluett	Bernard Evan-Cook
John & Pat Wilmshurst	M.J. Sparshatt Worley	Joseph John Murtagh
E.C. Moon	Thomas Baden Llewellyn	

John Spencer Gilks
B.L. James
Peter Jarvis
Rowan Cole
John Gabb
M. O'Donnell
Stephen Pawson
David Salway
Ron Sewell
Maj Paul R. Sheridan TD BA
Michael Power
Geoffrey Tyler
John Wells
Brig D.N. Locke
Maj S.W. Bennett TD RLC
R.N.T. Coles
Jim Cleary
Mary Cleary
Pat Smith
Robert R. Davies
Philip Sykes Ridgway
H.W.T. Saywell
J.A.T. Saywell
T.R.T. Saywell
Gerald Golder
David and Elizabeth Stoneham
M.E.G. Taylor
Simon Charles Collins
John H. Feltham
John G. Turner
Richard Springford
John Michael Guttridge
William Spiers
John Emms
Oliver Richard Gordon Sunderland
Richard G. Lovell
Gerry Long
Robert C. Wiseman
Bruce H. Owen FCA
Alan Jones OBE
Stephen G. Lane
Stanley Blum
Phillip J. Blum
K.A. Hatcher
Past Master S.A. Paige DFC
Adrian R. Sellars
Graham D. Miller OBE
Maj J.H. Burgess RLC
T.R. Sermon (Chairman, London Federation of Clubs for Young People)
E.C. Moon

Christopher J.R. Gotch
Maj Gen D.B.H. Colley CB CBE FCIT
The Rt Rev'd Bill Down
John W. Mitchell
Herbert F. Pennell
Maj L.C.W. Reason
D.J. Skinner
Paul Sutherland
Joan Isabel Taylor
Geoffrey William Drust
Richard Pollitzer
Professor Stuart Cole
Florence Pollard
D.G. ('Tiny') Milne CBE
Michael Woods
Michael A.O'N. Wallis
Robert Hawkins
Roy Gravestock
T.L. Beagley CB
Jack Henley
Geoffrey Simms
Alan Christopher Edwards
Donald Cleaver
Patrick J. O'Donnell
Micliael A. O'Donnell
Lt Col G.A. Hodkinson RA
Edward J. Black
K.W.A. Beaumont
D. Freedman
Brian L. Veale
C.A. Lawrence
John Silbermann
Sir Christopher Leaver
Peter Foden
C.J. Bourne
M.J.G. Linington
Bruce Hewett
Montague George Moss
Michael J. Gerson
Louis Schweitzer
R.M.F. Coles
C.J.A. Barrett
James A. Barrett
Lt Col R.G. Cross MBE
John W. Maddern
Susan A. Griggs
Hannah E.B. Edwards
Christine F. Maddern
Charles A.B. Edwards
Col G.T. Spate OBE TD DL
Robin D. Waite

Peter N. Acton
Sir Daniel Pettit
Frank E. Coxhead MBE, Senior Past Master
R.W. Mellor CBE
E.A. Lewis
Lt Col R.M. Wilkinson TD
Graham Merricks
Henry Raschen TD FCA
Ian Ramsay
M.L. Summers
Mrs G.C. Lloyd
Beryl Maureen Sumner
Peter Williams
Basil J. Hooper
R. Woolcock
Brig M.W. Betts CBE
P.A.C. Edwardes
Maj Gen M.S. White CB CBE DL
T.J.E. Price MBE FCIT
Christopher Salaman
E.R. Britt
Dr R.P. Britt
Prebendary Dr Chad Varah CBE MA
Mrs E. R. Adams
Andrew G. Jackson
Richard J. Lloyd
Stephen R. Britt
Charlotte L. Britt
Mercedes J. Buckle
K.W.A. Beaumont
Clive Hodson
Peter W. Baker OBE
Paul E. Britt
Jack A. Britt
John Palmer
Maj Patrick Marsland-Roberts TD
Robin Bawtree
Gordon C. Lees
A.J. Lucking
Norman Grundon
K.M.P. O'Shaughnessy
Richard Birch
Caroline Birch
James Birch
Emma Birch
Katie Doble-Birch
Jamie Birch
Hannah Redfearn
Christopher Redfearn

Remaining names unlisted

INDEX

All figures in *italics* refer to illustrations

AA 147
Acres, Thomas 36
Acts:
 Bank Charter 93
 City of London Traffic
  Regulation 1863 96
 Dock 88
 General Turnpike (Broad
  Wheels) 1773 .... 74, *83*
 Light Railways 98
 Local Government 1929 117
 London Traffic 1924 ... 117
 Metropolitan Street 1867 96
 Parcel Act 1799 76
 Road & Rail Traffic 1933 118
 Traffic 1930 117
 Thames Conservancy
  1857 95
 Trade Disputes 115
 Transport 1947 135
 1953 136
 1967 138
 Turnpike 1745 71
 1840 94
 Watermen 1700 64
 1859 95
 Workmen's Compensation
  115
Adams family 162
 F. 150
 William 76
Adelphi 154
Admiral ('buses) 117
Adrian, Phyllis 121
Albert Memorial 96
Alder's Gate 10
Aldershot 151, 156, *166*
Aldridge, Joe 154
Alfred, King 12, *15*
Allen, Thomas 118
Amersham *106*
Anderson, Robert 21, 22, 159
Anne, Queen 69
 Princess 148, 149, 150, 151,
  152, *165*
Applebee, William 90, 93
arms, coat of ... 117, 153, 192
 supporters to 119
Army 116, 117
Arnold, Edward 139, 141,
  146
Arundell, Christopher 21
Atlas & Waterloo Omnibus
  Assoc 93
Attlee, Maj the Countess 161
Austin, Herbert 116
Awbry, Mr 61
Aylesbury *106*

Back, Richard 96
Bailey, Capt 43
Baker Britt *143*
 Dennis 154, *166*
 John 57
Ball, Joseph 91
Balls, Austin 118, 119, 135
Banbury *85*
Bank 92, 96, *107*
 of England 61, 120
Barber, John 71
Barragan, Francis 141
Barrett, Colin *173*
 Mrs *173*
Batavier Line *101*
Bate, Maj-Gen William .. 140,
  145, 148, 149
Bateman, Samuel 96
 Thomas 96
Bates, Mrs 57
Bawtree, Cdr Robin 160, *174*
Bayliss, Alexander 97
 E.A. 97
Baynard's Castle 12
Bayswater *105*
Beare, Amy 47
 Edward 47
Bear Quay 73
Bede 12
Bedford 137
Beeching, Dr 138
Bendall, Robert 58
Bennett, Eric 119
Benson, Edward 49, 58
 Mrs 57
Bentley, Obediah 61
Benton, Woodroffe 142, *145*,
  151, 154
Berkhamsted *106*
Bermuda, Bishop of 154
Berry, Mr 59
Berryman 120
Bethnal Green *127*
Bevis Marks Synagogue . 157
Bezzant, Norman ... 152, 153
 Reginald 136, *143*
 Richard 136
Bible 35, 116, 136
Bicester, RCT 25 Freight Sqn
  140, 152, 158
Billings Gate 20, *24*, 60, 71, 73,
  80
 Dock 73
 Ward Club 138, 154
Bingham, Joseph 96
Birch (coachmaker) 100
Bros 115, 117, 118, 130, *131*,
  137, 139

Clive 141, 147 *et seq*, *165*, *166*,
  174
 James 150
 Jamie 150
 John *131*, 150
 John Manley 98
 Peter 150
 Raymond *131*, 136, 137, *144*,
  150
 Prize 137
 Richard 150
 Widow 93
 William 93
  Henry 93, 94, *131*
  Manley 93, *104*
  Samuel 93, *131*
Bird, Freddie . 148, 149, 150,
  164
Birkett, Norman, KC 119
Birmingham 117
Black Death 19
Blackfriars 48
Blackwall Tunnel *108*
Bleriot 116
Blinkorne, John 38
Bloomsbury 92
Bluett, David 162
Blunt, Maj-Gen Peter 140
Board of Green Cloth 27, 70
Bodleian Library 149
Boer War 99, 147
Bolland, William 89
Bonde, Thomas 21
Bonington, R.P. *103*
Borough Market 73
Boswell, James 69, 73
Boudica 11
Bourn, Daniel 72
Boutland, Charles 98
Bowles, Thomas 16
Bowyer, Mr 64
Braggins, Maj-Gen Derek 151
Brazen Rooms 70
Breden, Thomas 96
Bremell, John 28
Bridewell 36
bridges:
 Blackfriars 76, *104*, *112*, 115
 London 11, 17, 25, 37, 70, 76,
  95, *103*, *104*, 155
 Southwark . 87, 97, *101*, *104*
 Tower 98
 Waterloo 87, *104*
 Westminster 70, *104*
Briggs, John 21
Brighton 98
British Airways 147
 Carriage Manufacturers 100

Electric Traction .. 136, 139
 Petroleum 142, 155
 Rail 139, 147, 155
 Road Services 136
 Transport Commission 135
Britannic Tower 142, 155
Britt family 162
 Eric 156, 158, *168*, *173*, *174*
Broadbent, Michael 157
Broadbridge, Lord 119
Bronze Age 11
Brook's Wharf 76
Browne, Anthony 49
 Sir Richard 46
 Widow 70
Brussels 162
Brutus 11
Buckee, Elizabeth 93
Buckingham *85*
Bulychromp, John 20
Burgitt, Mr 57
Burke, Michael 141, 149, 150
 Ulick 141
Burlington House *129*
Burmese (horse) 156, *169*
buses etc, horsed:
 Birch *112*
 LNWR *106*
 Rothschild station *130*
 Tivoli, de *107*
 tram *111*
Byrde, William *41*, 137
Cabot 21
Caesar, Julius 11
Caines, John 49
Calais 25
Camden Town 87
Campeon, William 58
Carmen's Award of Merit 153
 Ball 150, 154, 155, 156,
  161, *166*, *172*
 banner 135, *143*, 148
 Banquet 118
 Benevolent Fund .. 118, 140,
  148, 150, 153, 157, 159, 161
 Trust 160, 161
 Car 150, *165*
 Courts 1943 .... *134*
 1959 .... *144*
 1981 .... *163*
 1997 .... *170*
 Fanfare 161
 flag 156, 158
 Freemen's Scheme 156
 Golf Society 159
 Hall *32*, 59
 Hymn 161
 Ladies' Festival 121, *132*

187

Carmen's (cont.)
  lectures 154
  Master's badge 98, 119, *132*, 155
  meeting 1668 .... *56*
  mission statement 158
  Mobility Scheme 155
  Motor Cycling Club 159
  Musick 137
  Oaths *32, 50, 176*
  Ordinances 1528 .... *31*
    1665 .... *53, 54*
    1787 .... *84*
  petition 1798 .... *86*
  Remonstrance 45, *51*
  Room 154, 158
  Sword of Honour . 140, 159
  trolley *94, 126*
  whistle 147
  widows 1668 .... *56*
  window 140, *146*, 153
Carpenters' School 99
Carpentum *12, 14*
carts *23, 24*, 52, 54
  A.C. Lloyd *125*
  automatic road sweeper *126*
  Carmen's trolley *126*
  costermonger's cart *127*
  Evan Cook handcart ... *113*
  General Service wagon 150, 165
  handcarts *127*
  mailvan *111*
  waggons *55, 83*
cart hiring 144
cart marking *166, 167*
Cart Horse Parade Soc .. 115
Catering Corps 157
Catesby 35
Caveat of Warening *34*
Cavallini, C. *128*
Confederation of British
  Industry 139
Celts 11
Chalstrey, (Sir) John 157
Channel Tunnel 158
Chapman, John 13, 94
Charing Cross 97, 98
Charity Commission . 99, 159
Charles I 44, *50*
  II 60, *64*
Charrington, John 116
Charter, 1605 ..... 35, *41*, 119
  1946 .... 121, *142*
  Coachmakers 1677 .... *64*
Chartered Institute of
  Transport 152
Chelsea 11
Chesham Coffee Tavern *112*
Chester 11
Chitwell, John 49, 69
Christ's Hospital 26 *passim*, 79
churches:
  St Dunstan's in the East . 58
    James, Garlickhythe .. 142, 148
    Laurence's 71
    Magnus 20, 37
    Mary-at-Hill 75, 154
    -le-Bow 81

  Woolnoth 120
Michael Paternoster Royal
  48, 55, 141, 161, *168*
Olave's 142, 149, 154
Paul's (Cathedral) *10*, 11, 48, 59, 61, 139
Stephen's, Walbrook 48, 118, 120, 141, *146*
Cicero 12
Cisium *12, 14*
City & Guilds of London Inst 99, 136
  of London Artillery 116
  School for Boys 151
  Motor Omnibus Co 117
  Police 92
  Press 136
  University 139
Civil War 13, *16*, 45
Clapton Common *111*
Clark, Rev Charles 118
  Frederick 105
Clarke, Bob 154, *168*
  John 49, 63
  Captain 59
  Richard 57
Clarkson, Geoffrey . 141, 142
  Thomas 115
Claudius 11
Clerke, Mr 58
Cnihtengild 12
Cnut 12
coaches 52, 54
  RCT coach No 2 167
Coal Board 121
Exchange 77, *82*, 92, *102*, 117, 118, 135
Cockaine, Sir William ... 39
coffee houses:
  Child's 59
  Edward Lloyd's 59
  Grecian 59
  Jonathan's *64*
  Pasqua Rosee's 59
  Truby's 59
coffin cab *101*
Cognet family 162
  George 162
Cohen, Sir John (Jack) ... 139, 145
Cold Harbour, Mansion of 48
Cole, Sir Colin *168*
College of Arms 151
  Heralds 119
Collet, Sir Christopher .. 166
Collins, Glennis 153, *171*
  Norman 153, 161, *171*
  Simon 161
Columbus 21
Commissioners for Licensing
  Hackey Coaches 71
  of Sewers 58
Common Hall 162
  Serjeant 69
Compagnie Generale des
  Omnibus de Londres . 93
Conductor, The *107*
Cook, Henry 20
Coosyn, Edward 28
Cornhill 11

Cornewell, William 27
Corp, Richard 89
Corporation of the Poor 46, 47
Cory, Wm 92, 99
Council of Europe 135
Court of Aldermen 20, 25, 27, 28, 44, 95
  Common Council 12, 20, 36, 37, 46, 58, 70, 77, 89, 90, 91, 95, 139
  Pleas 20, 35
  Exchequer 20
  Husting 12
  King's Bench 20, 29, 35, 37, 59
  Queen's Bench 70
  Star Chamber 35, 36, 37, 38, 44, 60
Court, Sarah Bingham 93
Courteous Carman, the *66*
Covent Garden 59, 73
Coxhead Award 161
  Dorothy *134*
  Ernest ... 116, 117, 120, 121, *130*, 136
  Fund 136
  Frank . 119 *et seq, 134, 136 et seq,* 149 *et seq, 166, 174*
Coxon, Sir William 119
Crawford, Col E.W. *132*
Crimean War 96
Cromwell, Oliver 46
Cross, Cheapside *16*
Crouch, Bob 153
Crow, Annie 137, 160
  Herbert 137, 151, 160
  Memorial Prize .. 137, 160
Cruikshank *101*
Cue, John 49
Cure, Thomas ... 21, 22, 159
Cursell, Hugh 58
Daily Advertiser 74
  Mail 117
  Telegraph 99
Dalton, Asst Commissary 152
Danes 12
Dash, Jackie 138
Davies, David 94
  Thomas 73
Day, Isaac 89, 90
  Samuel 71, 87, 90
  Thomas 69
  Thomas II .... 69 *et seq*, 157
Deighton, Ann 161
Dept of Transport 147
Deptford 48
docks:
  Albert 139
  King George 139
  London (Wapping) . 77, 88, 117
  St Katherine's 88
  Surrey & Commercial ... 88, 102
  Victoria 139
  West India 77, 88
Dock Transit Shed *123*
Dodds, George 88
Doe, Sir Charles 57

Donald, Murray 140, 141
Donaldson, Lady 148
Dormor, Rev Duncan 136
  Peter 136
  Rev William 136, 150
Dorsett, Elizabeth 93
Dover 46
Down, (Rt) Rev William . 141, 150, 154, *164*
Doyley, Henry 35, 36
Drane, Edward 27
Dulwich College 161
Duncombe, Sir Saunders . 43
Dunstall, John *52*
Dunstan, William 46, 55
Dutfield, Edward 140
  George 120
  Henry 120, 121, 140, *145*
  Owen 140
Dyson, R.A. *133*
Ealing 115
Earle, Henry 46, *55*
  John 49, 57, 58
  William 90
East India Company 72
Edinburgh 88
Edward the Confessor ... 12
  I 19
  II 19
  III 20, 62
Edwards, John 105
  Widow 58
Edwin, Sir Humphry 63
European Economic
  Community 138
European Free Trade Assoc 137
Ellard, J.G. 156
Ellerman Lines 147
English Cart Horse Soc .. 98
Elizabeth I 25, 28
  II 156, *169*
Elliott 120
Elton 162
Empire Wharf *143*
Essedum 12
Estell, J.H. *123*
Euston Station 96, 97
Evan Cook *113, 129*, 162
  Jack 137, *144*, 157
Evening Standard 156
Ewer, Albert *128*
Exchange 72
Exeter 93
Eyke, John 96
Falkland Islands 148
Fardell, C.E. 97, 99
  James 97
  J.R. 97
  Thomas 97
Fellows, William 48
Fellowship of Clerks 159
Felton 94
Fenny Stratford *103*
Ferrier, Lt 148
Fielding, Sir John 73
Finch (carter) 89
Finchley 93
Finsbury 9
Fletcher, Robert 28

Flexney, John 71
Ford 147
Forde, Eileen 156, *171*
Foundation Day . *18*, 21, 150, 161, *170*
   document *171*
Fountain, Joe 137
Fowler, William 46, 55
Fox, John 49
Franco-Prussian War 162
Frederick, Sir John 58
Freight Transport Assoc 138
French Revolution 76
Frithgild 12
Frost Fair 69, *79*
Froude 97
Fruchard, Philip *79*
Gama, Vasco da 21
Gay, John 70
Gazeteer 74
George VI 121
General Strike 1926 116
Gentleman's Magazine .. 16, 71, 85
Gerson, Michael 153, 162
Gibson, Rebecca 155, *170*
Gilbert 120
Gilbey, Walter 98
Gillingham, Rev Canon
   Frank Hay 118
Gladstone (Prime Minister) *108*
Glyn Thomas 162
Godfrey, Sir Edmund Berry 49, *67*
Golder family 162
   Gerald 159, *174*
Goldsmith, Oliver 73
Gotch, Jenny 149
   Jeremy .. 157, 160, *168, 169, 174*
Gracie, Christopher 120
   Duncan 120
   William 120
Grand Junction Canal .. *103*
   Remonstrance 45
Grays 48
Grayson, Thomas *109*
Gray, Thomas 73
Great Exhibition 1851 93, 96
   Fire 1666 . 13, 48, 49, 55, 61
   War 14
Greby, Sir George 63
Greenwich 88, 96
   Hospital 63
Greswell, Goodwife 27
Grinslade, George 96, 97
Groom, R.S. *102*
Guildhall *17*, 20, 22, 25, 48, 59, 71, 75, 95, 116, 139, 147, 157, 159, *164*, 167
   Old Library 148
   School of Music 155
   window 140, *146*, 153
Guilds & guildsmen:
   Accountants 154
   Arbitrators 141
   Bakers 138
   Brewer 21
   Bricklayer 91

Brown baker 21
Coachmakers 44, 60, 72, 74, 76, *81*, 94, 99, *113*, 116, 157
Coffermaker 21
Distiller 157
Fanmakers 157
Farmers 137, 138, 141
Farriers 20
Fuellers 142
Fuller 21
Glovers 153
Greytawer 21
Hackney Carriage Drivers 154
Horners 29
Innholder 21
Insurers 154
Loriners 19, 69
Paviors 20, 137
Saddlers 19, 21
Salter 21
Scriveners 69
Skinner 21
Tailor 21
Tallow Chandler 21
Watermen & Lightermen 29, 30, *39*, 43, 69, 71, 77, *79, 86, 133*
Weavers 19
Wheelwrights 44, 58, 60, 72, 74, *81*, 94, 99, *108, 113*, 154
Woodmongers .... 20 *passim*
Gummer, Rt Hon John .. 154
Gundry-White, Col L.A. .. *145*
   Livery Fund 139, 156
Gunpowder Plot 35
Gurney 94
Habeas Corpus 60
Haines, Thomas 49, 57, 58
halls:
   Apothecaries 141
   Blacksmiths 59
   Drapers 150
   Innholders ... 139, 148, 151
   Painter-Stainers 59, 154
   Plaisterers 162, *174, 175*
   Tallow Chandlers . 120, 139, 154
   Waterman's 48, 75
   Woodmongers 26, *32*
Hall, Sir Benjamin 96
Hammersmith 115
Hammond, Robert 21, 25
Hancock, Thomas 94
   Walter 94, *107*
Hansom 13, 94
   cab 94, *104*
Hardy, Robert 49
Harman, Thomas *34*
Harrington, Dr Ralph 154
Harris, Benjamin 89
   James 89
Harrison, James 36
Hart, Tony 140, *145*, 153
Hatton, John 21
Hayter 76
Hazlitt, William 92
Heartzell, James 98
Henderson, Alexander .. 100
Henley, Jack 162, *173*

Henry IV 20
   VIII 21
Henry Appleby (locomotive) *106*
Hicklenton & Phillips ... 140
Highway Code 118
Hill(s), John 21, 47, 49, 57
Hilton, William 95
Hinton, Michael 141, 142
Hobart, Lord 87
Hodgson 76
Holborn 48, *123*
Holder, William 58
Holloway 92, 93
Holmes, Sir Arthur 120
   John 88, 89, 90, 93
Home, Horses' 99
Holyland, William 71, 118
Hooker, Thomas 49
Hooper, Basil . 160, 162, *173, 174*
   George 99
   Report 160
Honourable Artillery
   Company 75
Hopkins, Thomas 69
Hore-Belisha 118
Horne, William 92
Horse Accident Prevention
   Soc 99
   Ferry 70, *86*
Horsemonger Lane Gaol . 96
House of Commons 37, 44, 77
Hughes, Christopher . *23, 24*
Hunt, Fred 117
Huntleigh-Smith, Alf 154
Hyde Park turnpike *85*
Hyndley, Lord 121
Ingersole, Henry 47, 57
inns, taverns etc:
   Angel, Islington 92
   Bible & Crown *64*
   Blue Anchor 97
   Brown Tavern 72
   Bull & Mouth *83*
   Cardinal Hat 29
   Falcon *34*
   George 46
   Green Dragon *64*
   Grosvenor House 121, 137, 154, 155
   InterContinental 161
   Mayfair *132*
   Swan Tavern 74
   Yorkshire Stingo 92
   Irish Chamber 59, 75
   Society 44
Iron Age 11
Irons, Mr 59
Isle of Dogs 77
Jacobs, A. & Sons 136
   H.A. 98
   T.C. 136, *144*
   Tingle & 136
James I 35, 36
   II 60
Jeffrys, Mr 138
Jempson, Edward 58
John, Prince 12
Johnson, Dr 71

   George 97
   Henry 98, 100
   Richard 96
Jones, Rev Canon Glyn .. 154
Jorrocks, Mr 94
Justices of the Peace 19
Kentish Town 97, 98, *113*
Kew 115
King Edward's School, Witley 151, 153, 154
   John 47
   Samuel 74
King's Cross 97
Kirketon, Richard de 20
Kitchen, Richard 36
Kotze 43
Knarisborough, Thomas .. 28
Knights of the Road 119, *131*
Laker 120
Lambeth 70
   Palace 137
Lancaster Herald 119
Landing Ship Logistic ... 155
Lane, Jno 73
   S.G. 156, 158
Langton (carter) 95
Lawrence, Sir John 62
'Lease-Lend' *134*
Leaver, Sir Christopher . 140, 147 *et seq*, *163, 174*
   Lady Helen *163*
Ledger 74
Legal Quays 25, *32*, *80*, 88
Leicester, Asst Bishop ... 154
Lemmer 162
Leominster 72
Letts, Norman 118, 120, 137, 138
Levene family 162
   Colin 158
   (Peter), Lord 152, 156, 157, 162, *173, 175*
Lewis, John, MP 136
Liber Custularum 19
Lincolns Inn 35
Lloyd family 162
   A.C. 93, 117
   cart *125*
   Amelia Charlotte 93
   Charles .. 117, 140, *145*, 155
   John 93, 120
   William 93, 120
   David 91
   David jnr 91
   Eric 117
   George (1) 100
   (2) 117
   Cullman 93, 120
   Henry 93, 118, 120
   H. 117
   John 120
   John 75, 91
   Keziah 93
   Richard 117
Lloyds 157
Londinium 11, 19
London Cartage Fund ... 135, 148, 159
   Cart Horse Parade .. 98, 137
   carts 94

London (*cont.*)
  County Council .. 115, 116, 117
  Electric Omnibus Co 99
  General Omnibus Co 93, 96, *109*, 115, 116, 117, *124*
  Passenger Transport Board 118, *131*, 135
  Road Car Co 98, 115
  (Slow Moving) Traffic Regulations 118
  Steam Omnibus Co 99
  Transport 14, 139
    Executive 135
Long, Barbara *174*
  Gerry 147, 149, 155, *173*, *174*
Longmate, B. 85
Lord Mayor's Banquet .. 147
  Fund 99
  Show 13, 119, 147, 162, *173*
Louterell Psalter 24
Lovers Lamentation *39*
Lowth, Lt Gemma .. 162, *175*
Lucar, Edward 49
Lucioni, John *166*
Ludgate 11, 12
Lunardi 75
Lundenwic 12
Lyly, John 26, 70
M1 Motorway 137
McAdam, John 13, 87
McAuley Gracie, W. *132*
McPhail, W.A. 140, 141
MacRea, Sir Charles 118, 135, *143*
Maberly, George 99
  Joseph 90, 95
Magic Circle 161
Magna Carta 12
mail coach *84*
mailvans 94, *111*
Maitland *81*
Manor Park *128*
Mansfield, Lord 74
Mansion House . *16*, 93, 120, 121, 137, 140, 147, 148, 162, *175*
maps:
  'Agas' 1562 ...... *30*, *32*, *192*
  Braun & Hogenburg 1575 *10*
  Leake, John *42*
  Rocque, John *68*, *80*
  Senex, John *85*
Marlborough, Duke of 69
March, Richard 72
Marmont, Victor 121
Marsom, Henry 47
Master of the Posts 13
Martin, Edward 58
Mary, Queen 25
Matchett, Clement *41*
Maw, James 49
May, Christopher 69
Maybury 120
  Edward 116
  jnr 116
Mayhew, Henry 98, 99
Mayor, Edward 72
Maypole (Strand) 43
Mellitus 12

Mencap 150
Mercantile General 139
Merriman, Thomas 76
Meteyard, Eliza (Silverpen) 92, 93
Metropolitan Electric Tramway 116
Middle Temple 57
Miles, John 72
Millbank 70
Ministry of Transport ... 116
Missions to Seamen 154
Monson, Bucks 57
Montagu, Lord Chief Justice 38
Montfichet 12
Moore, Henry 47
  John 69
  Sir John 62
Moorfields 75
Morley, Thomas *39*
Mormons 159
Morrison, Herbert 120
Moss 120
Motor & Cycle Trades Ben Fund 151
  Industry Research Assoc 139
  Traction Co 99
Mowlem, John 142
Mulberry Harbour *133*
Mumford, James 100
Murden, William 74
Murray, Ernie 119, 138
Napier, Diane-Elizabeth 161
Napoleon 78, 87, 88
National Bus Co 139, 141
  Coal Board 135
  Council of Coal Traders 116
  Debt 75
  Freight Consortium 148
    Corporation 138, 147, 148
  Health Service 121
  Safe Deposit Co 140
  Westminster Bank 140
Neal, H.O. *64*
Needham, Widow 58
Needle (carman) 95
Neolithic 11
Newcastle 30
Newman, Thomas 21
North Atlantic Treaty Organisation 135
  Metropolitan Tramways Co 98, *111*
Northey, Edward 69
Notting Hill Gate 96
Oates, Titus 49
Old Bailey 156
Options for Change 159, 160
Otway & Golder 159, 160
Outon, James 88
Owen, Richard 95
Oxford . 46, 98, 116, 149, 155
Oxlad, Edward 49
Paddington 97, *107*, 155, *167*
  Post Office 98, 116
paddle steamer *101*
Paice, John 93, 96
Palmer, John 75
P & O Road Services 118

Paris 93, 96
  Prefect of Police 93
Parker, Victor 137
Parry, Ken 147, 148, 152, 153, 156, 157
  William 57, 69
Passenger Vehicle Operators' Assoc 138, 139
Paterson's Roads *104*
Paulding, Mary *82*
  Richard *82*
Payne, Joseph 90
Pearce, Lt Col Geoffrey . 142, 149 *et seq*, *169*, *174*
  Jean 156, 160, *169*, *174*
Peckham *113*
Peel, Sir Robert 92
Peelers 92
Pentonville 87
Pepys, Samuel 46, 48
Perkins, Joseph 88
Petition of Right 44
Petulengro & Pattie 121
Philip, Prince 139, 141
Philipson, John 100
Pick, Frank 119
Pioneer Corps 157
Pitt, William 76
Plague, Great 47, 49, *52*
Plaustrum 12
Plymouth 93
Polehampton, Mr 61
Pollitzer, Sir Frank 120
  Joe . 120, 121, 137, 149, 150, 154, 155, *165*
  Richard 137
Pool of London 88, *101*
Pope, Thomas 90, 91
Popish Plot 149
Port of London 77, *123*, 138
  Authority 95
  Reeve 12
Portsmouth 46
Post Office 98, 157
post-chaise *85*
Power, Michael *174*
Pratt, Roger 48
Press, Joseph 91
Preston, Benjamin 118
  Isaac 49, 57
Price, Eddie 162
Priestley, Thomas .. 96, 97, 98
  Thomas Potter 97
Prince Regent 75
Princess Royal *4*, *167*, *175*
Privy Council 29, 35, 37, 119
Public Advertiser *74*
  Transport Assoc .. 138, 139
Pulvermacher, Mark 150
Purefoy, Geoffrey *80*
Pye, John .. 118, 136, 140, 148
Pyggott, Nicholas 25
quays *80*
Queen Hithe .. 11, 12, *15*, 73, 76, 99
  Steps *32*
Queen's Waterman 153
Quick-Smith, G.W. 120, 136 *et seq*, 148, 149, 151, *163*
Quo Warranto 60, 63

Royal Automobile Club . 147
railways:
  cable 96
  Central *110*
  District Line 115
  Docklands Light 162
  Great Western *107*
  London & Birmingham 96, *106*
  & Greenwich 96
  LNWR *106*
  Metropolitan .. 97, *106*, *108*
  pneumatic tube 96
  Stockton & Darlington Light 13
  twopenny tube *110*
Raleigh 147
Randall, Steven 27
Ranewyke, John 21
Rao, Karra Venkateswara 153
Ratcliff, John 161, *174*
  Marsha Rae *132*, *170*, *172*, *174*
Rawles, H.V. 118
Reading 115
Reave, Mr 63
Red Mick 138
Regents Park Barracks .. 137, 140, 153, 154
Reid, Sir Robert 155, 156, *167*
  David 141
  Janet 160
Renault 161
Richard II 20
  III 20
Richardson, James 21
Rickett, Cockerell & Co . 137
Ridley, Prof Tony 154
Riverbus 153
River Police 88, *100*
Rix, Brian 150
Road Board 116
  Haulage Assoc 118, 138, 139, 147
Robinson, Sir John 48
Roche, (Lady) Heather .. 161
Roll, Sir James 116, *128*
Romans 11, 14
Roomland 73, 77, *80*
Rorke's Drift 152
Rose, George 116
Rossiter 120
Rotherhithe *102*, 117, *133*
Rothschild *130*
Royal Army Ordance Corps 157
  Service Corps 137
  Commission 1854 97
  Corps of Transport 139, *145*, 148, 153, 157, *166*
  bandsmen *166*
  Corps Week 140
  Institution 140, 151
  Junior Leaders *165*
  Safety Award 149, 156
Exchange 93, *110*
Logistic Corps 157
Mail Yard 98, *113*
Society 48
  of Arts 137, 154
Waggon Train 153

Royce, Sir Henry, Memorial Foundation 149
Ruffhead, James 49, 57, 58
Ruskin College 138
Russen, Arthur 98
Russell & McIver 117
  Archibald 119
Safety Bicycle 98, *112*
St Katherine 22, 119, 151, 161
  Fraternity of 21, 26
  Martins-le-Grand GPO . 96, *108*
Samaritans 141
Sappers 157
Save the Children Fund . 149, *164*
Savoy Palace *23*
Sawyer (Attorney General) 63
Saxons 12
Saywell, Telfer . 162, *174, 175*
Scholes, Charles 99
  John 96
Schweitzer, Albert 161
  Louis 161, *171*
Scott, John 21, 22, 159
Scrivener, Charles 99
Scruttons Ltd 138
Sealing Day 75
sedan *80*
See Britain Tours 117
Selby, Sir Kenneth 147, 148, 150, 153, 154, 155, 156, 157, *164*
Services Club 121
Shadrack, Ernest A. 118, 120, *132*
  Ronold 120, 160
Shalstone Manor *80*
Shardlowe, Robert 27, 30
Sharman, Percy 137
Sharpe, James 72
Shaw, Frank 149
Sheddick, Gillian 161
Shepherd, A. *101*
  Thomas 82
Sheppard, Alexander 49
  Richard 58
Sherriff, 'Iain' 158
Shillibeer, George 92
Ship Money 44
ships, vessels:
  Anson, HMS 120
  Belfast, HMS 153
  Cardiff, HMS 161
  Rosie 120
  Thames, ps 88
Shire Reeve 12
Shoobert, Mary 93
Short, Jack 154
Silverpen 92
Slithurst 61
Smart's Key 46, 77, *82*
Smiles, Samuel 100
Smith, Adam 88
  Sir Bracewell 120, 121
  Sir Ben 120, 121
  Thomas 49
  William 58
  W.H. & Son 117
Smithfield 12, 19, 73, *114*

Society of Coal Buyers 77
  Factors 71, 116
  Coal Merchants 44, 142
Somers Town 87
South Sea Annuities 75
Southwark 26, 38, 70, 96
Sparshatts 162
Spitalfields 73
Spratt, Stephen 45, *51*
Springwell, Joseph 73, *82*, 118
Stafford, Lord 43
stage carriage licence 105
  coach, first 55
Stampe, Sir Thomas 63
Standford, John 49
Standley, William 49
Staunford, Robert 20
Steam Enterprise Omnibus 94
Stephenson, George 106
Stepney 88
Stone, Richard 153
  Thomas 58
Storm (horse) 137
Stow, John 26, 43
Stowe House 150, *166*
Stratford East 94
  Guy de 20
streets, roads:
  Aldermanbury 99
  Aldersgate 46
  Aldgate 29
  Archway Road 93
  Birchin Lane 29
  Blackfriars Road 87
  Botolph Lane 37
  Bread Street 12
    Hill 37
  Broad Street, Teddington *122*
  Budge Row 120
  Bush Lane 37
  Camomile Street 99
  Cannon Street 97
  Cheapside 25, 29, 75, *81*, *114*, 140
  Coleman Street 97
  Cripplegate 11
  Crutched Friars 37
  Dowgate Hill 99, 120
  East Cheap 19, 29
  Embankment *123*
  Farringdon Street 97
  Fenchurch Street 37
  Fish Street Hill 74
  Fleet Street *34*, 64, 70, 78, 97, *122*
  Garlick Hill 37
  Goswell Road 94, *128*
  Gracechurch 29
  Great Conduit 29
  Harp Lane *32*, 58
  Holborn Hill 97, *109*
    Viaduct 97, *109*
  Horseferry Road 93
  Huggin Lane 37
  Kingsway 115
  Knightrider Street 99
  Lawrence Pountney Hill 99
  Leadenhall Street 29, 72

  Leather Lane 94
  Lime Street 29
  Little Conduit 29, 37
  Liverpool Street 96
  Lombard Street 59
  Long Acre 117
  Lower Thames Street 70, 74
  Ludgate Circus *109*
    Hill 96, 142, 156
  Mark Lane 37
  Milk Street 99
  Mincing Lane 37
  Moorgate *111*
  New Road 87, 92
  Newgate Market 29
  Noble Street 69
  Norton Folgate 57
  Old Street *111*
  Petty Wales 20
  Philpot Lane 37
  Poultry 12
  Primrose Hill 49
  Pudding Lane 37
  Ryder Street *32*
  St Dunstan's Hill 37
    James' Place 99
    Lawrence Pountney Lane 37
    Magnus Corner . *32*, 37, 58
    Martin Outwich *83*
    Martin's Lane 37
    Mary at Hill 37
    Michael's Lane 37
  Sea-coal Lane 19
  Shoe Lane 64
  Strand 43
  Thames Street 20, 29, *30*, 37, 58, 60, 61, 62, *68*, 71 et seq, *82*, 95
  Tower Street 37
  Threadneedle Street 12, *83*
  Trinity Lane 37
  Upper Thames Street 19
  Vauxhall Bridge Road . 121
  Wardrobe Hill 37
  Water Lane 37
  Watling Street 99
  West Cheap 19
  Stuarts 12, 35
  Suirdale, Viscount 119
  Sumpter, Mr *64*
  Sunderland, Arthur 119, 120
    Gordon .. 119, 120, *132*, 138
    Oliver ... 136, 138, 141, 142, 152, 154
    Richard 161, *173*
  Surtees, William 94
  Surveyor Surveyed *51*
  Sutherland, Paul 161
  Sweet Charity (show) ... 161
  Swettman, John 47
  Tacitus 11
  Tail Cart-takers 70
  Talbot, Joseph 76
  Taylor, Eric *128*, *134*
    John 43, 44, *50*
    Michael 158, 159, *174*
  Teddington *122*
  Lock 95
  Telford 13, 93

telephone exchange 97
Temple 69
  Bar 20
Tesco 139
Transport & General
  Workers' Union 139
Thames Barrier 153
  Line 153
  Street Association 74
  Television 156
Thatcher, Sir Dennis 148, 149
Thomas, Brian 140
  William 69
Thompson, John 57
  William 70
Thrupp, George 99
Tilbury 138
Tilling, Thomas 115, 139
Tomlynson, Edward 21
Tough, Robert 118
Tower, The 12, 20, 25
  Dock 37
Town Clerk 138
Traffic Commissioners .. 117
Transport Consultative
  Panel 157
Treaty of Versailles 75
Trull, John 71
Tudors 12, 21
Tuesday Committee 62
Turner, Bernard 120
  Frederick 120
  James Thomas 120
  J.H. 118
  Joe 120
  William 49, 57, 63
Tyler, Wat 19
Tyson, Kathryn 155
Ulster 44
Union Lighterage 139
Unwin, Edward 88
Utah 159
Varah, Rev Canon Chad 141
Variety Club 161
vehicles:
  Albion lowloader *133*
  Alvis (model) 162
  Atkinson eight-wheeler *131*
  Bedford van 121
  Bluebird coach 162, *173*
  charabanc 117, *128*
  Clarkson steamer 115
  Commer *143*
  Daimler van 98
  Fischer omnibus 124
  Ford Model A *128*
    T (model) 147
    Prefect 121
  Hancock Automaton *107*
  Infanta 94
  Horbick car 122
  International *134*
  Isuzu 162
  Landrover 149, *164*
  Leyland Crossley 124
    Titan *130*
    removal van *129*
  Milnes-Daimler 'bus .. 115
  Rolls Royce 140
  Silver Ghost (model) 155

191

vehicles (*cont.*):	Sir Patience 62	Whipcord, Jack 71	Wilmshurst, John 157
Unic cab 14, 116, *125*	Wells, Aaron John ... 117, 120	Whitbread's Brewhouse,	Wilson, Mrs 92
Wells steam truck *129*	Arthur Edward 117, 120	Mr 76	Thomas 76
Venetian Ambassador 37	E. & Son 116, 117, *129*	*Whislinge Carman, the* *41,*	Winkworth, Mr 76
Vere, John 59	Ernest 120	*137*	World War II 14
Victoria 97, *105*	Sir Frederick . 120, 135, *143*	Whistler, J. McNeill *100*	Worrell, Bartholomew 21
Virginia 36	John Aaron 117	Whitechapel 115	*Worshipful Company of Carmen*
Viva Shield 136, 138, *143,*	John Peters .. 136, 138, 147,	Whitehall 28, 63	(locomotive) 155, *167*
147, 148	150 *et seq*, *165, 170, 174*	White Tower *15*	Wren, Christopher ... 48, 142
Walworth 19	Willie 120	Whittington Hall .. 141, 147,	Wright, William 96, 97
Wanstead Golf Club 142,	West Horsham 99	160	Wrytsam, John 21
151	India Dock Co 88	Wilcox, Mr 71	Wyatt, Richard 36
Sports Ground 154	Westminster 11, 20, 69	Wilkes, John 76	Thomas 25
Wapping 77, 88	Abbey 12	William I, the Bastard 12, *15*	Yelverton, Sir Henry 39
Tunnel 96, *108*	Omnibus Assoc 93	III 62	York 46
War of Independence 75	wharves *68*	Williams family 162	Young 120
Ward Electrical Co 99	Wheeler, Richard 57	Denise 161, *169*	Set 161, *172*
Ned 70	Thomas 57	Elaine 161, *169*	Zulu War 152

Illustrations by Alan Percy Walker

Chapter 1 Et tu Brute	6 Old King Coal
2 Country Carman	7 Just in time
3 Roll 'em, roll 'em, roll 'em	8 Wish you well to fare
4 Cavalier cast-off	9 Import/export
5 Strumpet in sedan	10 A cart well marked
11 Civic carr	

ABOVE: The arms and supporters of the Company were granted in 1929 and 1938: this is from the original grant, held at Guildhall. (GL) ENDPAPERS: The 1562 'Agas' map shows much of Thames Street, and the sparse development south of the Thames. (GL)

Blac... ...rdrop Knight Ryder streat 13
The ind... 12
S. Andrewes hyll ...tayn... S. Peter hyll Lambart hyll 7
S. Peter S. Mary Somerset
Castell hill
Baynardes Castel Poles Wharfe Byllasee Tryglane Broken Wharfe

The bolle bayting